CompTIA

Cloud+®

Certification Practice Exams
(Exam CV0-002)

CompTIA
Cloud+®

Certification Practice Exams
(Exam CV0-002)

Daniel Lachance

New York   Chicago   San Francisco
Athens   London   Madrid   Mexico City
Milan   New Delhi   Singapore   Sydney   Toronto

Cataloging-in-Publication Data is on file with the Library of Congress

McGraw-Hill Education books are available at special quantity discounts to use as premiums and sales promotions, or for use in corporate training programs. To contact a representative, please visit the Contact Us pages at www.mhprofessional.com.

CompTIA Cloud+® Certification Practice Exams (Exam CV0-002)

1 2 3 4 5 6 7 8 9   QFR   21 20 19 18

ISBN: 978-1-260-12227-5
MHID: 1-260-12227-1

Sponsoring Editor *Amy Stonebraker*	**Technical Editor** *Eric Vanderburg*	**Composition** *Cenveo Publisher Services*
Editorial Supervisor *Janet Walden*	**Copy Editor** *William McManus*	**Illustration** *Cenveo Publisher Services*
Project Editor/Manager *Ishan Chaudhary,* *Cenveo® Publisher Services*	**Proofreader** *Claire Splan*	**Art Director, Cover** *Jeff Weeks*
Acquisitions Coordinator *Claire Yee*	**Production Supervisor** *Lynn M. Messina*	

To my two amazing kids, Roman and Trinity—much love,
and to our dog Dori, I love you too!

ABOUT THE AUTHOR

Daniel Lachance, CompTIA Cloud+, CompTIA Server+, CompTIA A+, CompTIA Network+, CompTIA Security+, MCT, MCSA, MCITP, MCTS, is the owner of Lachance IT Consulting Inc., based in Halifax, Nova Scotia. Dan has delivered technical IT training for a wide variety of products for more than 20 years. He has recorded IT support videos related to security and various cloud-computing platforms. Dan has developed custom applications and planned, implemented, troubleshot, and documented various network configurations and conducted network security audits. Dan has worked as a technical editor on a number of certification titles and has authored titles including *CompTIA Server+ Certification All-in-One Exam Guide (Exam SK0-004)* and *CompTIA Security+ Certification Practice Exams, Second Edition (Exam SY0-401)*.

When not performing with the Halifax-based cover band Clusterfunk, Dan loves being around family and spending time outdoors.

About the Technical Editor

Eric Vanderburg is Vice President of Cybersecurity at TCDI and a well-known blogger, speaker, and thought leader. He is best known for his insights on cybersecurity, privacy, cloud, and storage. Vanderburg is also a licensed private investigator with an MBA and several undergraduate degrees. He is a continual learner and has earned over 40 technology certifications from Microsoft, Cisco, CompTIA, (ISC)^2, Rapid7, EMC, CWNP, and Hitachi Data Systems. Eric is passionate about sharing cybersecurity and technology news, insights, and best practices. He regularly presents on security topics and publishes insightful articles. You can find him throughout the day posting valuable and informative content on his social media channels:

Twitter: @evanderburg
LinkedIn: https://www.linkedin.com/in/evanderburg
Facebook: https://www.facebook.com/VanderburgE

Becoming a CompTIA Certified
IT Professional Is Easy

It's also the best way to reach greater professional opportunities and rewards.

Why Get CompTIA Certified?

Growing Demand

Labor estimates predict some technology fields will experience growth of more than 20 percent by the year 2020. (Source: CompTIA 9th Annual Information Security Trends study: 500 U.S. IT and Business Executives Responsible for Security.) CompTIA certification qualifies the skills required to join this workforce.

Higher Salaries

IT professionals with certifications on their résumé command better jobs, earn higher salaries, and have more doors open to new multi-industry opportunities.

Verified Strengths

Ninety-one percent of hiring managers indicate CompTIA certifications are valuable in validating IT expertise, making certification the best way to demonstrate your competency and knowledge to employers. (Source: CompTIA Employer Perceptions of IT Training and Certification.)

Universal Skills

CompTIA certifications are vendor neutral—which means that certified professionals can proficiently work with an extensive variety of hardware and software found in most organizations.

Learn	Certify	Work
Learn more about what the exam covers by reviewing the following:	Purchase a voucher at a Pearson VUE testing center or at CompTIAstore.com.	Congratulations on your CompTIA certification!

Learn

Learn more about what the exam covers by reviewing the following:

- Exam objectives for key study points.
- Sample questions for a general overview of what to expect on the exam and examples of question format.
- Visit online forums, like LinkedIn, to see what other IT professionals say about CompTIA exams.

Certify

Purchase a voucher at a Pearson VUE testing center or at CompTIAstore.com.

- Register for your exam at a Pearson VUE testing center.
- Visit pearsonvue.com/CompTIA to find the closest testing center to you.
- Schedule the exam online. You will be required to enter your voucher number or provide payment information at registration.
- Take your certification exam.

Work

Congratulations on your CompTIA certification!

- Make sure to add your certification to your résumé.
- Check out the CompTIA Certification Roadmap to plan your next career move.

Learn More: Certification.CompTIA.org/certifications/cloud

CompTIA Disclaimer

CONTENTS AT A GLANCE

1   Cloud Computing Concepts, Models, and Terminology   1

2   Disk Storage Systems   17

3   Storage Networking   35

4   Network Infrastructure   51

5   Virtualization Components   75

6   Virtualization and the Cloud   103

7   DevOps   121

8   Performance Tuning   139

9   Systems Management   159

10   Security in the Cloud   179

11   Security Best Practices   197

12   Business Continuity and Disaster Recovery   229

13   Testing, Automation, and Changes   253

14   Troubleshooting   277

A   About the Online Content   305

CONTENTS

Acknowledgments .... *xvii*

Introduction .... *xix*

Exam Readiness Checklist .... *xxii*

1   Cloud Computing Concepts, Models, and Terminology **1**

Questions 2

Quick Answer Key 7

In-Depth Answers 8

2   Disk Storage Systems **17**

Questions 18

Quick Answer Key 24

In-Depth Answers 25

3   Storage Networking **35**

Questions 36

Quick Answer Key 41

In-Depth Answers 42

4   Network Infrastructure **51**

Questions 52

Quick Answer Key 61

In-Depth Answers 62

5   Virtualization Components **75**

Questions 76

Quick Answer Key 87

In-Depth Answers 88

6 Virtualization and the Cloud **103**

Questions 104
Quick Answer Key 110
In-Depth Answers 111

7 DevOps **121**

Questions 122
Quick Answer Key 128
In-Depth Answers 129

8 Performance Tuning **139**

Questions 140
Quick Answer Key 147
In-Depth Answers 148

9 Systems Management **159**

Questions 160
Quick Answer Key 167
In-Depth Answers 168

10 Security in the Cloud **179**

Questions 180
Quick Answer Key 186
In-Depth Answers 187

11 Security Best Practices **197**

Questions 198
Quick Answer Key 210
In-Depth Answers 211

12 Business Continuity and Disaster Recovery **229**

Questions 230
Quick Answer Key 239
In-Depth Answers 240

13 Testing, Automation, and Changes **253**

    Questions 254
    Quick Answer Key 262
    In-Depth Answers 263

14 Troubleshooting **277**

    Questions 278
    Quick Answer Key 288
    In-Depth Answers 289

A About the Online Content **305**

    System Requirements 306
    Single User License Terms and Conditions 306
    Total Tester Online 307
    Performance-Based Questions 308
    Technical Support 308

ACKNOWLEDGMENTS

I would like to make known the stellar team that contributed to this book's existence. All of the following people were given raw materials that were forged into a refined product, this book.

To the amazingly skilled good people at McGraw-Hill Education including but not limited to: Amy Stonebraker, Claire Yee, Lynn Messina, Ishan Chaudhary, Janet Walden; thank you for getting this book off the ground and working with me to result in a great product!

To my superb technical editor Eric A. Vanderberg, your attention to detail contributed greatly to this project—thanks, Eric! Thanks to William McManus for the great copyediting performed on this book.

elcome to *CompTIA Cloud+ Certification Practice Exams*! This book serves as a preparation tool for the CompTIA Cloud+ certification exam (CV0-002) as well as for your work in the IT security field.

The CompTIA Cloud+ Certification Exam (Exam CV0-002)

The CompTIA Cloud+ certification exam (CV0-002) is a vendor-neutral exam that prepares candidates for configuring, managing, and supporting cloud computing environments. CompTIA recommends that exam candidates have a solid understanding of computer networking (CompTIA Network+, CompTIA Server+) and 24–36 months of IT experience related to computer networking, local and network storage technologies, or datacenter administration.

Because cloud computing depends on operating system virtualization, understanding hypervisors and virtualization is critical. Aside from cloud concepts such as cloud service models, candidates should also have experience deploying and managing a variety of cloud services through at least one public cloud provider. Most large cloud providers allow potential customers to sign up for a free trial account; if you haven't actually deployed public cloud services in the past, you should consider it as part of your exam preparation.

Exam CV0-002 consists of five categories, otherwise called "domains." CompTIA has assigned a percentage for each domain as it relates to the overall exam as follows:

Domain	Content Percentage for CV0-002
1.0 Configuration and Deployment	24 percent
2.0 Security	16 percent
3.0 Maintenance	18 percent
4.0 Management	20 percent
5.0 Troubleshooting	22 percent

Exam CV0-002 consists of multiple choice questions and performance-based questions. Multiple choice questions are designed to test your knowledge, or ability to retain information. The performance-based questions are designed to ensure you have the necessary skill to apply your knowledge to solve a business problem through cloud computing.

The performance-based questions may be on a single screen, or you may flip back and forth between two screens (most likely diagrams) to answer the question. Text will accompany any diagrams to guide you in solving a problem.

You may come across exam questions that show command-line output, performance metrics, and so on. Make sure you can interpret cloud-related performance statistics to determine where a problem might exist.

Watch the question wording carefully. It might seem all answer choices are correct for some questions, but the question might ask what is the FIRST, BEST, LAST, or NEXT thing that should be done—the sequence of how to perform tasks properly is important!

About This Book

The objective of this book is to prepare you for the CompTIA Cloud+ exam by familiarizing you with the technology and body of knowledge tested on the exam. Because the primary focus of this book is to help you pass the test, it doesn't always cover every aspect of the related technology. Some aspects of the technology are covered only to the extent necessary to help you understand what you need to know to pass the exam, but I hope this book will serve you as a valuable professional resource after your exam as well.

CompTIA Cloud+ Certification Practice Exams (Exam CV0-002) provides a battery of practice test questions organized by chapter topic. The 14 chapters contain 500 questions that cover all the objectives for the CV0-002 exam. Additionally, the accompanying website provides access to 200 more practice questions in an online, customizable test engine that enables you to take full-length practice exams in a simulated testing environment or customized quizzes by chapter or exam domain. A separate quiz of 10 performance-based questions simulates the interactive question types you are likely to encounter in the CV0-002 exam.

This book was developed and written in conjunction with the *CompTIA Cloud+ Certification Study Guide, Second Edition (Exam CV0-002)*, by Scott Wilson and Eric Vanderburg. The order the objectives are presented in is identical, as are the chapter titles.

The Exam Readiness Checklist included at the end of this introduction allows you to cross-reference the specific chapters and question numbers that cover each exam objective. These books were designed to work together as a comprehensive program for self-study.

In Every Chapter

This book is organized in such a way as to serve as an in-depth review for the CompTIA Cloud+ exam for both experienced IT security professionals and newcomers to security technologies. Each chapter covers a major aspect of cloud computing, with practice questions to test your knowledge of specific exam objectives.

Each chapter contains components that call your attention to important items and reinforce salient points. Take a look at what you'll find in every chapter:

- Every chapter begins with **Certification Objectives**—what you need to know in order to pass the section on the exam dealing with the chapter topics.
- Practice **Questions**, similar to those found on the actual exam, are included in every chapter. By answering these questions, you'll test your knowledge while becoming familiar with the structure of the exam questions.
- The **Quick Answer Key** section follows the questions and enables you easily to check your answers.
- **In-Depth Answers** at the end of every chapter include explanations for the correct and incorrect answer choices and provide an opportunity for reviewing the exam topics.

In the Online Content

Included with this book is access to the Total Tester, an online exam engine that contains even more practice questions with detailed explanations of the answers, as well as a separate quiz of performance-based questions (PBQs). Using this set of practice questions provided in the Total Tester exam engine and taking the PBQ quiz is another tool to help you prepare for the CompTIA Cloud+ exam. Please see the appendix for more information about accessing the online content.

Exam CV0-002

Exam Readiness Checklist

Domain and Objective	Ch #	Question #	Beginner	Intermediate	Expert
1.0 Configuration and Deployment					
1.1 Given a scenario, analyze system requirements to ensure successful system deployment.	1 3	1, 5, 6, 8, 10, 11, 13, 15, 16, 22 1–27			
1.2 Given a scenario, execute a provided deployment plan.	9 13	1–3, 15, 19, 23, 33 9–11, 24, 37, 46			
1.3 Given a scenario, analyze system requirements to determine if a given testing plan is appropriate.	4 11 12 13	13, 18, 21, 26–29, 30–35 3, 5–7, 15, 16, 20, 24–34 6, 9–11, 15, 17–19, 28, 29, 34, 37, 38, 40, 41, 45 1, 16–19, 21, 23, 24, 26, 28, 29, 31, 39, 40–43			
1.4 Given a scenario, analyze testing results to determine if the testing was successful in relation to given system requirements.	7 8 13 14	2–5, 7, 9, 10, 15, 27, 28, 32, 33 4, 8, 11, 13–15, 19, 21–23, 25, 31, 32, 35 1, 7, 8, 12, 18, 19, 21, 23, 24, 28–33, 39, 41, 46, 47 1, 7, 8, 12, 19, 23, 28, 29, 31–33, 41, 42, 45–47			
1.5 Given a scenario, analyze sizing, subnetting, and basic routing for a provided deployment of the virtual network.	4 9 10	7, 9, 11–13, 19, 20, 22, 24, 31, 32, 35 1, 5, 7, 13, 25, 31, 32 1, 21, 32			
1.6 Given a scenario, analyze CPU and memory sizing for a provided deployment.	5 6 13	3–6, 20, 22, 23, 27, 29, 30, 35 9–11, 13, 14, 16, 18–20, 22, 25 1, 4, 5, 8, 12, 15, 19, 20, 23, 25, 31–33, 37			
1.7 Given a scenario, analyze the appropriate storage type and protection capability for a provided deployment.	3 10 12	1, 2, 4–14, 16, 17, 21–24, 27 1, 2, 6–9, 11, 16, 21, 22, 24, 27, 30 3, 5, 6, 9–11, 19, 28–33, 37, 38, 42, 45, 46			

Exam Readiness Checklist

Domain and Objective	Ch #	Question #	Beginner	Intermediate	Expert
1.8 Given a scenario, analyze characteristics of the workload (storage, network, compute) to ensure a successful migration.	6	3–5, 7, 9, 10, 12, 17, 19, 20, 22, 25			
1.9 Given a scenario, apply elements required to extend the infrastructure into a given cloud solution.	4 5 10	1, 5, 6, 8–11, 13–15, 21, 29, 30, 33, 34 9, 10, 12–14, 25 1–5, 13–15, 17, 20, 23, 25, 26, 28, 33, 35			
2.0 Security					
2.1 Given a scenario, apply security configurations and compliance controls to meet given cloud infrastructure requirements.	9 10 11	1, 4, 7, 9, 31 1–12, 14, 16–18, 23, 26–31 3, 5–7, 9, 11–15, 17, 19–21, 27–29, 33, 42, 46			
2.2 Given a scenario, apply the appropriate ACL to the target objects to meet access requirements according to a security template.	10	15, 21–25, 27, 32–35			
2.3 Given a cloud service model, implement defined security technologies to meet given security requirements.	10 11	1, 2, 6–9, 11, 25, 33–35 3, 5–7, 11, 12, 20, 34, 36, 39, 43			
2.4 Given a cloud service model, apply the appropriate security automation technique to the target system.	10 13	20, 23, 28, 29 9, 24, 34, 35, 41			
3.0 Maintenance					
3.1 Given a cloud service model, determine the appropriate methodology to apply given patches.	9	8, 10–14, 16, 18, 19, 21, 22, 27, 28, 31, 33, 34			
3.2 Given a scenario, apply the appropriate automation tools to update cloud elements.	9 13	16, 19, 25, 27–29, 33 33, 34, 37, 38			
3.3 Given a scenario, apply an appropriate backup or restore method.	12	1, 3, 5, 7, 9–11, 14, 22–25, 29–31, 34–36, 46			

Exam Readiness Checklist

Domain and Objective	Ch #	Question #	Beginner	Intermediate	Expert
3.4 Given a cloud-based scenario, apply appropriate disaster recovery methods.	12	1, 2, 4–7, 9–11, 14, 20, 21, 26, 29, 32, 33, 36, 38–40, 43, 45			
3.5 Given a cloud-based scenario, apply the appropriate steps to ensure business continuity.	12	5, 7, 11–13, 15, 16, 18, 26, 28, 30, 32–34, 37, 39, 42, 43			
3.6 Given a scenario, apply the appropriate maintenance automation technique to the target objects.	8 11 13	2, 5, 12, 13, 15, 17, 21, 23, 24, 30 3, 10, 17, 18, 21, 39–41, 43, 44 9, 14, 34, 37, 42, 46			
4.0 Management					
4.1 Given a scenario, analyze defined metrics to determine the presence of an abnormality and/or forecast future needed cloud resources.	7	2, 3, 5, 6, 9, 10, 12–16, 31, 33			
4.2 Given a scenario, determine the appropriate allocation of cloud resources.	1 8 9 13	3, 8, 16, 20, 22–24 3–5, 22 5, 21, 22 7, 13, 14, 16, 36			
4.3 Given a scenario, determine when to provision/deprovision cloud resources.	6 7	1, 5, 14, 16, 21, 22, 25 1, 12–15, 22, 24–26, 32, 33			
4.4 Given a scenario, implement account provisioning techniques in a cloud environment to meet security and policy requirements.	10 11	1, 2, 13, 15, 21–24, 31–35 4, 8, 10, 13, 20–23, 34–42, 44			
4.5 Given a scenario, analyze deployment results to confirm they meet the baseline.	13	12, 15, 19, 21–23, 25, 26, 33, 34, 46			
4.6 Given a specific environment and related data (e.g., performance, capacity, trends), apply appropriate changes to meet expected criteria.	7 8 13	9, 10, 15, 27, 33 4, 6–8, 11, 19–23, 25, 27, 31–35 7, 14, 15, 18, 19, 21, 23, 24, 42			
4.7 Given SLA requirements, determine the appropriate metrics to report.	9	1–6, 20, 29			

Exam Readiness Checklist

Domain and Objective	Ch #	Question #	Beginner	Intermediate	Expert
5.0 Troubleshooting					
5.1 Given a scenario, troubleshoot a deployment issue.	14	20, 22, 33, 35–39			
5.2 Given a scenario, troubleshoot common capacity issues.	14	11, 14, 18, 19, 28, 36, 40–43, 47, 48			
5.3 Given a scenario, troubleshoot automation/orchestration issues.	14	36, 42, 44, 45, 47, 48			
5.4 Given a scenario, troubleshoot connectivity issues.	14	1–4, 7, 23, 24, 30, 38, 46			
5.5 Given a scenario, troubleshoot security issues.	14	20, 26, 27, 29, 35, 39, 42, 44			
5.6 Given a scenario, explain the troubleshooting methodology.	14	12, 15, 16, 32			

Chapter 1

Cloud Computing Concepts, Models, and Terminology

CERTIFICATION OBJECTIVES

1.01   Cloud Service Models

1.02   Cloud Deployment Models and Services

1.03   Cloud Characteristics and Terms

1.04   Object Storage Concepts

QUESTIONS

Cloud computing is attractive to many organizations because it puts the focus on business processes and the delivery of goods and services instead of on the underlying technology that makes it all happen.

The attraction also lies in not having to absorb up-front costs related to IT hardware, software, and licensing, as well as other costs related to IT system installation, configuration, and ongoing maintenance.

1. Your organization has decided to use cloud storage for long-term archiving of financial records. Which type of cloud service model is this?
   A. SaaS
   B. PaaS
   C. IaaS
   D. CaaS

2. Instead of hosting an on-premises PBX telephony solution, your organization has chosen to outsource this to a public cloud provider. Which category of cloud services does this apply to?
   A. CaaS
   B. SaaS
   C. PaaS
   D. IaaS

3. Marcia is an IT consultant for a medium-sized medical practice. She has been asked to determine which outsourced cloud solutions would best meet regulatory requirements for the health industry. Which type of cloud is best suited for this scenario?
   A. Private
   B. Public
   C. Health
   D. Community

4. Software developers are most likely to consume which type of cloud service model?
   A. SaaS
   B. PaaS
   C. CaaS
   D. IaaS

5. Your company stores budget forecasting data on a local file server at headquarters. An on-premises virtual machine periodically replicates file server data to the public cloud as an off-site backup. What type of cloud is used for this scenario?

   A. Community

   B. Private

   C. Hybrid

   D. Public

6. Which of the following are cloud computing characteristics? Choose two.

   A. Tracking the amount of hours a virtual machine has been running

   B. Running virtual machines on a hypervisor

   C. Centralized patch management

   D. Automatically adding virtual machines to meet application workload demands

7. Refer to the diagram in Figure 1-1. Which term best describes the scenario?

   A. Cloud reaching

   B. Active cloud computing

   C. Passive cloud computing

   D. Cloud bursting

FIGURE 1-1

Custom
application cloud
environment

Private Cloud	Public Cloud
On-premises custom application with occasional performance spikes	Additional virtual machines are provisioned as needed

8. A public website experiences unpredictable usage spikes that have historically slowed down the application to unacceptable levels. What should be configured to ensure performance is optimal during usage spikes?

   A. Faster Internet connection from on premises to the cloud

   B. Auto-scaling

   C. Reduced virtual machine logging

   D. Content delivery network

9. Your organization uses a private cloud for various departments. Resource usage is tracked for each department for the purpose of _____.

   A. Chargeback

   B. Depreciation

   C. Disaster recovery planning

   D. Penetration testing

10. Developers in your organization make improvements to various web applications regularly. Currently, the process involves the manual deployment of cloud-based virtual machines, web server configurations, and back-end databases. What should be used to streamline this workflow?

    A. Configuration management

    B. Operating system imaging

    C. Cloud bursting

    D. Orchestration

11. In Figure 1-2, match the terms on the left with the associated descriptions on the right.

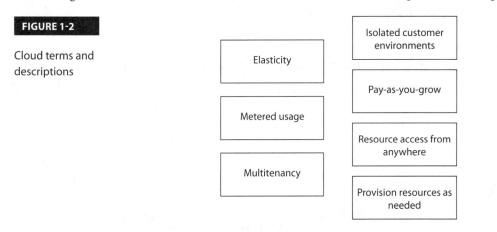

FIGURE 1-2

Cloud terms and descriptions

Elasticity

Metered usage

Multitenancy

Isolated customer environments

Pay-as-you-grow

Resource access from anywhere

Provision resources as needed

12. Project managers complain that storing files in the cloud for a variety of projects makes it difficult to locate files related to a single project. Which solution involves the least amount of administrative effort?

    A. Add project name metadata to cloud-stored files

    B. Configure each project in its own cloud tenancy

    C. Enable file auto-scaling

    D. Enable departmental chargeback

13. Which of the following statements regarding cloud computing are correct? Choose two.

    A. Infrastructure provisioning time is increased.

    B. IT capital expenditures are increased.

    C. Infrastructure provisioning time is decreased.

    D. IT capital expenditures are decreased.

14. In which cloud computing model does virtual machine operating system patching fall under the cloud provider's responsibility? Choose two.

    A. SaaS

    B. IaaS

    C. PaaS

    D. XaaS

15. Which type of document details baseline performance measurements for cloud resource performance?

    A. BIA

    B. BCP

    C. DRP

    D. SLA

16. You are responsible for the migration of an on-premises Human Resources department web application to the public cloud. Which of the following must you do? Choose two.

    A. Identify source hosts

    B. Enable cloud bursting

    C. Identify target hosts

    D. Encrypt all cloud content

17. Zoey, an executive, asks the IT team to provide a list of pros and cons related to the use of cloud computing. Which of the following are benefits of cloud computing? Choose two.

    A. Increased control of IT resources

    B. Rapid deployment of IT resources

    C. Focus on using technology instead of configuring it

    D. SLA created by the cloud tenant

18. Which cloud data option provides high availability?

    A. SLA

    B. Virtual machines

    C. Replicas

    D. BLOBs

19. Which statement regarding a single SaaS offering is true?

    A. Each cloud tenant runs an instance of the same application.

    B. Each cloud tenant runs an instance of a separate application.

    C. The cloud provider is responsible for data backup.

    D. Cloud tenant data is accessible to other tenants.

20. Which of the following statements are correct? Choose two.

    A. Cloud bursting relates to private and public cloud IT solutions.

    B. Cloud bursting must be performed manually on-demand.

    C. Elasticity allows for rapid resource provisioning.

    D. Elasticity must be performed manually on-demand.

21. Outsourcing VoIP IT systems to public cloud providers is a form of _____.

    A. SaaS

    B. PaaS

    C. CaaS

    D. IaaS

22. What is used by software developers to hook into cloud-provided programmatic libraries?

    A. Baseline

    B. Object ID

    C. API

    D. Auto-scaling

23. Cloud data replication falls under which type of cloud model?

    A. CaaS

    B. IaaS

    C. PaaS

    D. SaaS

24. Which benefit is realized by developers using public cloud PaaS?

    A. Quicker time to market

    B. More control than an on-premises equivalent solution

    C. No dependency on network connections

    D. Wider selection of programming tools than an on-premises equivalent solution

A QUICK ANSWER KEY

1. C
2. A
3. D
4. B
5. C
6. A, D
7. D

8. B
9. A
10. D
11. See "In-Depth Answers."
12. A
13. C, D

14. A, C
15. D
16. A, C
17. B, C
18. C
19. A
20. A, C

21. C
22. C
23. B
24. A

IN-DEPTH ANSWERS

1. Your organization has decided to use cloud storage for long-term archiving of financial records. Which type of cloud service model is this?
    A. SaaS
    B. PaaS
    C. IaaS
    D. CaaS

    ☑   **C.** Storage is considered Infrastructure as a Service (IaaS).
    ☒   **A, B,** and **D** are incorrect. Software as a Service (SaaS) allows thin client devices to access a network application running on cloud provider equipment. Platform as a Service (PaaS) refers to databases and tools made available to developers without setting up the underlying IT infrastructure. Communication as a Service (CaaS) offers hosted PBX, VoIP, and other communications configurations in the cloud.

2. Instead of hosting an on-premises PBX telephony solution, your organization has chosen to outsource this to a public cloud provider. Which category of cloud services does this apply to?
    A. CaaS
    B. SaaS
    C. PaaS
    D. IaaS

    ☑   **A.** Communication as a Service (CaaS) offers hosted PBX, VoIP, and other communications configurations in the cloud.
    ☒   **B, C,** and **D** are incorrect. Software as a Service (SaaS) allows thin client devices to access a network application running on cloud provider equipment. Platform as a Service (PaaS) refers to databases and tools made available to developers without setting up the underlying IT infrastructure. Infrastructure as a Service (IaaS) refers to cloud offerings such as storage, virtual machines, and network configurations.

3. Marcia is an IT consultant for a medium-sized medical practice. She has been asked to determine which outsourced cloud solutions would best meet regulatory requirements for the health industry. Which type of cloud is best suited for this scenario?

A. Private

B. Public

C. Health

D. Community

☑   **D.** Community clouds service the same set of needs across a group of organizations, often within the same industry.

☒   **A, B,** and **C** are incorrect. Private clouds are not outsourced and use hardware and software owned exclusively by a single organization. Public clouds are available to all Internet users and offer a wide variety of IT computing needs that run on cloud provider infrastructure. Health clouds are not a type of cloud model.

4. Software developers are most likely to consume which type of cloud service model?

A. SaaS

B. PaaS

C. CaaS

D. IaaS

☑   **B.** Platform as a Service (PaaS) refers to databases and tools made available to developers without setting up the underlying IT infrastructure.

☒   **A, C,** and **D** are incorrect. Software as a Service (SaaS) allows thin client devices to access a network application running on cloud provider equipment. Communication as a Service (CaaS) offers hosted PBX, VoIP, and other communications configurations in the cloud. Infrastructure as a Service (IaaS) refers to cloud offerings such as storage, virtual machines, and network configurations.

5. Your company stores budget forecasting data on a local file server at headquarters. An on-premises virtual machine periodically replicates file server data to the public cloud as an off-site backup. What type of cloud is used for this scenario?

A. Community

B. Private

C. Hybrid

D. Public

☑   **C.** Hybrid clouds allow organizations to benefit from both on-premises private cloud resources and public clouds, such as data being created on premises and replicated to the cloud for long-term storage. Remember that simply running virtual machines on premises does not constitute a private cloud.

☒   **A, B,** and **D** are incorrect. Community clouds service the same set of needs across a group of organizations, often within the same industry. Private clouds are not outsourced and use hardware and software owned exclusively by a single organization. Public clouds are available to all Internet users and offer a wide variety of IT computing needs that run on cloud provider infrastructure.

6. Which of the following are cloud computing characteristics? Choose two.

   A. Tracking the amount of hours a virtual machine has been running
   B. Running virtual machines on a hypervisor
   C. Centralized patch management
   D. Automatically adding virtual machines to meet application workload demands

   ☑ **A** and **D.** Tracking cloud resource usage is also called metering, similar to water or electricity, where you are charged based on usage. Auto-scaling can automatically add virtual machines to support an IT workload when usage increases. Both of these are cloud characteristics: metered usage and rapid/elastic provisioning.

   ☒ **B** and **C** are incorrect. Virtualization itself does not define cloud computing, although it does make cloud computing possible. While important, patch management is not a cloud computing characteristic.

7. Refer to the diagram in Figure 1-1. Which term best describes the scenario?

   A. Cloud reaching
   B. Active cloud computing
   C. Passive cloud computing
   D. Cloud bursting

FIGURE 1-1

Custom application cloud environment

Private Cloud	Public Cloud
On-premises custom application with occasional performance spikes	Additional virtual machines are provisioned as needed

   ☑ **D.** Cloud bursting provisions public cloud IT resources on demand when on-premises IT resources are depleted. This is often achieved with a secure connection from on premises to the public cloud provider through a site-to-site VPN, although this is not a requirement.

   ☒ **A, B,** and **C** are incorrect. Cloud reaching is not a valid cloud computing term. While active and passive could be applied to failover cluster node configurations, they do not apply to cloud computing.

8. A public website experiences unpredictable usage spikes that have historically slowed down the application to unacceptable levels. What should be configured to ensure performance is optimal during usage spikes?

   A. Faster Internet connection from on premises to the cloud
   B. Auto-scaling

C. Reduced virtual machine logging

D. Content delivery network

☑ **B.** Auto-scaling can provide additional virtual machines to handle heavy workloads. This can be triggered automatically, such as when the average existing CPU usage or network usage exceeds a configured value, or it can be scheduled for predictable workloads.

☒ **A, C,** and **D** are incorrect. A faster Internet connection from on premises to the cloud doesn't improve the user experience for a public website where users are connecting from other locations. Lessening virtual machine logging levels is not nearly as effective in responding to peak demands as auto-scaling is. Content delivery networks (CDNs) place website content geographically near the user base to reduce network latency. This will not make a difference during usage spikes as auto-scaling will.

9. Your organization uses a private cloud for various departments. Resource usage is tracked for each department for the purpose of _____.

A. Chargeback

B. Depreciation

C. Disaster recovery planning

D. Penetration testing

☑ **A.** Metered usage of cloud resources, including private clouds, allow departmental chargeback for the specific IT resources used by a particular department.

☒ **B, C,** and **D** are incorrect. Calculating depreciation, planning for disasters, and actively testing vulnerabilities are not directly related to the tracking of resource usage within a private cloud.

10. Developers in your organization make improvements to various web applications regularly. Currently, the process involves the manual deployment of cloud-based virtual machines, web server configurations, and back-end databases. What should be used to streamline this workflow?

A. Configuration management

B. Operating system imaging

C. Cloud bursting

D. Orchestration

☑ **D.** Orchestration tools automate repetitive workflows to reduce errors and increase efficiency.

☒ **A, B,** and **C** are incorrect. Configuration management often comes in the form of a centralized tool that manages the configuration of many managed devices. Operating system imaging is used for the mass deployment of the same operating system and settings from a reference image captured on a reference computer. Cloud bursting provisions public cloud IT resources on demand when on-premises IT resources are depleted. This is often achieved with a secure connection from on premises to the public cloud provider through a site-to-site VPN, although this is not a requirement.

11. In Figure 1-2, match the terms on the left with the associated descriptions on the right.

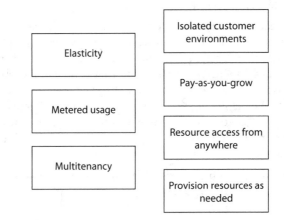

FIGURE 1-2

Cloud terms and descriptions

Figure 1-3 shows the correct matching of cloud terms and their descriptions. Elasticity allows cloud customers to provision and deprovision IT resources such as storage, or virtual machines, as needed. Metered usage adheres to the pay-as-you-go, or pay-as-you-grow, mentality where fees are charged only on usage. Multitenancy provides many customer computing environments within a single cloud provider, with each customer configuration settings and data kept isolated from other tenants.

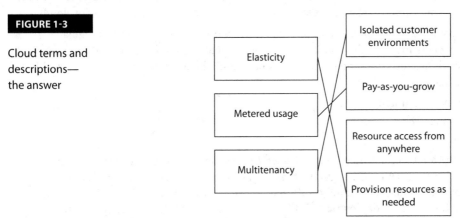

FIGURE 1-3

Cloud terms and descriptions— the answer

12. Project managers complain that storing files in the cloud for a variety of projects makes it difficult to locate files related to a single project. Which solution involves the least amount of administrative effort?

A.   Add project name metadata to cloud-stored files

B.   Configure each project in its own cloud tenancy

C. Enable file auto-scaling

D. Enable departmental chargeback

☑ **A.** Cloud resources can be "tagged," which means additional information, or metadata, can be associated with the resource. For example, tagging files related to ProjectX as "ProjectX" would facilitate searching and organization among many cloud-stored files.

☒ **B, C,** and **D** are incorrect. While each project manager could acquire their own cloud account, this involves more effort than tagging files with metadata. Auto-scaling can provide additional virtual machines to handle heavy workloads, but this does not solve the problem of organizing project files. Charging departments for cloud resource usage is a billing and cost management benefit but does not help with unorganized project files.

13. Which of the following statements regarding cloud computing are correct? Choose two.

A. Infrastructure provisioning time is increased.

B. IT capital expenditures are increased.

C. Infrastructure provisioning time is decreased.

D. IT capital expenditures are decreased.

☑ **C** and **D.** Cloud providers are responsible for ensuring that adequate resources can be provisioned on demand by customers; this is much quicker than provisioning resources on premises. Because equipment, software, and licenses need not be acquired with most public cloud computing resources, there is less up-front cost. Note that some cloud software such as databases can use existing licenses that have already been acquired; this is called Bring Your Own License (BYOL).

☒ **A** and **B** are incorrect. Provisioning resources is made more efficient with cloud computing, not less efficient. IT capital costs are not increased since cloud computing normally incurs a small monthly subscription fee plus any resource usage charges.

14. In which cloud computing model does virtual machine operating system patching fall under the cloud provider's responsibility? Choose two.

A. SaaS

B. IaaS

C. PaaS

D. XaaS

☑ **A** and **C.** SaaS and PaaS. With these cloud models, the underlying virtual machines are managed by the cloud provider.

☒ **B** and **D** are incorrect. With IaaS, cloud customers deploy virtual machines in the cloud and are responsible for the patching and configuration of those virtual machines. Anything as a Service (XaaS) is not a specific cloud model; it refers to the delivery of some kind of IT service in a cloud environment.

15. Which type of document details baseline performance measurements for cloud resource performance?

A. BIA

B. BCP

C. DRP

D. SLA

☑ **D.** The service level agreement (SLA) is a contract between a cloud provider and cloud consumer that details expected performance for a specific cloud service. Note that it is normal to have different SLAs for varying cloud services.

☒ **A, B,** and **C** are incorrect. A business impact analysis (BIA) identifies threats and the impact they could have against business continuity. A business continuity plan (BCP) relies on the BIA to determine what controls will be put in place to mitigate accepted threats. The disaster recovery plan (DRP) details how to return a failed system of some kind to a functional state with a minimum of downtime.

16. You are responsible for the migration of an on-premises Human Resources department web application to the public cloud. Which of the following must you do? Choose two.

A. Identify source hosts

B. Enable cloud bursting

C. Identify target hosts

D. Encrypt all cloud content

☑ **A** and **C.** The source hosts where existing web application components reside must be identified. Suitable targets, such as cloud-based virtual machines, must then be selected.

☒ **B** and **D** are incorrect. Cloud bursting and content encryption are not requirements for the migration of on-premises IT services to the public cloud.

17. Zoey, an executive, asks the IT team to provide a list of pros and cons related to the use of cloud computing. Which of the following are benefits of cloud computing? Choose two.

A. Increased control of IT resources

B. Rapid deployment of IT resources

C. Focus on using technology instead of configuring it

D. SLA created by the cloud tenant

☑ **B** and **C.** Cloud computing uses pooled underlying IT resources, which allows for the rapid deployment of cloud resources by cloud consumers. This way customers have more time to focus on their specific business functions instead of the supporting technology.

☒ **A** and **D** are incorrect. Cloud computing actually results in less control of IT resources, from a cloud consumer perspective, since much of the underlying complexities are managed by the cloud provider. While SLAs are sometimes negotiable, they are not created by cloud tenants.

18. Which cloud data option provides high availability?

A. SLA

B. Virtual machines

C. Replicas

D. BLOBs

☑ **C.** Having copies (replicas) of data, whether specific files, databases, and so on, results in high availability; if one copy of the data is unavailable, others will be.

☒ **A, B,** and **D** are incorrect. SLAs outline expected performance and availability values, but they do not themselves provide high availability. Virtual machines and Binary Large Objects (BLOBs) can benefit from replication, but they themselves do not provide high availability.

19. Which statement regarding a single SaaS offering is true?

A. Each cloud tenant runs an instance of the same application.

B. Each cloud tenant runs an instance of a separate application.

C. The cloud provider is responsible for data backup.

D. Cloud tenant data is accessible to other tenants.

☑ **A.** SaaS defines software used over a network that is provided and managed by a cloud provider. The provider ensures the software application is running and patched.

☒ **B, C,** and **D** are incorrect. Cloud tenants using the same SaaS cloud offering use the same software but different instances of that software. Cloud customers are responsible for managing data that results from SaaS application usage. Each cloud tenant then runs their own instance of the same app while their settings and data are isolated for other tenants.

20. Which of the following statements are correct? Choose two.

A. Cloud bursting relates to private and public cloud IT solutions.

B. Cloud bursting must be performed manually on-demand.

C. Elasticity allows for rapid resource provisioning.

D. Elasticity must be performed manually on-demand.

☑ **A and C.** Cloud bursting allows an organization to use public cloud resources when private cloud resources are depleted, where elasticity allows for quick provisioning and deprovisioning of resources.

☒ **B and D** are incorrect. Cloud bursting and elastic cloud resource provisioning can be automated.

21. Outsourcing VoIP IT systems to public cloud providers is a form of _____.

A. SaaS

B. PaaS

C. CaaS

D. IaaS

☑ **C.** Communication as a Service (CaaS) offers hosted PBX, VoIP, and other communications configurations in the cloud.

☒ **A, B,** and **D** are incorrect. Software as a Service (SaaS) allows thin client devices to access a network application running on cloud provider equipment. Platform as a Service (PaaS) refers to databases and tools made available to developers without setting up the underlying IT infrastructure. Infrastructure as a Service (IaaS) refers to cloud offerings such as storage, virtual machines, and network configurations.

22. What is used by software developers to hook into cloud-provided programmatic libraries?

    A. Baseline

    B. Object ID

    C. API

    D. Auto-scaling

    ☑ **C.** Application programming interfaces (APIs) expose functionality that can be automated, such as for the management of cloud-based virtual machines.

    ☒ **A, B,** and **D** are incorrect. Baselines establish a standard for configurations or performance against which future configurations or performance metrics are compared. Object IDs are unique values used to track cloud resources. Auto-scaling can provide additional virtual machines to handle heavy workloads.

23. Cloud data replication falls under which type of cloud model?

    A. CaaS

    B. IaaS

    C. PaaS

    D. SaaS

    ☑ **B.** Infrastructure as a Service (IaaS) refers to cloud offerings such as storage, virtual machines, and network configurations. Since replication applies to various forms of storage, it is considered IaaS.

    ☒ **A, C,** and **D** are incorrect. Communication as a Service (CaaS) offers hosted PBX, VoIP, and other communications configurations in the cloud. Platform as a Service (PaaS) refers to databases and tools made available to developers without setting up the underlying IT infrastructure. Software as a Service (SaaS) allows thin client devices to access a network application running on cloud provider equipment.

24. Which benefit is realized by developers using public cloud PaaS?

    A. Quicker time to market

    B. More control than an on-premises equivalent solution

    C. No dependency on network connections

    D. Wider selection of programming tools than an on-premises equivalent solution

    ☑ **A.** Because the underlying complexities (networking, virtual machines, database installation, etc.) are handled already, software development takes less time, which means a quicker time to market.

    ☒ **B, C,** and **D** are incorrect. Cloud solutions reduce the amount of control (and complexity) related to IT systems. A network connection is required to access public cloud services. PaaS solutions offer a limited set of programming tools compared to what could be chosen on premises.

Chapter 2

Disk Storage Systems

CERTIFICATION OBJECTIVES

2.01   Disk Types and Configurations

2.02   Tiering

2.03   File System Types

QUESTIONS

Cloud storage is based on technologies that have long been used, such as SCSI and SATA. The cloud provides self-provisioning, metered usage, and elasticity of storage resources based on these storage standards.

While public cloud providers take care of the underlying storage technologies, knowledge of disk types, interfaces, file systems, and RAID configurations is critical when setting up a private cloud.

1. What type of storage drive has no moving parts?
   A. DAS
   B. HDD
   C. NAS
   D. SSD

2. Which of the following network types is designed solely for storage traffic?
   A. SSD
   B. DAS
   C. NAS
   D. Fibre Channel

3. You are configuring an on-premises hypervisor host with storage connected locally to the server. What type of storage is this?
   A. SAN
   B. NAS
   C. DAS
   D. iSCSI

4. Your cloud provider allows frequently accessed data to reside on fast storage while less utilized data is migrated to slower storage. What type of configuration is this?
   A. RAID 1
   B. Storage tiers
   C. IOPS
   D. SSD

5. Which of the following is not a hard disk drive (HDD) interface?

    A. NAS

    B. SAS

    C. SCSI

    D. SATA

6. Which RAID level uses mirroring to duplicate data?

    A. RAID 0

    B. RAID 1

    C. RAID 5

    D. RAID 6

7. You are responsible for the configuration of a storage array for a private cloud. Performance is the highest priority in order to support a heavily used database transaction system. Which level of RAID should you configure in the array?

    A. RAID 0

    B. RAID 1

    C. RAID 5

    D. RAID 6

8. Which RAID level combines striping with mirroring?

    A. RAID 0

    B. RAID 1

    C. RAID 10

    D. RAID 6

9. Which RAID level can tolerate the loss of two disks in the array?

    A. RAID 0

    B. RAID 1

    C. RAID 5

    D. RAID 6

10. Your Windows server holds contract documents on an NTFS disk volume. Users make revisions to documents before they are finalized. You need to ensure previous versions of files are available to users. What should you configure?

    A. Journaling

    B. Volume shadow copies

    C. File classification

    D. System restore points

11. What of the following is *not* a benefit of using a Fibre Channel network compared to SCSI?

A. Shared storage devices

B. Distance

C. Cost

D. Number of devices

12. Which of the following terms is associated with hierarchical storage management?

A. Fibre Channel

B. Virtualization

C. iSCSI

D. Storage tier

13. Your on-premises users synchronize cloud files to their Windows laptops. Corporate security policies dictate that locally stored files must be encrypted for the user. What should be configured on user laptops?

A. BitLocker

B. EFS

C. PKI

D. TPM

14. Which storage tier should be used for long-term data archiving?

A. Tier 1

B. Tier 2

C. Tier 3

D. Tier 4

15. Which statements regarding SSDs are true? Choose two.

A. They withstand vibrations better than hard disk drives.

B. They are quieter than hard disk drives.

C. They are slower than hard drives.

D. They use rotating platters.

16. What statement relates to a disadvantage of using SSDs?

A. They are more expensive than hard disk drives.

B. They are louder than hard disk drives.

C. They are slower than hard drives.

D. They do not withstand vibrations as well as hard disk drives.

17. What term describes the time it takes for a hard disk actuator arm to move to the correct location?

A. IOPS value

B. Rotational latency

C. Seek time

D. Transfer rate

18. Which term describes the time it takes for a hard disk platter to spin to the correct location?
  - A. IOPS value
  - B. Rotational latency
  - C. Seek time
  - D. Transfer rate

19. Which RAID level is depicted in Figure 2-1?
  - A. RAID 0
  - B. RAID 1
  - C. RAID 5
  - D. RAID 6

FIGURE 2-1

Disk striping

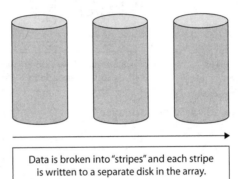

Data is broken into "stripes" and each stripe
is written to a separate disk in the array.

20. Which RAID level is depicted in Figure 2-2?
  - A. RAID 0
  - B. RAID 1
  - C. RAID 5
  - D. RAID 6

FIGURE 2-2

Disk mirroring

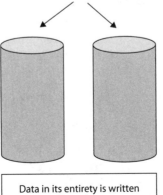

Data in its entirety is written
to two separate disks.

21. Which RAID level is depicted in Figure 2-3?

    A. RAID 0

    B. RAID 1

    C. RAID 5

    D. RAID 6

FIGURE 2-3

Disk striping
with parity

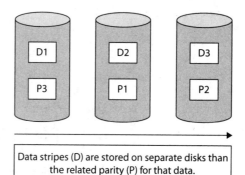

Data stripes (D) are stored on separate disks than
the related parity (P) for that data.

22. Which data tier has the best performance?

    A. Tier 1

    B. Tier 2

    C. Tier 3

    D. Tier 4

23. RAID 1 requires a minimum of how many disks?

    A. Two

    B. Three

    C. Four

    D. Five

24. Which RAID level provides no redundancy?

    A. RAID 0

    B. RAID 1

    C. RAID 5

    D. RAID 6

25. You are planning the storage requirements for a two-disk mirror of a server operating system disk partition. How much disk space is usable in the mirrored volume?

A. 10 percent

B. 30 percent

C. 50 percent

D. 75 percent

26. RAID 5 requires a minimum of how many disks?

A. Two

B. Three

C. Four

D. Five

27. RAID 6 requires a minimum of how many disks?

A. Two

B. Three

C. Four

D. Five

28. Which user key decrypts EFS data?

A. Private

B. Public

C. Symmetric

D. Asymmetric

QUICK ANSWER KEY

1. D	**8.** C	**15.** A, B	**22.** A
2. D	**9.** D	**16.** A	**23.** A
3. C	**10.** B	**17.** C	**24.** A
4. B	**11.** C	**18.** B	**25.** C
5. A	**12.** D	**19.** A	**26.** B
6. B	**13.** B	**20.** B	**27.** C
7. A	**14.** D	**21.** C	**28.** A

IN-DEPTH ANSWERS

1. What type of storage drive has no moving parts?
   A. DAS
   B. HDD
   C. NAS
   D. SSD

   ☑ **D.** Solid state drive (SSD) storage drives do not have moving parts as traditional hard disk drives do, which results in faster access times, less power consumption and heat, and less noise.
   ☒ **A, B,** and **C** are incorrect. Direct attached storage (DAS) devices are locally accessible by a machine without traversing a network. Hard disk drives (HDDs) have rotating platters with an actuator arm that is used to read and write data to and from the platters. Network attached storage (NAS) provides storage over a standard computer network using standard file sharing protocols such as CIFS and NFS; it is not a type of storage drive.

2. Which of the following network types is designed solely for storage traffic?
   A. SSD
   B. DAS
   C. NAS
   D. Fibre Channel

   ☑ **D.** Fibre Channel networks are designed to transmit disk commands between hosts and storage arrays at high speeds. This type of network does not support any other type of traffic including TCP/IP.
   ☒ **A, B,** and **C** are incorrect. Solid state drive (SSD) storage devices do not have moving parts as traditional hard disk drives do, which results in faster access times, less power consumption and heat, and less noise. Direct attached storage (DAS) devices are locally accessible by a machine without traversing a network. Network attached storage (NAS) provides storage over a standard computer network using standard file sharing protocols such as CIFS and NFS.

3. You are configuring an on-premises hypervisor host with storage connected locally to the server. What type of storage is this?
   A. SAN
   B. NAS
   C. DAS
   D. iSCSI

   ☑ **C.** Direct attached storage (DAS) devices are locally accessible by a machine without traversing a network.
   ☒ **A, B,** and **D** are incorrect. A storage area network (SAN) allows hosts to read and write from storage over a network as if that storage were available to the host locally. Network attached storage (NAS) provides storage over a standard computer network using standard file sharing protocols such as CIFS and NFS. iSCSI places standard SCSI disk commands into TCP/IP packets, which are then sent to network storage devices where the SCSI commands are exposed and executed.

4. Your cloud provider allows frequently accessed data to reside on fast storage while less utilized data is migrated to slower storage. What type of configuration is this?
   A. RAID 1
   B. Storage tiers
   C. IOPS
   D. SSD

   ☑ **B.** Storage tiers use policies to determine what type of data is stored on specific types of storage for the purposes of performance, high availability, and archiving.
   ☒ **A, C,** and **D** are incorrect. RAID 1 (disk mirroring) uses a minimum of two disks to write a copy of data to a separate disk, which provides fault tolerance. Input/output operations per second (IOPS) is a unit of performance measurement related to on-premises and cloud storage. Solid state drive (SSD) storage devices do not have moving parts as traditional hard disk drives do, which results in faster access times, less power consumption and heat, and less noise.

5. Which of the following is not a hard disk drive (HDD) interface?
   A. NAS
   B. SAS
   C. SCSI
   D. SATA

   ☑ **A.** Network attached storage (NAS) provides storage over a standard computer network using standard file sharing protocols such as CIFS and NFS. It is a storage network standard, not a hard disk drive interface type.
   ☒ **B, C,** and **D** are incorrect. Serial Attached SCSI (SAS) supersedes the old SCSI parallel data transmission standard. Small Computer System Interface (SCSI) is a standard stemming from the late 1970s that places devices such as printers and hard disks with configured unique IDs on a parallel data bus. The Serial ATA (SATA) disk interface supersedes PATA and allows very large disks to be used at higher speeds while using a smaller cable.

6. Which RAID level uses mirroring to duplicate data?

   A. RAID 0

   B. RAID 1

   C. RAID 5

   D. RAID 6

   ☑ **B.** RAID 1 (disk mirroring) uses a minimum of two disks to write a copy of data to a separate disk, which provides fault tolerance.

   ☒ **A, C,** and **D** are incorrect. RAID 0 (disk striping) uses a minimum of two disks where each data write is spread out among the drives, which results in a performance benefit. RAID 5 (disk striping with distributed parity) uses a minimum of three disks to spread out data and recovery information across the disks in the array, which increases fault tolerance and performance. RAID 5 can tolerate the failure of one disk. RAID 6 enhances RAID 5 by using two parity blocks written across the array, which increases fault tolerance such that the array remains stable even if two disks fail.

7. You are responsible for the configuration of a storage array for a private cloud. Performance is the highest priority in order to support a heavily used database transaction system. Which level of RAID should you configure in the array?

   A. RAID 0

   B. RAID 1

   C. RAID 5

   D. RAID 6

   ☑ **A.** RAID 0 (disk striping) uses a minimum of two disks where each data write is spread out among the drives, which results in a performance benefit.

   ☒ **B, C,** and **D** are incorrect. RAID 1 (disk mirroring) uses a minimum of two disks to write a copy of data to a separate disk, which provides fault tolerance. RAID 5 (disk striping with distributed parity) uses a minimum of three disks to spread out data and recovery information across the disks in the array, which increases fault tolerance and performance. RAID 5 can tolerate the failure of one disk. RAID 6 enhances RAID 5 by using two parity blocks written across the array, which increases fault tolerance such that the array remains stable even if two disks fail.

8. Which RAID level combines striping with mirroring?

   A. RAID 0

   B. RAID 1

   C. RAID 10

   D. RAID 6

   ☑ **C.** RAID 10, or 1+0, requires a minimum of four disks (two groups of two) where within each group data is mirrored, then that mirrored group data is striped to (written across) another set of disks.

   ☒ **A, B,** and **D** are incorrect. RAID 0 (disk striping) uses a minimum of two disks where each data write is spread out among the drives, which results in a performance benefit. RAID 1 (disk mirroring) uses a minimum of two disks to write a copy of data to a separate disk, which provides fault tolerance. RAID 6 enhances RAID 5 by using two parity blocks written across the array, which increases fault tolerance such that the array remains stable even if two disks fail.

9. Which RAID level can tolerate the loss of two disks in the array?

A. RAID 0

B. RAID 1

C. RAID 5

D. RAID 6

☑ **D.** RAID 6 enhances RAID 5 by using two parity blocks written across the array, which increases fault tolerance such that the array remains stable even if two disks fail.

☒ **A, B,** and **C** are incorrect. RAID 0 (disk striping) uses a minimum of two disks where each data write is spread out among the drives, which results in a performance benefit. RAID 1 (disk mirroring) uses a minimum of two disks to write a copy of data to a separate disk, which provides fault tolerance. RAID 5 (disk striping with distributed parity) uses a minimum of three disks to spread out data and recovery information across the disks in the array, which increases fault tolerance and performance. RAID 5 can tolerate the failure of one disk.

10. Your Windows server holds contract documents on an NTFS disk volume. Users make revisions to documents before they are finalized. You need to ensure previous versions of files are available to users. What should you configure?

A. Journaling

B. Volume shadow copies

C. File classification

D. System restore points

☑ **B.** The Windows volume shadow copy service (VSS) tracks changes to files at the block level. It is used as a backup source and can be used to restore both deleted files and previous versions of files.

☒ **A, C,** and **D** are incorrect. Journaling tracks file system transactions and is used upon remounting of the file system for recovery in case of a disk problem or power loss. File classification assigns to certain files metadata that can be used to control access to those files; for example, the Executive group might have read and write access to files classified, or flagged, with the word "contract." On Windows client operating systems, system restore points allow the configuration of the machine to be set back to an earlier point in time.

11. What of the following is *not* a benefit of using a Fibre Channel network compared to SCSI?

A. Shared storage devices

B. Distance

C. Cost

D. Number of devices

☑ **C.** Fibre Channel networks are more expensive due to specialized equipment. Other network storage solutions such as iSCSI are less expensive because they can use standard network equipment along with the TCP/IP protocol suite.

☒ **A, B,** and **D** are incorrect. Fibre Channel allows storage devices to be shared by multiple hosts, unlike SCSI, which is local to a host. Fibre Channel transmits light pulses, which increases the transmission distance, and it allows more storage devices than a traditional SCSI bus.

12. Which of the following terms is associated with hierarchical storage management?

A. Fibre Channel

B. Virtualization

C. iSCSI

D. Storage tier

☑ **D.** Hierarchical storage management (HSM) systems organize storage into tiers using policies. Tier 1 (the fastest) is used to store frequently accessed data, whereas tier 4 (the slowest) is more suitable for long-term storage of infrequently accessed data.

☒ **A, B,** and **C** are incorrect. Fibre Channel (FC) is a standard for sending storage commands over a dedicated network using specialized FC equipment. Virtualization is used to allow multiple operating systems or applications (containers) to run simultaneously on shared hardware. iSCSI uses standard network equipment to send SCSI storage commands over a TCP/IP network where shared storage is used among multiple hosts.

13. Your on-premises users synchronize cloud files to their Windows laptops. Corporate security policies dictate that locally stored files must be encrypted for the user. What should be configured on user laptops?

A. BitLocker

B. EFS

C. PKI

D. TPM

☑ **B.** Encrypting File System (EFS) lets Windows users encrypt files and folders. The default behavior is such that the specific user that encrypted a file must be logged on to decrypt that same file.

☒ **A, B,** and **C** are incorrect. BitLocker is a Windows solution that is used to encrypt entire disk volumes and is not in any way tied to a user account. Public key infrastructure (PKI) is a hierarchy of issued security certificates for users, devices, and apps that provides authentication and confidentiality capabilities. Trusted Platform Module (TPM) is computer firmware used to stored decryption keys and machine startup hashes; BitLocker can be used with TPM.

14. Which storage tier should be used for long-term data archiving?

A. Tier 1

B. Tier 2

C. Tier 3

D. Tier 4

☑ **D.** Tier 4 uses the slowest and least expensive storage devices and is used for long-term storage.

☒ **A, B,** and **C** are incorrect. Tier 1 uses the fastest storage media for frequently accessed critical data. Tier 2 balances response time and cost for less critical data access. Tier 3 is for infrequently accessed data, but not archived data.

15.   Which statements regarding SSDs are true? Choose two.
   A.   They withstand vibrations better than hard disk drives.
   B.   They are quieter than hard disk drives.
   C.   They are slower than hard drives.
   D.   They use rotating platters.

   ☑   **A** and **B.** Because SSDs lack moving parts, they require less power, which means they generate less heat and do not require loud fans, and they are less likely to be damaged due to vibrations or being dropped than hard disk drives, which use moving parts.
   ☒   **C** and **D** are incorrect. SSDs do not use rotating platters, so, because there are no mechanical moving parts, SSDs provide quicker data access times.

16.   What statement relates to a disadvantage of using SSDs?
   A.   They are more expensive than hard disk drives.
   B.   They are louder than hard disk drives.
   C.   They are slower than hard drives.
   D.   They do not withstand vibrations as well as hard disk drives.

   ☑   **A.** On a per-gigabyte (GB) basis, SSDs are more expensive than traditional hard disk drives.
   ☒   **B, C,** and **D** are incorrect. SSDs use less power, which means they generate less heat, which means they don't require fans; they are quiet. Because there are no mechanical moving parts, SSDs provide quicker data access times than hard disks. SSDs are less likely to be damaged due to vibrations or being dropped than hard disk drives, which use moving parts.

17.   What term describes the time it takes for a hard disk actuator arm to move to the correct location?
   A.   IOPS value
   B.   Rotational latency
   C.   Seek time
   D.   Transfer rate

   ☑   **C.** Seek time measures how long it takes in milliseconds (ms) for a disk actuator arm to move over the correct disk platter position to read data.
   ☒   **A, B,** and **D** are incorrect. Input/output operations per second (IOPS) is a unit of performance measurement related to on-premises and cloud storage. Rotational latency measures how long it takes for a hard disk platter to spin to the correct location to read data. The transfer rate measures how much data can be moved to and from storage devices within a given timeframe; it is normally specified in megabits per second (Mbps) and megabytes per second (MBps).

18.   Which term describes the time it takes for a hard disk platter to spin to the correct location?
   A.   IOPS value
   B.   Rotational latency
   C.   Seek time
   D.   Transfer rate

☑ **B.** Rotational latency measures how long it takes for a hard disk platter to spin to the correct location to read data.

☒ **A, C,** and **D** are incorrect. Input/output operations per second (IOPS) is a unit of performance measurement related to on-premises and cloud storage. Seek time measures how long it takes in milliseconds (ms) for a disk actuator arm to move over the correct disk platter position to read data. The transfer rate measures how much data can be moved to and from storage devices within a given timeframe; it is normally specified in megabits per second (Mbps) and megabytes per second (MBps).

19. Which RAID level is depicted in Figure 2-1?
    A. RAID 0
    B. RAID 1
    C. RAID 5
    D. RAID 6

FIGURE 2-1

Disk striping

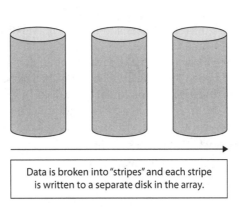

Data is broken into "stripes" and each stripe
is written to a separate disk in the array.

☑ **A.** RAID 0 (disk striping) uses a minimum of two disks where each data write is spread out among the drives, which results in a performance benefit.

☒ **B, C,** and **D** are incorrect. RAID 1 (disk mirroring) uses a minimum of two disks to write a copy of data to a separate disk, which provides fault tolerance. RAID 5 (disk striping with distributed parity) uses a minimum of three disks to spread out data and recovery information across the disks in the array, which increases fault tolerance and performance. RAID 6 enhances RAID 5 by using two parity blocks written across the array, which increases fault tolerance such that the array remains stable even if two disks fail.

20. Which RAID level is depicted in Figure 2-2?
    A. RAID 0
    B. RAID 1
    C. RAID 5
    D. RAID 6

FIGURE 2-2

Disk mirroring

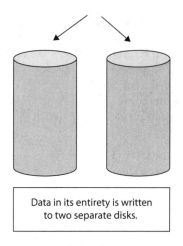

Data in its entirety is written
to two separate disks.

☑ **B.** RAID 1 (disk mirroring) uses a minimum of two disks to write a copy of data to a separate disk, which provides fault tolerance.

☒ **A, C,** and **D** are incorrect. RAID 0 (disk striping) uses a minimum of two disks where each data write is spread out among the drives, which results in a performance benefit. RAID 5 (disk striping with distributed parity) uses a minimum of three disks to spread out data and recovery information across the disks in the array, which increases fault tolerance and performance. RAID 6 enhances RAID 5 by using two parity blocks written across the array, which increases fault tolerance such that the array remains stable even if two disks fail.

21. Which RAID level is depicted in Figure 2-3?

    A.   RAID 0

    B.   RAID 1

    C.   RAID 5

    D.   RAID 6

FIGURE 2-3

Disk striping
with parity

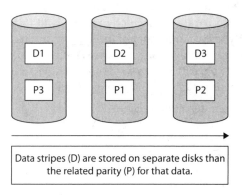

Data stripes (D) are stored on separate disks than
the related parity (P) for that data.

☑ **C.** RAID 5 (disk striping with distributed parity) uses a minimum of three disks to spread out data and recovery information across the disks in the array, which increases fault tolerance and performance.

☒ **A, B,** and **D** are incorrect. RAID 0 (disk striping) uses a minimum of two disks where each data write is spread out among the drives, which results in a performance benefit. RAID 1 (disk mirroring) uses a minimum of two disks to write a copy of data to a separate disk, which provides fault tolerance. RAID 6 enhances RAID 5 by using two parity blocks written across the array, which increases fault tolerance such that the array remains stable even if two disks fail.

22. Which data tier has the best performance?

    A.   Tier 1

    B.   Tier 2

    C.   Tier 3

    D.   Tier 4

☑ **A.** Tier 1 uses the fastest (and most expensive) storage media for frequently accessed critical data.

☒ **B, C,** and **D** are incorrect. Tier 2 balances response time and cost for less critical data access. Tier 3 is for infrequently accessed data, but not archived data. Tier 4 uses the slowest and least expensive storage devices and is used for long-term storage.

23. RAID 1 requires a minimum of how many disks?

    A.   Two

    B.   Three

    C.   Four

    D.   Five

☑ **A.** RAID 1 requires at least two disks where the second disk is used to mirror the data on the first.

☒ **B, C,** and **D** are incorrect. These do not represent the minimum required number of disks to configure RAID 1.

24. Which RAID level provides no redundancy?

    A.   RAID 0

    B.   RAID 1

    C.   RAID 5

    D.   RAID 6

☑ **A.** RAID 0 (disk striping) improves performance but does not provide redundancy; a single disk failure makes all data on the array inaccessible.

☒ **B, C,** and **D** are incorrect. RAID 1 (mirroring) uses additional disks to mirror data for redundancy. RAID 5 and 6 use distributed parity, which is used to recover data in the case of one (RAID 5) or two (RAID 6) failed disks.

25. You are planning the storage requirements for a two-disk mirror of a server operating system disk partition. How much disk space is usable in the mirrored volume?
   A. 10 percent
   B. 30 percent
   C. 50 percent
   D. 75 percent

   ☑ **C.** Because all data on mirrored disk partitions is duplicated on the second disk, only 50 percent of the original total disk capacity can be used.
   ☒ **A, B,** and **D** are incorrect. These percentages do not represent the amount of available space in the mirror.

26. RAID 5 requires a minimum of how many disks?
   A. Two
   B. Three
   C. Four
   D. Five

   ☑ **B.** RAID 5 requires a minimum of three disks in the array, although more can be added.
   ☒ **A, C,** and **D** are incorrect. These do not represent the minimum required number of disks to implement RAID 5.

27. RAID 6 requires a minimum of how many disks?
   A. Two
   B. Three
   C. Four
   D. Five

   ☑ **C.** RAID 6 requires a minimum of four disks in the array.
   ☒ **A, B,** and **D** are incorrect. These do not represent the minimum required number of disks for RAID 6.

28. Which user key decrypts EFS data?
   A. Private
   B. Public
   C. Symmetric
   D. Asymmetric

   ☑ **A.** The user private key is used to decrypt the file encryption key, which in turn is used to decrypt the file.
   ☒ **B, C,** and **D** are incorrect. EFS uses the user public key to encrypt the file encryption key. Although the file encryption key is symmetric and user public and private keys are asymmetric, these answers are not as specific as option A.

Chapter 3

Storage Networking

CERTIFICATION OBJECTIVES

3.01   Storage Types and Technologies

3.02   Storage Access Protocols

3.03   Storage Provisioning

3.04   Storage Protection

QUESTIONS

Shared storage allows multiple hosts to use storage capacity, and it's used on-premises as well as in cloud environments. Network storage is accessible using standards such as iSCSI, NAS, and Fibre Channel.

Configuring connected storage includes understanding settings related to object storage, thin provisioning, and deduplication. Time-sensitive applications and cross-region data synchronization benefit from synchronous replication to ensure data changes are written to all replicas.

1. Your private cloud consists of a server containing a total of 6TB of local storage. Each of the seven departments in the region require 1TB of space. Additional storage will not be purchased. Which option allows seven 1TB disk volumes to be created on the local storage?

   A. Compression
   B. Overcommitting
   C. Deduplication
   D. Snapshots

2. Which of the following NAS and SAN statements is correct?

   A. A SAN uses network sharing protocols such as CIFS.
   B. A SAN shares the network with TCP/IP traffic.
   C. NAS does not share the network with TCP/IP traffic.
   D. NAS uses network sharing protocols such as CIFS.

3. Which standard provides the automated discovery of iSCSI and Fibre Channel storage devices?

   A. Internet Storage Name Service
   B. Domain Name Service
   C. Dynamic Host Configuration Protocol
   D. Network Attached Storage

4. Refer to the diagram in Figure 3-1. Your cloud-deployed web application is not performing well. Which item in the diagram requires attention?

   A. vCPU Utilization
   B. Vnet Traffic In
   C. Vnet Traffic Out
   D. IOPS % Utilization

FIGURE 3-1		Aggregated Performance Metrics			
		vCPU Utilization	Vnet Traffic In	Vnet Traffic Out	IOPS % Utilization
Aggregated performance metrics	Week1	33	474,838	663,179	80
	Week2	45	66,699	185,758	76
	Week3	21	388,142	263,730	73
	Week4	54	370,231	115,122	69

5. Cloud providers allow the storage of files of almost any size using _____.
   A. Object storage
   B. RAID 0
   C. Storage tiers
   D. Deduplication

6. Regulations dictate that specific types of documents be stored permanently. Metadata must be added to each stored item to facilitate retrieval. Which term best describes this storage system?
   A. Content addressed storage
   B. Cloud backup
   C. Storage area network
   D. Storage tiers

7. Users in the marketing department normally share an original document that then gets saved with a different name for each user that modifies the file. You need to conserve disk space. What should you do to minimize consumed disk space?
   A. Enable compression
   B. Enable block-level deduplication
   C. Enable file-level deduplication
   D. Enable volume shadow copies

8. You are the storage administrator for a large enterprise. You need to implement granular security to separate shared storage between servers over the SAN. What should you configure?
   A. LUN masking
   B. File system ACLs
   C. Zoning
   D. VLAN

9. Where is storage zoning configured?
   A. FC switch
   B. Storage controller
   C. NIC
   D. TPM

10. An intranet website uses a backend SQL database stored on the SAN. You need to ensure that the website can access the SQL database at all times. What should you configure?

   A. SQL mirroring

   B. Zoning

   C. LUN masking

   D. Multipathing

11. Refer to this table. Which of the following statements about the SLA is true?

Cloud Storage – Service Level Agreement
99.999% annual uptime
Data is replicated to two separate data centers
Supports Tier 1 and 2 storage
SSD backed

   A. There is approximately 6 minutes of downtime each year.

   B. Synchronous replication is being used.

   C. The solution is suitable for data archiving.

   D. Performance will not be as good as HDDs.

12. Which type of replication does not notify the application of a successful write until all replicas have acknowledged the change?

   A. Asynchronous

   B. Passive

   C. Complacent

   D. Synchronous

13. Your virtual machine has 2TB of available storage. In the VM, you have created three 1TB disk volumes. Which option was used in this configuration?

   A. Thin provisioning

   B. Compression

   C. Deduplication

   D. Thick provisioning

14. Your colleague, Lain, mentions a new app being developed in-house that uses a storage tokenization system. What is Lain talking about?

   A. A method of authentication using a central identity provider that digitally signs tokens

   B. Configuring Windows pass-through authentication for access to storage

   C. A system whereby access to sensitive data is gained by providing a placeholder token to a tokenization system

   D. An iSCSI shared storage solution using the IBM Token Ring logical topology

15. Which term is used to describe a unique storage identifier?

    A. iSCSI target

    B. WWN

    C. MAC address

    D. Port number

16. Servers require a(n) _____ to connect to a SAN.

    A. NIC

    B. MAC address

    C. FC switch

    D. HBA

17. You are planning cross-regional replication between public cloud provider sites and your on-premises network. Periodic spikes in the amounts of transmitted data must be accommodated over the connection. What must you consider?

    A. Bursting

    B. Network compression

    C. Network deduplication

    D. Network snapshots

18. Which standard places Fibre Channel frames within Ethernet frames?

    A. FC

    B. iSCSI

    C. FCoE

    D. VLAN

19. A storage administrator has configured iSCSI storage on host storage1.fakedomain.local. You need to configure a virtual machine that will use some of that shared storage. What piece of information is required?

    A. IP address

    B. Partition ID

    C. LUN

    D. Disk interface type

20. Which component normally lies between an HBA and a storage array?

    A. FCoE

    B. TPM

    C. FC switch

    D. Multipath device

21. All of the following use LUN identifiers except _____.
    A. SCSI
    B. Ethernet
    C. SAN
    D. iSCSI

22. A medium-sized corporation requires the fastest solution for reading and writing database transactions to shared storage. Which solution should be used?
    A. NAS
    B. SAN
    C. iSCSI
    D. DAS

23. Which of the following phrases best describes DAS?
    A. Shared storage
    B. SAS
    C. SATA
    D. Local storage

24. Which storage protocols are used with DAS? Choose two.
    A. Fibre Channel
    B. SATA
    C. SAS
    D. Fibre Channel over Ethernet

25. You would like the ability to migrate virtual machines from one hypervisor to another with zero downtime. What is required for this?
    A. Virtual machine guest tools
    B. IPv6
    C. Shared storage
    D. Dedicated VLAN

26. An HBA World Wide Name consists of _____ bytes.
    A. 4
    B. 8
    C. 16
    D. 32

27. Which SAN configuration groups Fibre Channel switch ports together to form a virtual fabric?
    A. LUN masking
    B. Zoning
    C. Multipathing
    D. VSAN

A QUICK ANSWER KEY

1.	B	**8.**	A	**15.**	B	**22.**	B
2.	D	**9.**	A	**16.**	D	**23.**	D
3.	A	**10.**	D	**17.**	A	**24.**	B, C
4.	D	**11.**	A	**18.**	C	**25.**	C
5.	A	**12.**	D	**19.**	C	**26.**	B
6.	A	**13.**	A	**20.**	C	**27.**	D
7.	B	**14.**	C	**21.**	B		

IN-DEPTH ANSWERS

1. Your private cloud consists of a server containing a total of 6TB of local storage. Each of the seven departments in the region require 1TB of space. Additional storage will not be purchased. Which option allows seven 1TB disk volumes to be created on the local storage?

    A. Compression
    B. Overcommitting
    C. Deduplication
    D. Snapshots

    ☑ **B.** Overcommitting allows the creation of disk volumes whose total capacity exceeds physically available storage space. This allows the volumes to grow dynamically as needed.

    ☒ **A, C,** and **D** are incorrect. Compression removes duplicate file content to save space. Deduplication can track disk block-level changes to keep unique copies of only changed blocks. Volume snapshots are incremental block change copies of a disk volume.

2. Which of the following NAS and SAN statements is correct?

    A. A SAN uses network sharing protocols such as CIFS.
    B. A SAN shares the network with TCP/IP traffic.
    C. NAS does not share the network with TCP/IP traffic.
    D. NAS uses network sharing protocols such as CIFS.

    ☑ **D.** Network attached storage (NAS) presents network storage that is accessible from hosts using file sharing protocols such as CIFS

    ☒ **A, B,** and **C** are incorrect. Storage area networks (SANs) use iSCSI or Fibre Channel standards, not file sharing protocols. SANs are not used to transmit TCP/IP traffic, only storage traffic. NAS can present its storage on a TCP/IP network.

3. Which standard provides the automated discovery of iSCSI and Fibre Channel storage devices?

    A. Internet Storage Name Service
    B. Domain Name Service
    C. Dynamic Host Configuration Protocol
    D. Network Attached Storage

☑ **A.** Internet Storage Name Service (ISNS) is a network storage discovery protocol.

☒ **B, C,** and **D** are incorrect. Domain Name Service (DNS) is commonly used to translate friendly names into IP addresses. Dynamic Host Configuration Protocol (DHCP) is a central network configuration service that provides TCP/IP configuration settings to clients. Network attached storage (NAS) presents network storage that is accessible from hosts using file sharing protocols.

4. Refer to the diagram in Figure 3-1. Your cloud-deployed web application is not performing well. Which item in the diagram requires attention?
    A. vCPU Utilization
    B. Vnet Traffic In
    C. Vnet Traffic Out
    D. IOPS % Utilization

FIGURE 3-1	Aggregated Performance Metrics			
	vCPU Utilization	Vnet Traffic In	Vnet Traffic Out	IOPS % Utilization
Aggregated	Week1	33	474,838	663,179	80
performance	Week2	45	66,699	185,758	76
metrics	Week3	21	388,142	263,730	73
	Week4	54	370,231	115,122	69

☑ **D.** Input/output per second (IOPS) measures disk performance. Unless a performance baseline dictates otherwise, the only potential listed problem is the IOPS % utilization.

☒ **A, B,** and **C** are incorrect. The other metrics are average relative to the other listed performance metrics other than IOPS. The other listed metrics are not related to measuring disk performance.

5. Cloud providers allow the storage of files of almost any size using _____.
    A. Object storage
    B. RAID 0
    C. Storage tiers
    D. Deduplication

☑ **A.** Object storage assigns each stored item a unique ID. Metadata can also be added to facilitate searching and security. The object metadata is stored along with the data itself as opposed to being written to disk in blocks.

☒ **B, C,** and **D** are incorrect. RAID 0 (striping) writes data across multiple disks to increase disk performance. Storage tiers use policies to control which type of data is stored on different storage mediums, such as frequently accessed data being stored on the fastest disks (Tier 1). Deduplication can track disk block-level changes to keep unique copies of only changed blocks.

6. Regulations dictate that specific types of documents be stored permanently. Metadata must be added to each stored item to facilitate retrieval. Which term best describes this storage system?
    A. Content addressed storage
    B. Cloud backup
    C. Storage area network
    D. Storage tiers

☑ **A.** Content addressed storage (CAS) is designed for archiving and uses IDs for stored items as opposed to filenames. Metadata can facilitate searching for the item.

☒ **B, C,** and **D** are incorrect. Cloud backup stores backed-up data in the cloud but is not specifically related to archiving. Storage area networks (SANs) use iSCSI or Fibre Channel standards, not file sharing protocols. Storage tiers use policies to control which type of data is stored on different storage mediums, such as frequently accessed data being stored on the fastest disks (Tier 1).

7. Users in the marketing department normally share an original document that then gets saved with a different name for each user that modifies the file. You need to conserve disk space. What should you do to minimize consumed disk space?

   A. Enable compression
   B. Enable block-level deduplication
   C. Enable file-level deduplication
   D. Enable volume shadow copies

   ☑ **B.** Deduplication can track disk block-level changes to keep unique copies of only changed blocks.

   ☒ **A, C,** and **D** are incorrect. Compression removes duplicate file content to save space. File-level deduplication tracks changes to entire files, not blocks that compose a file. Volume shadow copies are used to track only changed disk blocks for the purposes of backup, file restoration, and file versioning.

8. You are the storage administrator for a large enterprise. You need to implement granular security to separate shared storage between servers over the SAN. What should you configure?

   A. LUN masking
   B. File system ACLs
   C. Zoning
   D. VLAN

   ☑ **A.** LUN masking provides more granular control to isolate shared storage between storage consumers over the network.

   ☒ **B, C,** and **D** are incorrect. File system access control lists (ACLs) list security principles and their permissions to files and folders. Zoning does not provide the same level of detailed control for storage isolation that LUN masking does. Virtual local area networks (VLANs) use criteria such as switch port to group devices together for traffic isolation purposes.

9. Where is storage zoning configured?

   A. FC switch
   B. Storage controller
   C. NIC
   D. TPM

☑ **A.** Zoning is used to isolate network storage on a SAN between hosts and is configured at the Fibre Channel (FC) switch.

☒ **B, C,** and **D** are incorrect. LUN masking is configured at the storage controller, not zoning. Network interface cards (NICs) and Trusted Platform Module (TPM) are not related to SAN configuration.

10. An intranet website uses a backend SQL database stored on the SAN. You need to ensure that the website can access the SQL database at all times. What should you configure?

    A. SQL mirroring
    B. Zoning
    C. LUN masking
    D. Multipathing

☑ **D.** Multipathing uses redundancy, such as multiple host bus adapters (HBAs) in each host connected to different Fibre Channel switches to remove single points of failure.

☒ **A, B,** and **C** are incorrect. SQL mirroring is used to synchronize data across multiple database replicas, but this will not work over a SAN (it needs TCP/IP). Zoning and LUN masking isolate shared network storage between consuming hosts.

11. Refer to this table. Which of the following statements about the SLA is true?

Cloud Storage – Service Level Agreement
99.999% annual uptime
Data is replicated to two separate data centers
Supports Tier 1 and 2 storage
SSD backed

    A. There is approximately 6 minutes of downtime each year.
    B. Synchronous replication is being used.
    C. The solution is suitable for data archiving.
    D. Performance will not be as good as HDDs.

☑ **A.** 99.999 percent uptime means about 6 minutes of downtime per year.

☒ **B, C,** and **D** are incorrect. There is no indication that synchronous replication will be used. Tiers 1 and 2 are not used for archiving. Solid state drives (SSDs) provide much better performance than hard disk drives (HDDs).

12. Which type of replication does not notify the application of a successful write until all replicas have acknowledged the change?

    A. Asynchronous
    B. Passive
    C. Complacent
    D. Synchronous

☑ **D.** Synchronous replication ensures all replicas have received changes before moving on.

☒ **A, B,** and **C** are incorrect. Asynchronous replication does not wait for an acknowledgment that all replicas have received a synchronization change. Passive and complacent are not common replication types.

13. Your virtual machine has 2TB of available storage. In the VM, you have created three 1TB disk volumes. Which option was used in this configuration?

A. Thin provisioning

B. Compression

C. Deduplication

D. Thick provisioning

☑ **A.** Thin provisioning allows administrators to overcommit physical storage space by creating multiple disk volumes whose sum exceeds available space.

☒ **B, C,** and **D** are incorrect. Compression removes duplicate file content to save space. Deduplication can track disk block-level changes to keep unique copies of only changed blocks. Thick provisioning consumes disk space immediately when the disk volume is created.

14. Your colleague, Lain, mentions a new app being developed in-house that uses a storage tokenization system. What is Lain talking about?

A. A method of authentication using a central identity provider that digitally signs tokens

B. Configuring Windows pass-through authentication for access to storage

C. A system whereby access to sensitive data is gained by providing a placeholder token to a tokenization system

D. An iSCSI shared storage solution using the IBM Token Ring logical topology

☑ **C.** Tokenization systems allow data access through a unique token that serves as a data placeholder.

☒ **A, B,** and **D** are incorrect. Central identity providers are used for single sign-on (SSO) and identity federation. Windows pass-through authentication is not related to storage tokenization, nor are iSCSI and IBM Token Ring.

15. Which term is used to describe a unique storage identifier?

A. iSCSI target

B. WWN

C. MAC address

D. Port number

☑ **B.** The World Wide Name (WWN) is a unique identifier used for SAN storage.

☒ **A, C,** and **D** are incorrect. iSCSI targets are devices hosting shared storage over the iSCSI protocol. MAC addresses are unique 48-bit addresses assigned to network interface cards. Port numbers identify a running network service.

16. Servers require a(n) _____ to connect to a SAN.

   A. NIC
   B. MAC address
   C. FC switch
   D. HBA

   ☑ **D.** A host bus adapter (HBA) enables SAN connectivity, much like a network interface card allows network connectivity.

   ☒ **A, B,** and **C** are incorrect. Network interface cards (NICs) enable connectivity to a network. MAC addresses are unique 48-bit addresses assigned to network interface cards. Fibre Channel (FC) switches connect host bus adapters (HBAs) to storage.

17. You are planning cross-regional replication between public cloud provider sites and your on-premises network. Periodic spikes in the amounts of transmitted data must be accommodated over the connection. What must you consider?

   A. Bursting
   B. Network compression
   C. Network deduplication
   D. Network snapshots

   ☑ **A.** Bursting allows for occasional usage spikes and accommodates these periodic changes.

   ☒ **B, C,** and **D** are incorrect. Network compression is not applied periodically when usage spikes. There are no such things as network deduplication and network snapshots.

18. Which standard places Fibre Channel frames within Ethernet frames?

   A. FC
   B. iSCSI
   C. FCoE
   D. VLAN

   ☑ **C.** Fibre Channel over Ethernet (FCoE) places FC frames into Ethernet frames to allow storage traffic on an Ethernet network.

   ☒ **A, B,** and **D** are incorrect. Fibre Channel (FC) does not use Ethernet framing. iSCSI and VLANs are not related to Fibre Channel.

19. A storage administrator has configured iSCSI storage on host storage1.fakedomain.local. You need to configure a virtual machine that will use some of that shared storage. What piece of information is required?

   A. IP address
   B. Partition ID
   C. LUN
   D. Disk interface type

   ☑ **C.** The logical unit number (LUN) is a unique identifier that is required by storage consumers.

   ☒ **A, B,** and **D** are incorrect. Since the DNS name is given, the IP address is not needed. The partition ID and disk interface type are not relevant when accessing network storage.

20. Which component normally lies between an HBA and a storage array?
    A. FCoE
    B. TPM
    C. FC switch
    D. Multipath device

    ☑ **C.** Fibre Channel (FC) switches connect host bus adapters (HBAs) to storage.
    ☒ **A, B,** and **D** are incorrect. Fibre Channel over Ethernet (FCoE) places FC frames into Ethernet frames to allow storage traffic on an Ethernet network. Trusted Platform Module (TPM) is a firmware security chip unrelated to a SAN fabric. There is no such thing as a multipath device.

21. All of the following use LUN identifiers except _____.
    A. SCSI
    B. Ethernet
    C. SAN
    D. iSCSI

    ☑ **B.** Ethernet networking is not related to LUN storage identifiers.
    ☒ **A, C,** and **D** are incorrect. Logical unit numbers (LUNs) uniquely identify storage for SCSI, SANs, and iSCSI.

22. A medium-sized corporation requires the fastest solution for reading and writing database transactions to shared storage. Which solution should be used?
    A. NAS
    B. SAN
    C. iSCSI
    D. DAS

    ☑ **B.** Storage area networks (SANs) provide the best network storage performance.
    ☒ **A, C,** and **D** are incorrect. Network attached storage (NAS) uses file sharing protocols for shared storage accessibility. iSCSI place SCSI storage commands into IP packets. Direct attached storage provides local access to storage from a host.

23. Which of the following phrases best describes DAS?
    A. Shared storage
    B. SAS
    C. SATA
    D. Local storage

    ☑ **D.** Direct attached storage provides local access to storage from a host.
    ☒ **A, B,** and **C** are incorrect. DAS is not shared storage since the storage is available only to the host it is attached to. Serial Attached SCSI (SAS) and Serial ATA (SATA) are disk interface types.

24. Which storage protocols are used with DAS? Choose two.

    A. Fibre Channel

    B. SATA

    C. SAS

    D. Fibre Channel over Ethernet

    ☑ **B** and **C.** Serial Attached SCSI (SAS) and Serial ATA (SATA) are disk interface types used with locally attached storage.

    ☒ **A** and **D** are incorrect. Fibre Channel (FC) is a standard designed specifically for the transmission of storage traffic. Fibre Channel over Ethernet (FCoE) places FC frames into Ethernet frames to allow storage traffic on an Ethernet network.

25. You would like the ability to migrate virtual machines from one hypervisor to another with zero downtime. What is required for this?

    A. Virtual machine guest tools

    B. IPv6

    C. Shared storage

    D. Dedicated VLAN

    ☑ **C.** Virtual machine files can reside on shared storage, which allows zero downtime when migrating VMs between hosts. A temporary VM memory contents file is also written to the shared storage for VM integrity.

    ☒ **A, B,** and **D** are incorrect. Virtual machine guest tools, IPv6, and VLANs do not enable VM migration.

26. An HBA World Wide Name consists of _____ bytes.

    A. 4

    B. 8

    C. 16

    D. 32

    ☑ **B.** World Wide Names (WWNs) consist of 8 bytes.

    ☒ **A, C,** and **D** are incorrect. These are not the correct number of bytes within a WWN.

27. Which SAN configuration groups Fibre Channel switch ports together to form a virtual fabric?

    A. LUN masking

    B. Zoning

    C. Multipathing

    D. VSAN

    ☑ **D.** Virtual storage area networks (VSANs) create an isolated virtual storage fabric similar to how VLANs are used to isolate traffic from other networks.

    ☒ **A, B,** and **C** are incorrect. The listed options are not used to create a virtual SAN fabric.

Chapter 4

Network Infrastructure

CERTIFICATION OBJECTIVES

4.01   Network Types

4.02   Network Optimization

4.03   Routing and Switching

4.04   Network Ports and Protocols

QUESTIONS

On-premises network components such as firewalls, routers, and switches have similar types of configurations in the cloud. Understanding their roles and configurations is crucial to successful cloud deployments over time.

Network services listen for client connections on specific port numbers, which must be allowed by firewalls. Devices must have a valid IP configuration to fully participate on a network. Port numbers and IP addresses have the same relevance in cloud computing environments.

1. Which network type allows authorized external users to access a controlled set of internal resources?
   A. Intranet
   B. Internet
   C. Extranet
   D. Federation

2. A university campus consists of many buildings populating a large property. All buildings are linked together through underground fiber-optic cables, creating a private network infrastructure. What type of network is this?
   A. MAN
   B. LAN
   C. WAN
   D. SAN

3. Which network topology has a potential central point of failure?
   A. Mesh
   B. Bus
   C. Ring
   D. Star

4. Which of the following is a disadvantage of network compression?
   A. Higher storage requirements
   B. Longer transmission time
   C. Higher compute requirements
   D. Shorter transmission time

5. Refer to Figure 4-1. Devices B and C have numerous computers plugged into them that can all access the Internet. In all likelihood, what is device A?
   A. Firewall
   B. Switch
   C. Router
   D. Hub

FIGURE 4-1

Network diagram

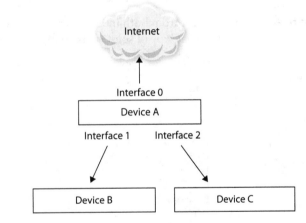

6. Refer to Figure 4-2. Devices B and C have numerous computers plugged into them. What type of devices are they?
   A. Firewall
   B. Switch
   C. Router
   D. VPN concentrator

FIGURE 4-2

Network diagram

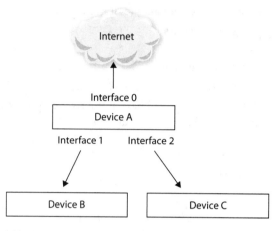

7. Refer to Figure 4-3. Internet traffic from both internal servers assumes an IP address of 200.1.1.1 when traversing the Internet. What type of solution is configured on device A?
   A. Routing
   B. Switching
   C. PAT
   D. NAT

FIGURE 4-3

Internal servers

Internal Windows Server
192.168.1.200

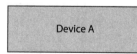

Public IP
200.1.1.1

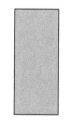

Internal Linux Server
192.168.1.210

8. Refer to Figure 4-4. What is wrong with the Windows TCP/IPv4 configuration?

    A. The default gateway is not reachable.

    B. The alternate DNS server is on a different subnet.

    C. The IP address is invalid.

    D. The subnet mask is invalid.

FIGURE 4-4

Windows TCP/
IPv4 settings

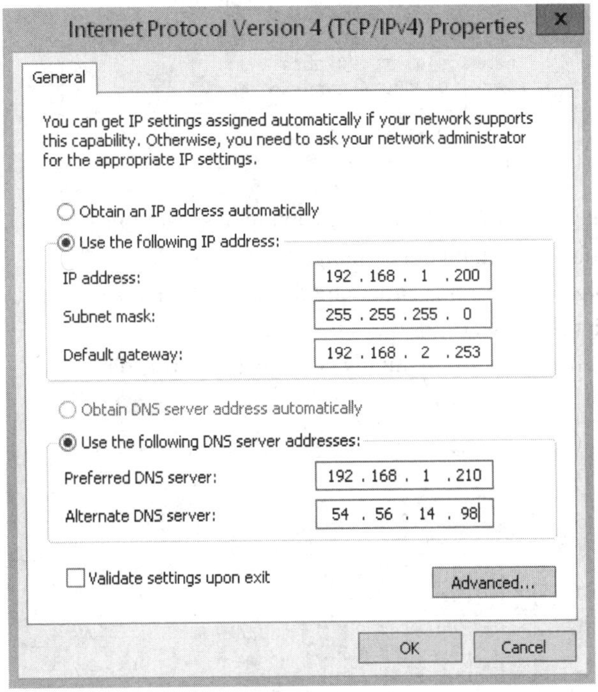

9. Refer to the packet capture in Figure 4-5. What type of network traffic is this?

    A. Web browser connecting to a web server

    B. User authentication

    C. Client DNS query to DNS server

    D. Ping request

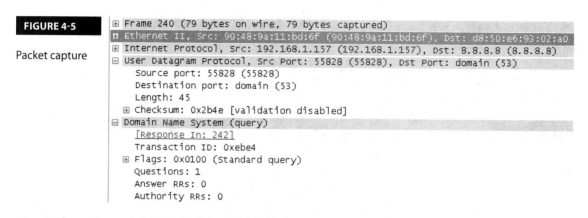

FIGURE 4-5

Packet capture

10. Refer to Figure 4-6. Which of the following observations is correct?

    A. The subnet mask must be changed.

    B. The physical address is not valid for a Wi-Fi adapter.

    C. The first DNS server entry is invalid.

    D. IP settings were not manually configured on this device.

FIGURE 4-6

Windows
ipconfig
command output

```
Wireless LAN adapter Wi-Fi:

   Connection-specific DNS Suffix  . : silversides.local
   Description . . . . . . . . . . . : Qualcomm Atheros AR956x Wireless Network
Adapter
   Physical Address. . . . . . . . . : 90-48-9A-11-BD-6F
   DHCP Enabled. . . . . . . . . . . : Yes
   Autoconfiguration Enabled . . . . : Yes
   IPv4 Address. . . . . . . . . . . : 192.168.1.157(Preferred)
   Subnet Mask . . . . . . . . . . . : 255.255.255.0
   Lease Obtained. . . . . . . . . . : Thursday, June 9, 2016 12:30:00 PM
   Lease Expires . . . . . . . . . . : Saturday, June 11, 2016 7:14:38 AM
   Default Gateway . . . . . . . . . : 192.168.1.1
   DHCP Server . . . . . . . . . . . : 192.168.1.1
   DNS Servers . . . . . . . . . . . : 8.8.8.8
                                       192.168.1.1
   Primary WINS Server . . . . . . . : 192.168.1.1
   NetBIOS over Tcpip. . . . . . . . : Enabled
```

11. You need to connect through a firewall to remotely administer a Windows server using RDP. Which firewall allowance must be configured?

    A. UDP 123

    B. TCP 22

    C. TCP 389

    D. TCP 3389

12. A client web browser connects to an HTTPS web server. Which port does the server use to communicate back to the client?

    A. 81

    B. 444

    C. Any port below 1024

    D. Any port above 1024

13. You are responsible for a web application running in the public cloud. Recent performance metrics indicate that the average user wait time for page loads is four seconds due to the high number of HTTP requests. What should you configure?

    A. Compression

    B. Load balancing

    C. Proxying

    D. PKI

14. Petaire is a cloud network sysadmin. Cloud-based virtual machines hosting a custom web application have been deployed to a single cloud virtual network that currently has no Internet access. Each virtual machine must have Internet access, while incoming connections initiated from the Internet must be blocked. Which solution should Petaire deploy?

    A. Forward proxy host

    B. Packet filtering firewall

    C. Web application firewall

    D. NAT

15. Users complain that Internet access has been intermittent. You check the configuration of a user system and discover it has an IP address beginning with 169.254. What is the problem?

    A. The DHCP server cannot be reached.

    B. The default gateway cannot be reached.

    C. The DNS server cannot be reached.

    D. The proxy server cannot be reached.

16. The _____ determines which portion of the IPv4 address identifies the network.

    A. Translation table

    B. Subnet mask

    C. MAC address

    D. IP address suffix

17. You are reviewing a network diagram for a client. The diagram has numerous references to /22. What does this mean?

    A. The maximum number of hosts per network is 22.

    B. The average network compression ratio is 1:22.

    C. IP addresses can be divided in 22 subordinate addresses.

    D. There are 22 bits in the subnet mask.

18. Your organization plans to use iSCSI for shared network storage. Which technique should be used to ensure that iSCSI traffic is kept separate from other IP traffic?

    A. LUN masking

    B. VLANs

    C. Zoning

    D. Load balancing

19. What is commonly used in cloud environments to separate network traffic between cloud tenants?
    A. VXLAN
    B. Router
    C. VLAN
    D. Switch

20. Which protocol is used to secure SFTP sessions?
    A. FTP
    B. IPSec
    C. SSH
    D. PKI

21. DHCP functionality across subnets is configured using a _____.
    A. Router
    B. DNS name
    C. DHCP relay agent
    D. Private IP address

22. Time synchronization traffic needs to traverse a firewall. Which port must be opened?
    A. TCP 123
    B. TCP 25
    C. UDP 123
    D. TCP 443

23. What does PAT use to track individual outbound connections?
    A. Private IP address
    B. MAC address
    C. Private IP address and port
    D. MAC address and port

24. Which port is used for standard SMTP mail transfer?
    A. 110
    B. 25
    C. 123
    D. 80

25. Which network topology uses a central cable to which network nodes are attached?
    A. Bus
    B. Straight-through
    C. Star
    D. Ring

26. Which two factors are related to network performance?

    A. IP address

    B. Bandwidth

    C. Network latency

    D. PKI

27. While network compression to the cloud reduces the size of transmitted data, what is increased?

    A. Storage space consumption

    B. Monthly cloud fees

    C. Processor utilization

    D. Security

28. What increases as compression reduces the size of transmitted data?

    A. Routing complexity

    B. Available bandwidth

    C. Cloud ingress network traffic costs

    D. Cloud egress network traffic costs

29. Which term describes distributing incoming application requests across multiple back-end servers?

    A. Load balancing

    B. Compressing

    C. Forward proxying

    D. NATting

30. What is another name for a forward proxy server?

    A. Layer 4 firewall

    B. Limiting host

    C. Redirection host

    D. Caching server

31. Which of the following is a valid class B private IP address range?

    A. 10.0.0.0–10.255.255.255

    B. 172.16.0.0–172.31.255.255

    C. 192.168.0.0–192.168.255.255

    D. 210.0.0.1–223.255.255.255

32. Which of the following are benefits of using PAT? Choose two.

    A. Less storage space consumption

    B. Increased network performance

    C. Increased security

    D. Less required public IP addresses

33. What type of IP address is given to a device when a DHCP server is unreachable?

   A.   APIPA

   B.   IPv6

   C.   Public

   D.   Class C

34. Which benefit is derived from supernetting?

   A.   Increased amount of available addresses

   B.   Increased router security

   C.   Reduced routing table size

   D.   Increased router performance

35. Which benefits can be realized from the use of VLANs? Choose two.

   A.   Security

   B.   Performance

   C.   Reduced costs

   D.   Reduced network complexity

A QUICK ANSWER KEY

1.	C	**10.**	D	**19.**	A	**28.**	B
2.	A	**11.**	D	**20.**	C	**29.**	A
3.	D	**12.**	D	**21.**	C	**30.**	D
4.	C	**13.**	B	**22.**	C	**31.**	B
5.	C	**14.**	D	**23.**	C	**32.**	C, D
6.	B	**15.**	A	**24.**	B	**33.**	A
7.	C	**16.**	B	**25.**	A	**34.**	C
8.	A	**17.**	D	**26.**	B, C	**35.**	A, B
9.	C	**18.**	B	**27.**	C		

A IN-DEPTH ANSWERS

1. Which network type allows authorized external users to access a controlled set of internal resources?
   A. Intranet
   B. Internet
   C. Extranet
   D. Federation

   ☑ **C.** An extranet allows authorized external users to access a controlled set of internal resources.

   ☒ **A, B,** and **D** are incorrect. Intranets are internal privately owned TCP/IP networks that use common Internet protocols such as HTTP to access internal web servers. The Internet is a global collection of interconnected networks using TCP/IP that is not owned by a corporation or government. Federation allows central identity providers to authenticate internal and external users and devices, but it is not a network type.

2. A university campus consists of many buildings populating a large property. All buildings are linked together through underground fiber-optic cables, creating a private network infrastructure. What type of network is this?
   A. MAN
   B. LAN
   C. WAN
   D. SAN

   ☑ **A.** A metropolitan area network (MAN) is larger than a local area network (LAN) and encompasses more than a single building, such as a university campus.

   ☒ **B, C,** and **D** are incorrect. A local area network (LAN) shares resources on a network normally contained within a single building. A wide area network (WAN) covers long distances. A storage area network (SAN) is an isolated network designed to transmit only storage-related traffic as opposed to TCP/IP traffic.

3. Which network topology has a potential central point of failure?
   A. Mesh
   B. Bus
   C. Ring
   D. Star

☑   **D.** Star network topologies use a central wiring location, normally in the form of one or more network switches. A switch failure means nodes plugged into that switch cannot communicate at all.

☒   **A, B,** and **C** are incorrect. Mesh networks provide connections between every node on a network, which increases resiliency as well as complexity and cost compared to other topologies. Bus networks use a single cable or trunk to which all network nodes are attached. Ring networks connect nodes to their previous and next neighbors; logical ring topologies provide the circular ring within the cabling even though physically they can be wired as a star.

4. Which of the following is a disadvantage of network compression?
    A. Higher storage requirements
    B. Longer transmission time
    C. Higher compute requirements
    D. Shorter transmission time

☑   **C.** Compression requires more processing power on both the sending and receiving devices than would otherwise be required without compression.

☒   **A, B,** and **D** are incorrect. Network compression is not related to storage, and it's advantage is that it decreases transmission time.

5. Refer to Figure 4-1. Devices B and C have numerous computers plugged into them that can all access the Internet. In all likelihood, what is device A?
    A. Firewall
    B. Switch
    C. Router
    D. Hub

FIGURE 4-1

Network diagram

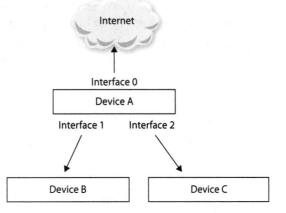

☑   **C.** A router allows internally connected devices to connect to the Internet.

☒   **A, B,** and **D** are incorrect. While firewalls can allow outbound traffic to the Internet, routers are absolutely required where firewalls are not. Switches and hubs allow multiple devices to be plugged into the same network, thus providing internal network communication, although switches isolate network conversations, which better utilizes network bandwidth.

6. Refer to Figure 4-2. Devices B and C have numerous computers plugged into them. What type of devices are they?

   A. Firewall
   B. Switch
   C. Router
   D. VPN concentrator

FIGURE 4-2

Network diagram

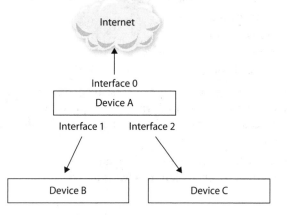

☑ **B.** Switches allow multiple devices to be plugged into the same network, thus providing internal network communication.

☒ **A, C,** and **D** are incorrect. Firewalls use rulesets to allow or deny network traffic. Routers use memory-resident routing tables to control network traffic flow. VPN concentrators are used to allow encrypted tunnel communication over an untrusted network. Unlike network switches, none of these devices is normally used to plug in multiple computers.

7. Refer to Figure 4-3. Internet traffic from both internal servers assumes an IP address of 200.1.1.1 when traversing the Internet. What type of solution is configured on device A?

   A. Routing
   B. Switching
   C. PAT
   D. NAT

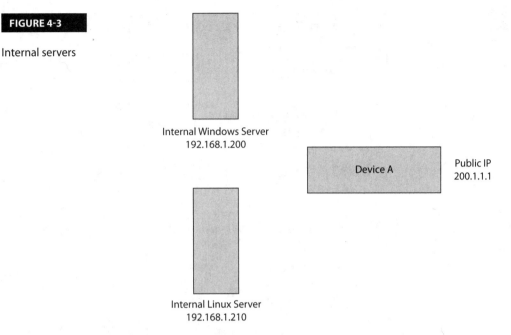

FIGURE 4-3

Internal servers

Internal Windows Server
192.168.1.200

Device A

Public IP
200.1.1.1

Internal Linux Server
192.168.1.210

☑ **C.** Port address translation (PAT) allows multiple internal hosts to use a single public IP address to gain Internet access. PAT tracks the source internal IP address and a unique port for outgoing connections.

☒ **A, B,** and **D** are incorrect. Routers use memory-resident routing tables to control network traffic flow. Switches have multiple ports for device network connections and make efficient use of network bandwidth by isolating network conversations. Network address translation is similar to PAT but differs technically in that there is a one-to-one mapping for public IP addresses to private internal IP addresses.

8. Refer to Figure 4-4. What is wrong with the Windows TCP/IPv4 configuration?

A. The default gateway is not reachable.

B. The alternate DNS server is on a different subnet.

C. The IP address is invalid.

D. The subnet mask is invalid.

Windows TCP/
IPv4 settings

Internet Protocol Version 4 (TCP/IPv4) Properties ☒

General

You can get IP settings assigned automatically if your network supports this capability. Otherwise, you need to ask your network administrator for the appropriate IP settings.

○ Obtain an IP address automatically
◉ Use the following IP address:

IP address: 192 . 168 . 1   . 200
Subnet mask: 255 . 255 . 255 . 0
Default gateway: 192 . 168 . 2   . 253

○ Obtain DNS server address automatically
◉ Use the following DNS server addresses:

Preferred DNS server: 192 . 168 . 1 . 210
Alternate DNS server: 54 . 56 . 14 . 98

☐ Validate settings upon exit   Advanced...

OK   Cancel

☑   **A.** The default gateway, or router, allows LAN traffic to get to other networks through a router; therefore, the default gateway must be configured to be on the same IP subnet as the host.
☒   **B, C,** and **D** are incorrect. DNS servers do not have to be configured on the same IP subnet as the host as long as the default gateway is set correctly. The IP address and subnet mask are valid.

9. Refer to the packet capture in Figure 4-5. What type of network traffic is this?

A. Web browser connecting to a web server
B. User authentication
C. Client DNS query to DNS server
D. Ping request

FIGURE 4-5

Packet capture

```
⊞ Frame 240 (79 bytes on wire, 79 bytes captured)
⊟ Ethernet II, Src: 90:48:9a:11:bd:6f (90:48:9a:11:bd:6f), Dst: d8:50:e6:93:02:a0
⊞ Internet Protocol, Src: 192.168.1.157 (192.168.1.157), Dst: 8.8.8.8 (8.8.8.8)
⊟ User Datagram Protocol, Src Port: 55828 (55828), Dst Port: domain (53)
     Source port: 55828 (55828)
     Destination port: domain (53)
     Length: 45
   ⊞ Checksum: 0x2b4e [validation disabled]
⊟ Domain Name System (query)
     [Response In: 242]
     Transaction ID: 0xebe4
   ⊞ Flags: 0x0100 (standard query)
     Questions: 1
     Answer RRs: 0
     Authority RRs: 0
```

☑ **C.** Client DNS queries occur on UDP port 53; this is listed in the capture as the destination port in the User Datagram Protocol (UDP) header.

☒ **A, B,** and **D** are incorrect. Traffic to a web server would normally be destined for TCP ports 80 or 443. User authentication traffic could occur using many different protocols; none of them would use UDP port 53. Ping traffic uses ICMP, not UDP, and it does not use a port number.

10. Refer to Figure 4-6. Which of the following observations is correct?

    A. The subnet mask must be changed.

    B. The physical address is not valid for a Wi-Fi adapter.

    C. The first DNS server entry is invalid.

    D. IP settings were not manually configured on this device.

FIGURE 4-6

Windows
ipconfig
command output

```
Wireless LAN adapter Wi-Fi:

   Connection-specific DNS Suffix  . : silversides.local
   Description . . . . . . . . . . . : Qualcomm Atheros AR956x Wireless Network
Adapter
   Physical Address. . . . . . . . . : 90-48-9A-11-BD-6F
   DHCP Enabled. . . . . . . . . . . : Yes
   Autoconfiguration Enabled . . . . : Yes
   IPv4 Address. . . . . . . . . . . : 192.168.1.157(Preferred)
   Subnet Mask . . . . . . . . . . . : 255.255.255.0
   Lease Obtained. . . . . . . . . . : Thursday, June 9, 2016 12:30:00 PM
   Lease Expires . . . . . . . . . . : Saturday, June 11, 2016 7:14:38 AM
   Default Gateway . . . . . . . . . : 192.168.1.1
   DHCP Server . . . . . . . . . . . : 192.168.1.1
   DNS Servers . . . . . . . . . . . : 8.8.8.8
                                        192.168.1.1
   Primary WINS Server . . . . . . . : 192.168.1.1
   NetBIOS over Tcpip. . . . . . . . : Enabled
```

☑ **D.** DHCP server and lease settings are shown in Figure 4-6, which means IP settings were not configured manually.

☒ **A, B,** and **C** are incorrect. The subnet mask is valid. MAC (physical) addresses are in no way impacted when using Wi-Fi. DNS servers can be on any subnet as long as the default gateway is set properly.

11. You need to connect through a firewall to remotely administer a Windows server using RDP. Which firewall allowance must be configured?

   A.   UDP 123

   B.   TCP 22

   C.   TCP 389

   D.   TCP 3389

   ☑   **D.** Remote Desktop Protocol (RDP) listens on TCP port 3389.

   ☒   **A, B,** and **C** are incorrect. UDP 123 is used by the Network Time Protocol (NTP). TCP 22 is used for Secure Shell (SSH) encrypted remote admin sessions. TCP 389 is used to connect to a network database using the Lightweight Directory Access Protocol (LDAP).

12. A client web browser connects to an HTTPS web server. Which port does the server use to communicate back to the client?

   A.   81

   B.   444

   C.   Any port below 1024

   D.   Any port above 1024

   ☑   **D.** Network services communicate back to clients on higher port numbers above 1024.

   ☒   **A, B,** and **C** are incorrect. Ports 81 and 444 are not used as client-side communication ports. Values above 1024 are used.

13. You are responsible for a web application running in the public cloud. Recent performance metrics indicate that the average user wait time for page loads is four seconds due to the high number of HTTP requests. What should you configure?

   A.   Compression

   B.   Load balancing

   C.   Proxying

   D.   PKI

   ☑   **B.** Load balancing distributes requests for a network service to multiple back-end hosts where the least busy host will respond.

   ☒   **A, C,** and **D** are incorrect. Compression removes duplicate file content to save space. Proxying is normally used to fetch Internet content requested by internal clients. Public key infrastructure (PKI) is a hierarchy of digital security certificates.

14. Petaire is a cloud network sysadmin. Cloud-based virtual machines hosting a custom web application have been deployed to a single cloud virtual network that currently has no Internet access. Each virtual machine must have Internet access, while incoming connections initiated from the Internet must be blocked. Which solution should Petaire deploy?

   A.   Forward proxy host

   B.   Packet filtering firewall

   C.   Web application firewall

   D.   NAT

☑ **D.** Network address translation (NAT) not only provides Internet access for internal hosts, it also blocks connections initiated from the Internet.

☒ **A, B,** and **C** are incorrect. Forward proxies fetch Internet content requested by internal clients. Packet filtering firewalls examine packet headers (not payloads) to allow or deny traffic. Web application firewalls monitor HTTP conversations and look for HTTP-specific attacks against web apps.

15. Users complain that Internet access has been intermittent. You check the configuration of a user system and discover it has an IP address beginning with 169.254. What is the problem?

    A. The DHCP server cannot be reached.
    B. The default gateway cannot be reached.
    C. The DNS server cannot be reached.
    D. The proxy server cannot be reached.

    ☑ **A.** Automatic IP addresses (APIPAs) are assigned by an operating system when a device configured to use DHCP cannot reach the DHCP server. The address will have a 169.254 prefix.

    ☒ **B, C,** and **D** are incorrect. The inability to reach a default gateway, DNS server, or proxy server does not result in a 169.254 address.

16. The _____ determines which portion of the IPv4 address identifies the network.

    A. Translation table
    B. Subnet mask
    C. MAC address
    D. IP address suffix

    ☑ **B.** The subnet mask determines how many bits of the IP address are allocated to the host versus the subnet.

    ☒ **A, C,** and **D** are incorrect. Translation tables, MAC addresses, and IP address suffixes do not determine the network portion of an IPv4 address.

17. You are reviewing a network diagram for a client. The diagram has numerous references to /22. What does this mean?

    A. The maximum number of hosts per network is 22.
    B. The average network compression ratio is 1:22.
    C. IP addresses can be divided in 22 subordinate addresses.
    D. There are 22 bits in the subnet mask.

    ☑ **D.** Classless inter-domain routing (CIDR) is commonly used to specify the number of bits in a subnet mask, such as /22.

    ☒ **A, B,** and **C** are incorrect. /22 is CIDR notation for the number of bits in a subnet mask and does not relate to the other listed items.

18. Your organization plans to use iSCSI for shared network storage. Which technique should be used to ensure that iSCSI traffic is kept separate from other IP traffic?
    A. LUN masking
    B. VLANs
    C. Zoning
    D. Load balancing

    ☑ **B.** Virtual local area networks (VLANs) logically subdivide a physical network into smaller networks for the purposes of network isolation to reduce network traffic and to increase security.
    ☒ **A, C,** and **D** are incorrect. LUN masking and zoning keep shared network storage visible only to certain hosts. Load balancing distributes requests for a network service to multiple back-end hosts where the least busy host will respond.

19. What is commonly used in cloud environments to separate network traffic between cloud tenants?
    A. VXLAN
    B. Router
    C. VLAN
    D. Switch

    ☑ **A.** Virtual extensible local area networks (VXLANs) are used in the cloud to keep cloud tenant traffic separate.
    ☒ **B, C,** and **D** are incorrect. While routers and switches are an important underlying part of the cloud infrastructure, VXLAN is a more specific answer. VLAN configurations are commonly used on premises.

20. Which protocol is used to secure SFTP sessions?
    A. FTP
    B. IPSec
    C. SSH
    D. PKI

    ☑ **C.** Secure Shell (SSH) is used with SFTP to secure FTP sessions.
    ☒ **A, B,** and **D** are incorrect. File Transfer Protocol (FTP), IPSec, and PKI do not secure FTP sessions.

21. DHCP functionality across subnets is configured using a _____.
    A. Router
    B. DNS name
    C. DHCP relay agent
    D. Private IP address

    ☑ **C.** DCHP relay agents are hosts or router configurations that listen for local subnet DHCP broadcasts seeking a DHCP server and forward that traffic to a DHCP server on a remote network.
    ☒ **A, B,** and **D** are incorrect. While routers connect networks and DHCP relay can be configured on a router, this is not as specific as DHCP relay agent. DNS names and private IPs have no direct relationship with DHCP.

22. Time synchronization traffic needs to traverse a firewall. Which port must be opened?
   A. TCP 123
   B. TCP 25
   C. UDP 123
   D. TCP 443

   ☑ **C.** The Network Time Protocol (NTP) communicates using UDP port 123.
   ☒ **A, B,** and **D** are incorrect. TCP 123 is not used for time synchronization. TCP 25 is used for SMTP mail transfer. TCP 443 is used for HTTP traffic.

23. What does PAT use to track individual outbound connections?
   A. Private IP address
   B. MAC address
   C. Private IP address and port
   D. MAC address and port

   ☑ **C.** Outbound connections are uniquely tracked in memory on the PAT device by using the private IP address of the initiating station along with a unique PAT port number.
   ☒ **A, B,** and **D** are incorrect. The private IP address is only one part of what is tracked by PAT. MAC addresses are not tracked by PAT.

24. Which port is used for standard SMTP mail transfer?
   A. 110
   B. 25
   C. 123
   D. 80

   ☑ **B.** Simple Mail Transfer Protocol (SMTP) communicates, by default, on TCP port 25.
   ☒ **A, C,** and **D** are incorrect. Post Office Protocol (POP) uses port 110, Network Time Protocol (NTP) uses port 123, and Hypertext Transfer Protocol (HTTP) uses port 80.

25. Which network topology uses a central cable to which network nodes are attached?
   A. Bus
   B. Straight-through
   C. Star
   D. Ring

   ☑ **A.** Bus topologies use a central trunk to which network nodes are attached. Bus topologies are rarely used.
   ☒ **B, C,** and **D** are incorrect. Straight-through is a standard twisted pair type of network cabling, not a topology. Star topologies use a central wiring device such as a switch, and ring topologies connect each node to its previous and next neighbors.

26. Which two factors are related to network performance?

    A. IP address

    B. Bandwidth

    C. Network latency

    D. PKI

☑ **B** and **C.** Network bandwidth measures how quickly data can travel between two points within a time frame, such as 10 Gbps. Network latency refers to delays in network transmission, such as due to a weak Wi-Fi signal.

☒ **A** and **D** are incorrect. IP addresses and public key infrastructure (PKI) do not influence network performance.

27. While network compression to the cloud reduces the size of transmitted data, what is increased?

    A. Storage space consumption

    B. Monthly cloud fees

    C. Processor utilization

    D. Security

☑ **C.** Compressing and decompressing data requires more CPU processing power than not participating in compression.

☒ **A, B,** and **D** are incorrect. Network compression does not increase storage space consumption, cloud fees, or security.

28. What increases as compression reduces the size of transmitted data?

    A. Routing complexity

    B. Available bandwidth

    C. Cloud ingress network traffic costs

    D. Cloud egress network traffic costs

☑ **B.** Network compression decreases the amount of data to be sent, thus increasing the amount of available network bandwidth.

☒ **A, C,** and **D** are incorrect. Routing complexity and inbound and outbound traffic costs are not influenced as described by network compression.

29. Which term describes distributing incoming application requests across multiple back-end servers?

    A. Load balancing

    B. Compressing

    C. Forward proxying

    D. NATting

☑ **A.** Load balancing distributes requests for a network service to multiple back-end hosts where the least busy host will respond.

☒ **B, C,** and **D** are incorrect. Compression, forward proxying, and NAT do not process incoming application requests.

30. What is another name for a forward proxy server?
   A. Layer 4 firewall
   B. Limiting host
   C. Redirection host
   D. Caching server

   ☑ **D.** Forward proxies not only fetch Internet content requested by internal clients, but also can cache the fetched data for a period of time to speed up subsequent requests for the same content.
   ☒ **A, B,** and **C** are incorrect. Layer 4 firewalls are not proxies; they are packet filtering firewalls. Neither limiting host nor redirection host is another name for a proxy server.

31. Which of the following is a valid class B private IP address range?
   A. 10.0.0.0–10.255.255.255
   B. 172.16.0.0–172.31.255.255
   C. 192.168.0.0–192.168.255.255
   D. 210.0.0.1–223.255.255.255

   ☑ **B.** RFC 1928 specifies that 172.16.0.0–172.31.255.255 is the class B internal IP address range not routed by Internet routers.
   ☒ **A, C,** and **D** are incorrect. The listed IP address ranges are not class B private IP address ranges.

32. Which of the following are benefits of using PAT? Choose two.
   A. Less storage space consumption
   B. Increased network performance
   C. Increased security
   D. Less required public IP addresses

   ☑ **C** and **D.** Port address translation (PAT) increases security by hiding internal IP addresses of requesting clients as well as blocking inbound connections initiated by the Internet. PAT also allows multiple internal IP addresses to access the Internet through a single public IP address.
   ☒ **A** and **B** are incorrect. PAT is not related to storage or increased network performance.

33. What type of IP address is given to a device when a DHCP server is unreachable?
   A. APIPA
   B. IPv6
   C. Public
   D. Class C

   ☑ **A.** Automatic IP addresses (APIPAs) are assigned by an operating system when a device configured to use DHCP cannot reach the DHCP server. The address will have a 169.254 prefix.
   ☒ **B, C,** and **D** are incorrect. Unreachable DHCP servers do not result in the configuration of a public, IPv6, or class C IP address.

34. Which benefit is derived from supernetting?

    A. Increased amount of available addresses

    B. Increased router security

    C. Reduced routing table size

    D. Increased router performance

    ☑ **C.** Supernetting allows multiple adjacent IPv4 networks to be expressed in a single routing table entry, thus reducing the size of routing tables.

    ☒ **A, B,** and **D** are incorrect. The listed items are not benefits resulting from supernetting.

35. Which benefits can be realized from the use of VLANs? Choose two.

    A. Security

    B. Performance

    C. Reduced costs

    D. Reduced network complexity

    ☑ **A** and **B.** Virtual local area networks (VLANs) logically subdivide a physical network into smaller networks for the purposes of network isolation to reduce network traffic and to increase security.

    ☒ **C** and **D** are incorrect. VLANs do not result in reduced costs; their configuration increases network complexity.

Chapter 5

Virtualization Components

CERTIFICATION OBJECTIVES

5.01   Hypervisor

5.02   Virtualization Host

5.03   Virtual Machine

5.04   Virtualized Infrastructure Service Elements

QUESTIONS

Virtualization is used on premises as well as in public cloud environments. In fact, cloud computing would not be possible without virtualization, which allows for the rapid provisioning of virtual machines and the sharing of pooled hardware compute resources.

Hypervisors are the foundation of operating system virtualization. Virtual machine guests have memory, processor, and network configurations that can efficiently share hypervisor resources.

1. Which type of hypervisor does not require an existing operating system?
   A. Type A
   B. Type 1
   C. Type 2
   D. Type B

2. Software developers in your organization currently use Windows 10 desktops. Custom apps are being built and tested using test servers. Developers have asked for an operating system virtualization solution they can run on their desktops. What would you recommend?
   A. Type A hypervisor
   B. Type 1 hypervisor
   C. Type 2 hypervisor
   D. Type B hypervisor

3. Which hardware standard supersedes BIOS?
   A. SAN
   B. SATA
   C. VT-x
   D. UEFI

4. Which memory management technique takes unused memory from virtual machines and allocates it where it is needed by other virtual machines?

A. Ballooning

B. Overcommitting

C. Compressing

D. Sharding

5. Your hypervisor has the ability to deduplicate virtual machine memory pages for optimal memory usage. What is this called?

A. Page swapping

B. Transparent page sharing

C. Ballooning

D. Overcommitting

6. Which NIC feature allows for a larger individual Ethernet packet size?

A. Checksum off-load

B. TCP segmentation off-load

C. NIC teaming

D. Jumbo frames

7. You are the virtualization administrator for a specific hypervisor host. There is limited disk space and you do not know how much disk space each virtual machine will require over time. Which virtual disk type should you employ?

A. Differencing

B. Dynamically expanding

C. Fixed

D. Thin provisioning

8. You need to configure a virtual machine so that it can communicate on the physical corporate LAN. Which hypervisor component sits between the virtual NIC and the physical network?

A. Ethernet switch

B. Twisted pair cabling

C. Virtual router

D. Virtual switch

9. Digital signatures are created with the _____ key.
- A. Symmetric
- B. Asymmetric
- C. Public
- D. Private

10. Digital signatures are verified with the _____ key.
- A. Symmetric
- B. Asymmetric
- C. Public
- D. Private

11. In a PKI, network data is normally encrypted with the recipient's _____ key.
- A. Symmetric
- B. Asymmetric
- C. Public
- D. Private

12. Your organization has numerous newly deployed virtual machines (VMs) in a public cloud. You are responsible for ensuring the VMs are malware free. What is the FIRST item you should configure?
- A. Malware definition updates
- B. Virtual machine antivirus extension
- C. Cloud packet filtering firewall
- D. Cloud web application firewall

13. What does an IPS do that an IDS does not?
- A. Report abnormal activity
- B. Block suspicious activity
- C. Notify administrators of abnormal activity
- D. Check for known attack signatures

14. A customer service tracking application runs on an internal web server. You need to ensure any suspicious activity related to the server and the app are logged, and administrators are notified. Which solution should you deploy?
- A. HIDS
- B. HIPS
- C. NIDS
- D. NIPS

15. You are preparing a host's hardware settings so that it can be a hypervisor. Which setting are you most likely to enable?

   A. Guest tools

   B. Boot sequence

   C. Power-on password

   D. Hardware-assisted virtualization

16. _____ is another name for a hypervisor.

   A. Virtual machine

   B. Guest

   C. Virtualization host

   D. vHost

17. What is required before installing a type 2 hypervisor?

   A. NIC teaming software

   B. Operating system

   C. Class C IP address

   D. Smartcard

18. Virtual machine disks can be provisioned using _____ or _____ provisioning. Choose two.

   A. Scaled out

   B. Thin

   C. Scaled up

   D. Thick

19. Which term describes grouping multiple network storage devices into a single storage unit?

   A. LUN masking

   B. Zoning

   C. SAN

   D. Storage virtualization

20. A _____ is a piece of software that runs virtual machines.

   A. Balloon driver

   B. TPM

   C. Guest

   D. Hypervisor

21. What type of virtualization solution is depicted in Figure 5-1?

A. Type 1 hypervisor

B. Type 2 hypervisor

C. Type 3 hypervisor

D. Type 4 hypervisor

FIGURE 5-1 Virtualization software

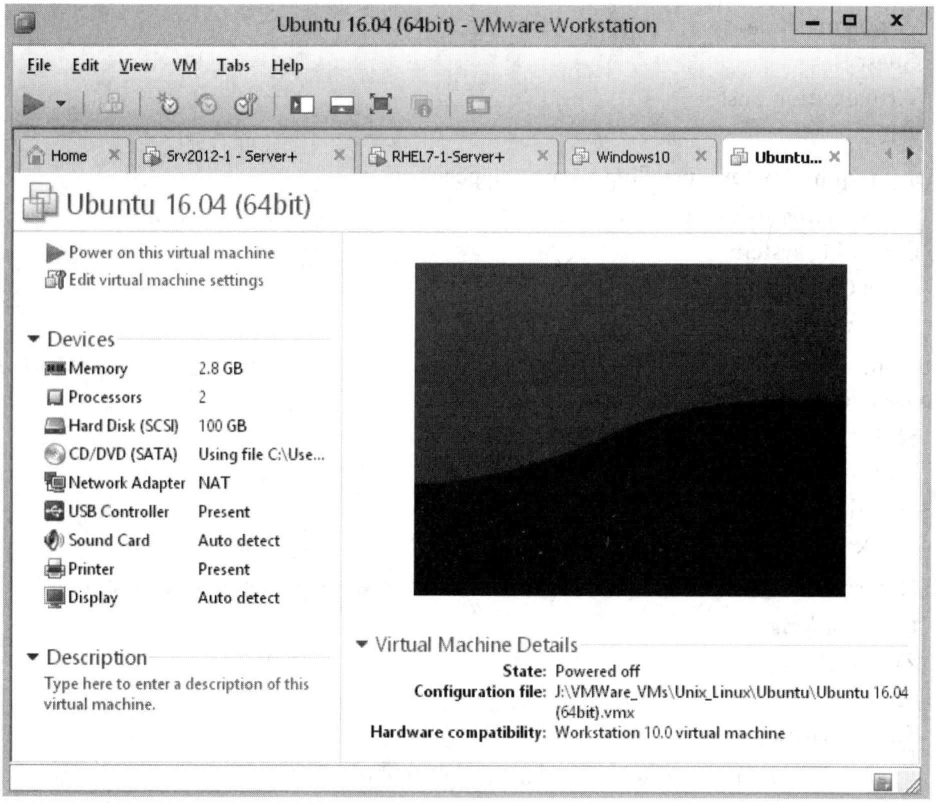

22. Which of the following statements regarding Figure 5-2 is correct?

A. Connections initiated from other networks will not reach the virtual machine.

B. The virtual machine memory configuration exceeds allowable thresholds.

C. The number of vCPUs should be increased to four.

D. NIC teaming is enabled on the host.

| FIGURE 5-2 | VMware Workstation virtual machine settings |

23. Refer to Figure 5-3. Which setting allows virtual machine memory to be increased and decreased while it is running?
    A. Memory weight set low
    B. RAM set high
    C. Memory weight set high
    D. Dynamic memory enabled

FIGURE 5-3   Microsoft Hyper-V virtual machine settings

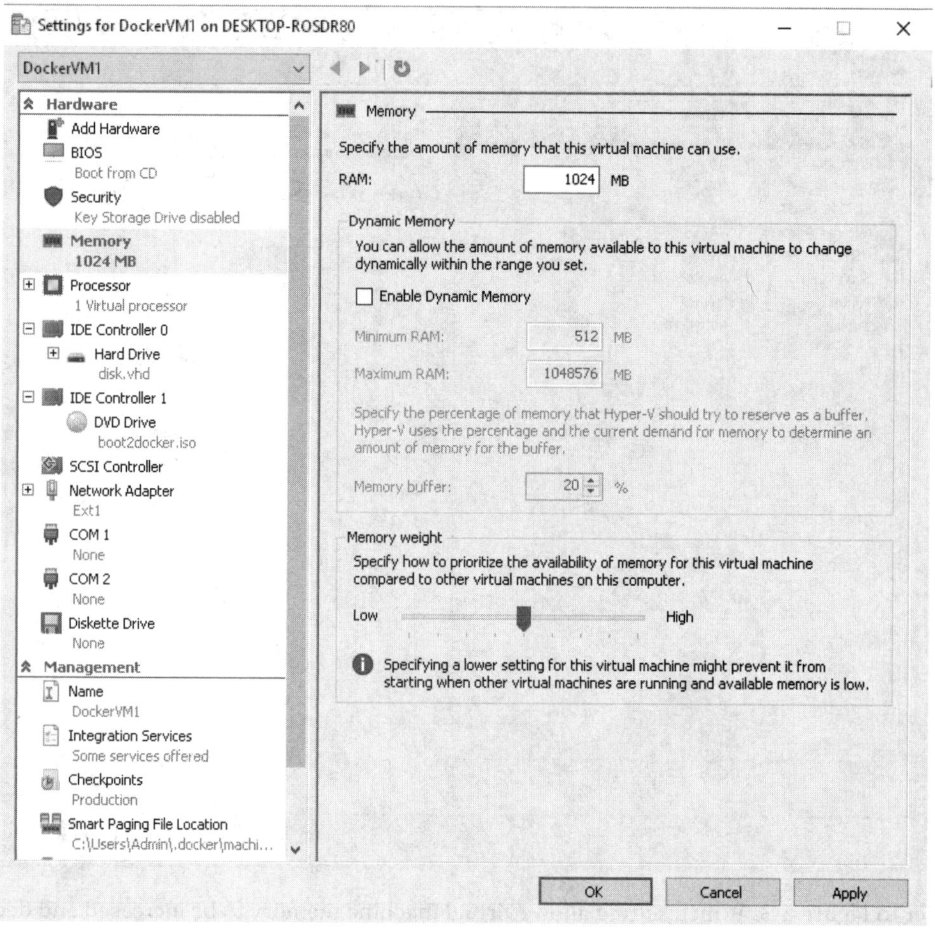

24. Refer to Figure 5-4. Which option will thinly provision the new virtual disk?
    A. Fixed size
    B. Dynamically expanding
    C. Differencing
    D. None of them, because the disk cannot be thinly provisioned

| FIGURE 5-4 | New virtual disk creation |

New Virtual Hard Disk Wizard   ✕

Choose Disk Type

Before You Begin
Choose Disk Format
Choose Disk Type
Specify Name and Location
Configure Disk
Summary

What type of virtual hard disk do you want to create?

○ Fixed size

This type of disk provides better performance and is recommended for servers running applications with high levels of disk activity. The virtual hard disk file that is created initially uses the size of the virtual hard disk and does not change when data is deleted or added.

◉ Dynamically expanding

This type of disk provides better use of physical storage space and is recommended for servers running applications that are not disk intensive. The virtual hard disk file that is created is small initially and changes as data is added.

○ Differencing

This type of disk is associated in a parent-child relationship with another disk that you want to leave intact. You can make changes to the data or operating system without affecting the parent disk, so that you can revert the changes easily. All children must have the same virtual hard disk format as the parent (VHD or VHDX).

< Previous   Next >   Finish   Cancel

25. You are configuring virtual network settings as per Figure 5-5. Virtual machines connected to VMnet1 must receive their TCP/IP settings automatically. Which option should you enable?

A. Bridged

B. NAT

C. Connect a host virtual adapter to this network

D. Use local DHCP service to distribute IP address to VMs

FIGURE 5-5   Virtual network settings

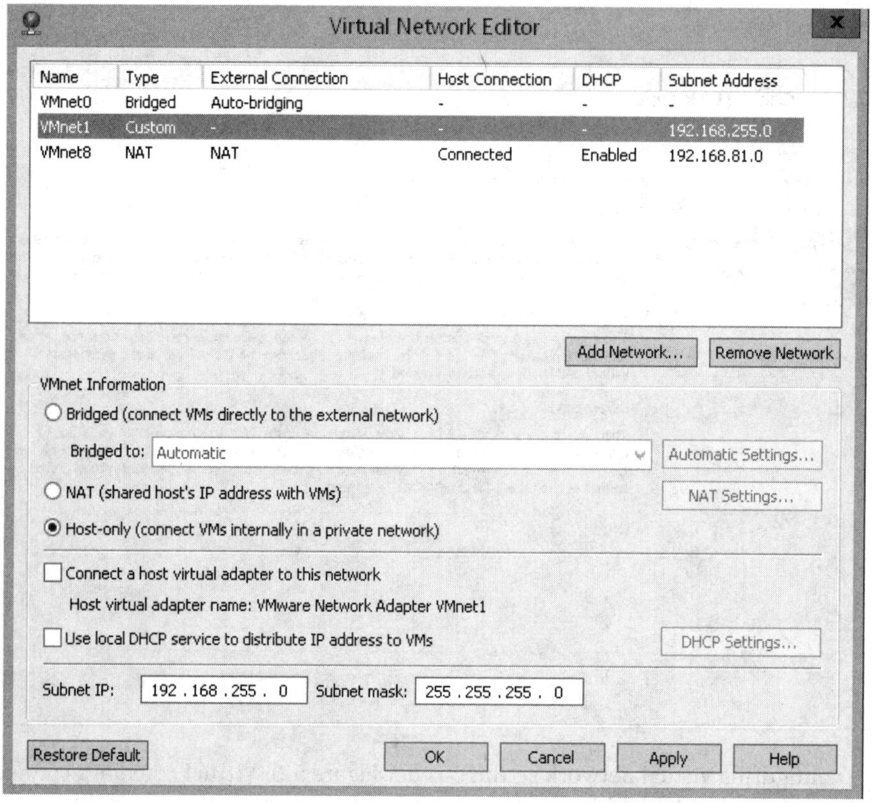

26. A virtual machine no longer properly synchronizes its time with the hypervisor host. Other virtual machines on the same host have no problems. Which menu option in Figure 5-6 should you select?

    A. Send Ctrl+Alt+Del
    B. Grab Input
    C. Reinstall VMware Tools
    D. Pause

FIGURE 5-6

Virtual machine
menu

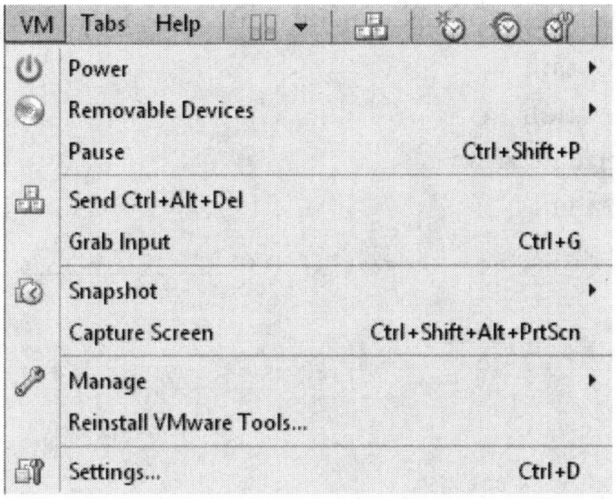

VM	Tabs	Help						

Power ▶

Removable Devices ▶

Pause   Ctrl+Shift+P

Send Ctrl+Alt+Del

Grab Input   Ctrl+G

Snapshot ▶

Capture Screen   Ctrl+Shift+Alt+PrtScn

Manage ▶

Reinstall VMware Tools...

Settings...   Ctrl+D

27. Which of the following hypervisor products are open source? Choose two.

    A. VMware ESXi

    B. Xen

    C. Xen Server

    D. KVM

28. You are configuring a hypervisor clustered solution consisting of three hypervisors using shared storage: Hv1, Hv2, and Hv3. Hv1 hosts three virtual machines, Hv2 hosts two virtual machines, and Hv3 hosts four virtual machines that all have network connectivity. Assuming the cluster will continue running with two failed nodes, what consideration must you account for?

    A. Shared storage

    B. Virtual machine IP addressing

    C. All virtual machines running on one host

    D. Storage space

29. Which hardware option allows for higher overcommitment ratios of vCPUs to physical CPUs?

    A. Hyperthreading

    B. Ballooning

    C. UEFI

    D. CPU NAT

30. It is generally safe to allocate up to _____ vCPU(s) for each physical CPU.

    A. One

    B. Two

    C. Three

    D. Four

31. Which term describes a virtual machine that is aware it is virtualized?
  A.   Full virtualization
  B.   Paravirtualization
  C.   Dynamic virtualization
  D.   Containerization

32. VMware virtual disks use a file extension of _____.
  A.   .vmdk
  B.   .vhd
  C.   .vhdx
  D.   .esx

33. Microsoft Hyper-V virtual disks use a file extension of _____.
  A.   .vmdk
  B.   .dhx
  C.   .vhdx
  D.   .esx

34. Which type of Microsoft Hyper-V disk reduces disk space consumption?
  A.   Differencing
  B.   Fixed
  C.   Dynamic
  D.   Compressed

35. What is the maximum amount of RAM supported by Citrix XenServer 6.1?
  A.   64GB
  B.   96GB
  C.   128GB
  D.   192GB

A
QUICK ANSWER KEY

1.	B	**10.**	C	**19.**	D	**28.**	C
2.	C	**11.**	C	**20.**	D	**29.**	A
3.	D	**12.**	B	**21.**	B	**30.**	C
4.	A	**13.**	B	**22.**	A	**31.**	B
5.	B	**14.**	A	**23.**	D	**32.**	A
6.	D	**15.**	D	**24.**	B	**33.**	C
7.	B	**16.**	C	**25.**	D	**34.**	A
8.	D	**17.**	B	**26.**	C	**35.**	C
9.	D	**18.**	B, D	**27.**	B, D		

IN-DEPTH ANSWERS

1. Which type of hypervisor does not require an existing operating system?
    A. Type A
    B. Type 1
    C. Type 2
    D. Type B

    ☑ **B.** Type 1 hypervisors are operating systems that support the running of virtual machines on shared hardware.

    ☒ **A, C,** and **D** are incorrect. Type A and Type B are not valid hypervisor types. Type 2 hypervisors must be installed on an existing operating system.

2. Software developers in your organization currently use Windows 10 desktops. Custom apps are being built and tested using test servers. Developers have asked for an operating system virtualization solution they can run on their desktops. What would you recommend?
    A. Type A hypervisor
    B. Type 1 hypervisor
    C. Type 2 hypervisor
    D. Type B hypervisor

    ☑ **C.** Type 2 hypervisors must be installed on an existing operating system.

    ☒ **A, B,** and **D** are incorrect. Type A and Type B are not valid hypervisor types. Type 1 hypervisors are operating systems that support the running of virtual machines on shared hardware.

3. Which hardware standard supersedes BIOS?
    A. SAN
    B. SATA
    C. VT-x
    D. UEFI

    ☑ **D.** Unified Extensible Firmware Interface (UEFI) is a replacement for BIOS.

    ☒ **A, B,** and **C** are incorrect. A storage area network (SAN) is a network dedicated to storage traffic. Serial ATA (SATA) is a hard disk interface standard. VT-x is a virtualization standard built into CPUs.

4. Which memory management technique takes unused memory from virtual machines and allocates it where it is needed by other virtual machines?

A. Ballooning
B. Overcommitting
C. Compressing
D. Sharding

☑ **A.** Memory ballooning occurs when a hypervisor receives an urgent request from a virtual machine for memory that is not available. Other virtual machine guests temporarily "lend" unused memory to the hypervisor through the ballooning driver.

☒ **B, C,** and **D** are incorrect. Overcommitting refers to overallocating resources, such as creating disk volumes whose total size exceeds physically available storage space. Compressing removes duplicates to reduce space consumption. Sharding is a database partitioning scheme used to improve performance.

5. Your hypervisor has the ability to deduplicate virtual machine memory pages for optimal memory usage. What is this called?

A. Page swapping
B. Transparent page sharing
C. Ballooning
D. Overcommitting

☑ **B.** Transparent page sharing removes duplicate virtual machine memory pages, which results in more efficient hypervisor memory utilization.

☒ **A, C,** and **D** are incorrect. Page swapping occurs when an operating system does not have enough memory pages; older memory pages are swapped to disk, thus freeing memory for current instructions. Memory ballooning occurs when a hypervisor receives an urgent request from a virtual machine for memory that is not available. Other virtual machine guests temporarily "lend" unused memory to the hypervisor through the ballooning driver. Overcommitting refers to overallocating resources, such as creating disk volumes whose total size exceeds physically available storage space.

6. Which NIC feature allows for a larger individual Ethernet packet size?

A. Checksum off-load
B. TCP segmentation off-load
C. NIC teaming
D. Jumbo frames

☑ **D.** Jumbo frames allow Ethernet frames to reach up to 9,000 bytes instead of the normal maximum of 1,514 bytes.

☒ **A, B,** and **C** are incorrect. Checksum off-load uses the NIC to process TCP traffic instead of the CPU. TCP segmentation off-load breaks large TCP transmissions into smaller units for traversal over a network. NIC teaming joins two or more NICs for increased bandwidth and resiliency to failure.

7. You are the virtualization administrator for a specific hypervisor host. There is limited disk space and you do not know how much disk space each virtual machine will require over time. Which virtual disk type should you employ?

   A. Differencing
   B. Dynamically expanding
   C. Fixed
   D. Thin provisioning

   ☑ **B.** Dynamically expanding disks grow over time as space is needed.

   ☒ **A, C,** and **D** are incorrect. Differencing disks use a parent-child relationship where a parent virtual disk holds files that are inherited by its children; changes are written to the differencing disk. Fixed virtual disks allocate the entire amount of specified storage at creation time. Thin provisioning optimizes available disk space by allowing virtual disks to allocate and commit storage space on demand.

8. You need to configure a virtual machine so that it can communicate on the physical corporate LAN. Which hypervisor component sits between the virtual NIC and the physical network?

   A. Ethernet switch
   B. Twisted pair cabling
   C. Virtual router
   D. Virtual switch

   ☑ **D.** Virtual machine virtual NICs connect to a virtual switch, which in turn can be connected (bridged) to a physical network.

   ☒ **A, B,** and **C** are incorrect. Ethernet switches, twisted pair cabling, and virtual routers are not hypervisor components.

9. Digital signatures are created with the _____ key.

   A. Symmetric
   B. Asymmetric
   C. Public
   D. Private

   ☑ **D.** Private keys are available only to their owner and are used to create digital signatures to prove authenticity of messages.

   ☒ **A, B,** and **C** are incorrect. Symmetric means the same key is used for operations such as encrypting and decrypting. Asymmetric keys are mathematically related, such as public and private key pairs. Public keys are used to verify digital signatures created with private keys.

10. Digital signatures are verified with the _____ key.

    A. Symmetric
    B. Asymmetric
    C. Public
    D. Private

☑ **C.** Public keys are used to verify digital signatures created with private keys.

☒ **A, B,** and **D** are incorrect. Symmetric means the same key is used for operations such as encrypting and decrypting. Asymmetric keys are mathematically related, such as public and private key pairs. Private keys are available only to their owner and are used to create digital signatures to prove authenticity of messages.

11. In a PKI, network data is normally encrypted with the recipient's _____ key.

A. Symmetric
B. Asymmetric
C. Public
D. Private

☑ **C.** A message is encrypted with the recipient's public key.

☒ **A, B,** and **D** are incorrect. Symmetric means the same key is used for operations such as encrypting and decrypting. Asymmetric keys are mathematically related, such as public and private key pairs. Private keys are available only to their owner and are used to create digital signatures to prove authenticity of messages.

12. Your organization has numerous newly deployed virtual machines (VMs) in a public cloud. You are responsible for ensuring the VMs are malware free. What is the FIRST item you should configure?

A. Malware definition updates
B. Virtual machine antivirus extension
C. Cloud packet filtering firewall
D. Cloud web application firewall

☑ **B.** Public cloud providers use virtual machine extensions to add functionality to virtual machines, such as with an antivirus extension.

☒ **A, C,** and **D** are incorrect. Malware definition updates are useless without an antimalware engine. Packet filtering and web application firewalls do not check for malware. Packet filters examine packet headers to allow or deny traffic. Web application firewalls examine HTTP conversations looking for anomalies.

13. What does an IPS do that an IDS does not?

A. Report abnormal activity
B. Block suspicious activity
C. Notify administrators of abnormal activity
D. Check for known attack signatures

☑ **B.** Intrusion prevention systems (IPSs) not only can detect and report suspicious behavior, but can also take steps to block the behavior.

☒ **A, C,** and **D** are incorrect. Both intrusion detection systems (IDSs) and IPSs can report, notify, and check for abnormal activity.

14. A customer service tracking application runs on an internal web server. You need to ensure any suspicious activity related to the server and the app are logged, and administrators are notified. Which solution should you deploy?

   A. HIDS
   B. HIPS
   C. NIDS
   D. NIPS

   ☑ **A.** A host-based intrusion detection system (HIDS) runs on a machine and examines not only incoming and outgoing network traffic, but host processes and logs.

   ☒ **B, C,** and **D** are incorrect. A host-based intrusion prevention system (HIPS) has the added capability of blocking suspicious activity. A network-based intrusion detection system (NIDS) monitors network traffic looking for anomalies. A network-based intrusion prevention system (NIPS) is similar to a NIDS but can also block suspicious activity.

15. You are preparing a host's hardware settings so that it can be a hypervisor. Which setting are you most likely to enable?

   A. Guest tools
   B. Boot sequence
   C. Power-on password
   D. Hardware-assisted virtualization

   ☑ **D.** Hardware-assisted virtualization is a firmware option that must be enabled on a hypervisor host.

   ☒ **A, B,** and **C** are incorrect. Guest tools provide functionality between virtual machines and the hypervisor, such as the ability to synchronize time, but this relates to guests, not the host. A machine's boot sequence and power-on password are not normally changed when preparing a hypervisor host computer.

16. _____ is another name for a hypervisor.

   A. Virtual machine
   B. Guest
   C. Virtualization host
   D. vHost

   ☑ **C.** Hypervisor and virtualization host are synonymous.

   ☒ **A, B,** and **D** are incorrect. Virtual machine and guest are synonymous. vHost is not a common virtualization term.

17. What is required before installing a type 2 hypervisor?

   A. NIC teaming software
   B. Operating system
   C. Class C IP address
   D. Smartcard

☑ **B.** Type 2 hypervisors are software applications that get installed on top of an existing operating system.

☒ **A, C,** and **D** are incorrect. NIC teaming, IP address configuration, and smartcard usage are not directly related to installing a type 2 hypervisor.

18. Virtual machine disks can be provisioned using _____ or _____ provisioning. Choose two.

    A. Scaled out

    B. Thin

    C. Scaled up

    D. Thick

☑ **B** and **D.** Virtual machine disk thin provisioning does not allocate all of the space upon creation as thick provisioning does; instead space is allocated as needed.

☒ **A** and **C** are incorrect. Scaling out adds more computing nodes to support an increased IT workload. Scaling up increases the power of existing nodes.

19. Which term describes grouping multiple network storage devices into a single storage unit?

    A. LUN masking

    B. Zoning

    C. SAN

    D. Storage virtualization

☑ **D.** Storage virtualization presents units of storage to storage consumers where the actual storage could consist of many storage devices grouped together.

☒ **A, B,** and **C** are incorrect. LUN masking and zoning are used to control host access to shared storage. A storage area network (SAN) is a network dedicated to the transmission of only storage traffic.

20. A _____ is a piece of software that runs virtual machines.

    A. Balloon driver

    B. TPM

    C. Guest

    D. Hypervisor

☑ **D.** Hypervisors run and manage virtual machine guests.

☒ **A, B,** and **C** are incorrect. Memory ballooning occurs when a hypervisor receives an urgent request from a virtual machine for memory that is not available. Other virtual machine guests temporarily "lend" unused memory to the hypervisor through the ballooning driver. Trusted Platform Module (TPM) is a firmware standard used to store decryption keys and to ensure boot sequences have not been tampered with. Guest is another term for virtual machine.

21. What type of virtualization solution is depicted in Figure 5-1?

A. Type 1 hypervisor

B. Type 2 hypervisor

C. Type 3 hypervisor

D. Type 4 hypervisor

Virtualization software

☑ **B.** Type 2 hypervisors are software applications that run on top of an existing operating system.

☒ **A, C,** and **D** are incorrect. Type 1 hypervisors are operating systems that can run and manage virtual machines. Type 3 and Type 4 are not valid types of hypervisors.

22. Which of the following statements regarding Figure 5-2 is correct?

A. Connections initiated from other networks will not reach the virtual machine.

B. The virtual machine memory configuration exceeds allowable thresholds.

C. The number of vCPUs should be increased to four.

D. NIC teaming is enabled on the host.

FIGURE 5-2   VMware Workstation virtual machine settings

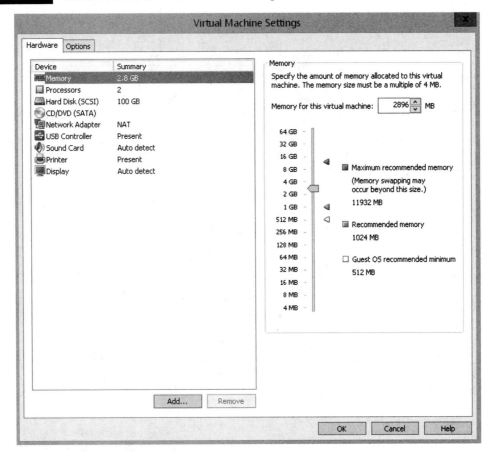

☑   **A.** While network address translation (NAT) allows outgoing Internet connections, it blocks connections initiated from outside the network.

☒   **B, C,** and **D** are incorrect. The listed items are not implied based on the information shown in Figure 5-2.

23.   Refer to Figure 5-3. Which setting allows virtual machine memory to be increased and decreased while it is running?

A.   Memory weight set low

B.   RAM set high

C.   Memory weight set high

D.   Dynamic memory enabled

FIGURE 5-3 Microsoft Hyper-V virtual machine settings

☑ **D.** Dynamic memory allows a virtual machine to change its memory allocation while running.

☒ **A, B,** and **C** are incorrect. Memory weight settings compare to other running virtual machines on the same hypervisor; higher weights receive memory over lower weights when hypervisor memory is limited. Setting the RAM amount high does not allow allocated memory to be changed.

24. Refer to Figure 5-4. Which option will thinly provision the new virtual disk?

A. Fixed size

B. Dynamically expanding

C. Differencing

D. None of them, because the disk cannot be thinly provisioned

FIGURE 5-4   New virtual disk creation

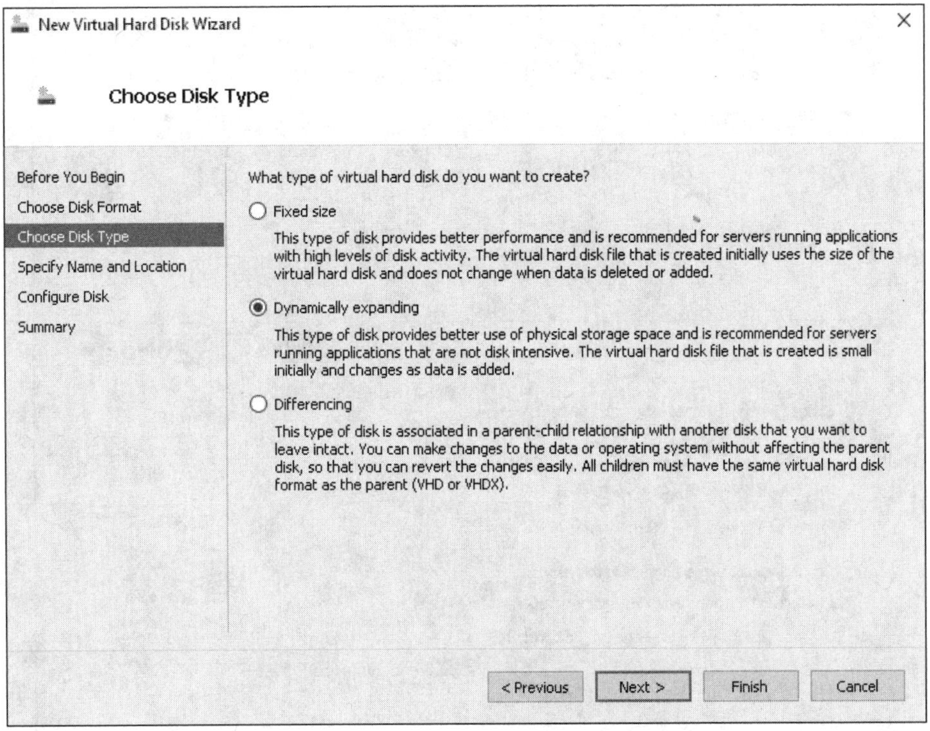

     ☑ **B.** Dynamically expanding disks are said to be thinly provisioned.

     ☒ **A, C,** and **D** are incorrect. Fixed-size disks allocate all specified storage space upon creation. Differencing disks use a parent-child relationship where a parent virtual disk holds files that are inherited by its children; changes are written to the differencing disk. The configuration in Figure 5-4 does allow thin provisioning.

25. You are configuring virtual network settings as per Figure 5-5. Virtual machines connected to VMnet1 must receive their TCP/IP settings automatically. Which option should you enable?

    A. Bridged

    B. NAT

    C. Connect a host virtual adapter to this network

    D. Use local DHCP service to distribute IP address to VMs

FIGURE 5-5   Virtual network settings

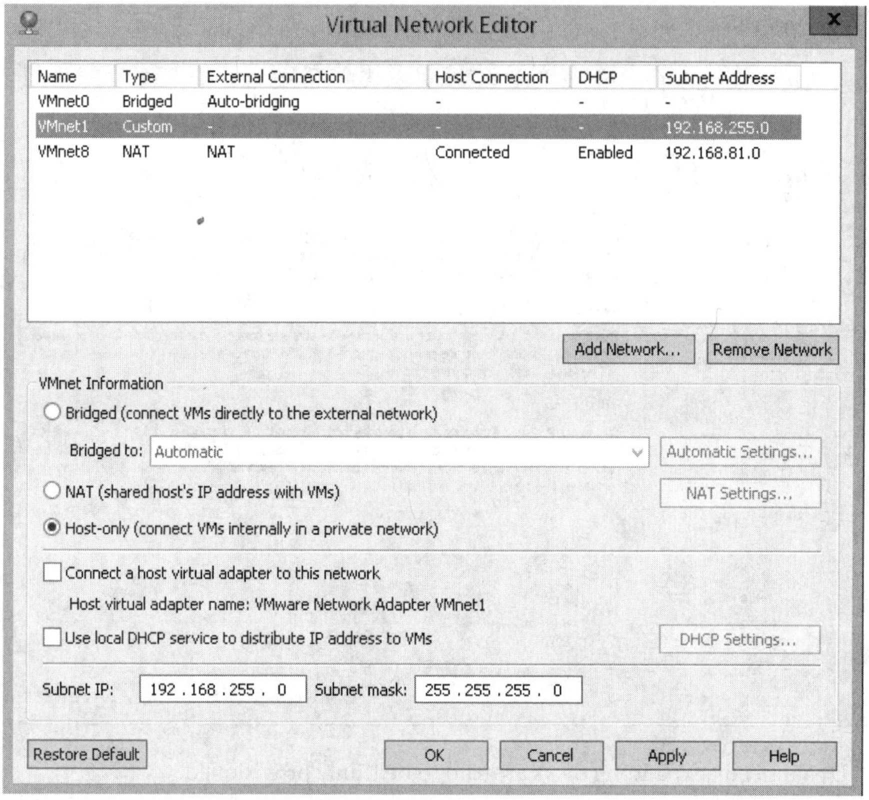

☑ **D.** Dynamic Host Configuration Protocol (DHCP) provides IP configuration settings to hosts over the network.

☒ **A, B,** and **C** are incorrect. Bridged and NAT virtual network type and connecting host virtual adapters will not provide TCP/IP settings to devices on VMnet1.

26. A virtual machine no longer properly synchronizes its time with the hypervisor host. Other virtual machines on the same host have no problems. Which menu option in Figure 5-6 should you select?

A.   Send Ctrl+Alt+Del

B.   Grab Input

C.   Reinstall VMware Tools

D.   Pause

FIGURE 5-6

Virtual machine menu

VM	Tabs Help	⏸ ▾	🖧	⏱ ⏲ ⚙
⏻	Power	▸
⊙	Removable Devices	▸
	Pause	Ctrl+Shift+P
🖧	Send Ctrl+Alt+Del	
	Grab Input	Ctrl+G
🔄	Snapshot	▸
	Capture Screen	Ctrl+Shift+Alt+PrtScn
🔧	Manage	▸
	Reinstall VMware Tools...	
🖳	Settings...	Ctrl+D

    ☑   **C.** The best course of action in this scenario is to reinstall VMware tools.

    ☒   **A, B,** and **D** are incorrect. Ctrl+Alt+Delete displays the Windows Task Manager or starts the logon sequence on Windows virtual machines. Grabbing screen input and pausing the virtual machine will not help with time sync issues.

27. Which of the following hypervisor products are open source? Choose two.

    A.   VMware ESXi

    B.   Xen

    C.   Xen Server

    D.   KVM

    ☑   **B** and **D.** Xen and KVM are both open source hypervisor solutions. Open source normally means free, or a low cost, along with the ability to see and modify the source code.

    ☒   **A** and **C** are incorrect. VMware ESXi and Xen Server are proprietary, not open source.

28. You are configuring a hypervisor clustered solution consisting of three hypervisors using shared storage: Hv1, Hv2, and Hv3. Hv1 hosts three virtual machines, Hv2 hosts two virtual machines, and Hv3 hosts four virtual machines that all have network connectivity. Assuming the cluster will continue running with two failed nodes, what consideration must you account for?

    A.   Shared storage

    B.   Virtual machine IP addressing

    C.   All virtual machines running on one host

    D.   Storage space

    ☑   **C.** If two nodes fail, all virtual machines need to be able to fail over to the last remaining node, which must have the hardware to accommodate all concurrently running virtual machines.

    ☒   **A, B,** and **D** are incorrect. Shared storage is already mentioned in the scenario. Virtual machine IP addresses remain unchanged after failover. Storage space is not an issue since the virtual machines are already running.

29. Which hardware option allows for higher overcommitment ratios of vCPUs to physical CPUs?
    A. Hyperthreading
    B. Ballooning
    C. UEFI
    D. CPU NAT

    ☑ **A.** Hyperthreading runs parallel instructions more efficiently than if the option were not enabled. This means a higher CPU overcommitment ratio is possible.

    ☒ **B, C,** and **D** are incorrect. Memory ballooning occurs when a hypervisor receives an urgent request from a virtual machine for memory that is not available. Other virtual machine guests temporarily "lend" unused memory to the hypervisor through the ballooning driver. Unified Extensible Firmware Interface (UEFI) is a replacement for BIOS. CPU NAT is an invalid term.

30. It is generally safe to allocate up to _____ vCPU(s) for each physical CPU.
    A. One
    B. Two
    C. Three
    D. Four

    ☑ **C.** General IT wisdom states that up to three vCPUs per physical CPU should be allocated to one or more virtual machines.

    ☒ **A, B,** and **D** are incorrect. The listed numeric values do not correspond with the general standard of vCPU to physical CPU ratio.

31. Which term describes a virtual machine that is aware it is virtualized?
    A. Full virtualization
    B. Paravirtualization
    C. Dynamic virtualization
    D. Containerization

    ☑ **B.** Paravirtualized operating systems are aware they are virtualized and can take advantage of this fact to increase efficiencies when talking to the hypervisor.

    ☒ **A, C,** and **D** are incorrect. Full virtualization means the operating system has no knowledge of being virtualized. Dynamic virtualization is not a valid term. Containerization is normally used to describe isolated application environments that do not include the operating system.

32. VMware virtual disks use a file extension of _____.
    A. .vmdk
    B. .vhd
    C. .vhdx
    D. .esx

    ☑ **A.** .vmdk is the file extension for VMware virtual disks.

    ☒ **B, C,** and **D** are incorrect. .vhd and .vhdx file extensions are used by Hyper-V (.vhdx is a newer and more robust file format). .esx is not a valid virtual disk file extension.

33. Microsoft Hyper-V virtual disks use a file extension of _____.

    A.   .vmdk

    B.   .dhx

    C.   .vhdx

    D.   .esx

    ☑   **C.** .vhdx is the newest Hyper-V virtual disk format.

    ☒   **A, B,** and **D** are incorrect. The listed file extensions are not used by Microsoft Hyper-V.

34. Which type of Microsoft Hyper-V disk reduces disk space consumption?

    A.   Differencing

    B.   Fixed

    C.   Dynamic

    D.   Compressed

    ☑   **A.** Differencing disks use a parent-child relationship where a parent virtual disk holds files that are inherited by its children; changes are written to the differencing disk.

    ☒   **B, C,** and **D** are incorrect. Fixed virtual disks allocated the entire amount of specified storage at creation time, unlike dynamic disks, which grow as needed. Compressed is not a type of Hyper-V virtual disk.

35. What is the maximum amount of RAM supported by Citrix XenServer 6.1?

    A.   64GB

    B.   96GB

    C.   128GB

    D.   192GB

    ☑   **C.** Citrix XenServer 6.1 supports a maximum of 128GB of RAM.

    ☒   **A, B,** and **D** are incorrect. The listed RAM values are incorrect.

Chapter 6

Virtualization and the Cloud

CERTIFICATION OBJECTIVES

6.01   Benefits of Virtualization in a Cloud Environment

6.02   Virtual Resource Migrations

6.03   Migration Considerations

QUESTIONS

Cloud computing relies heavily on virtualization. The rapid and elastic nature of server provisioning in the cloud is only possible with cloud provider hypervisors. Organizations must consider any existing on-premises physical or virtual servers that would benefit from running in the cloud. Migration types such as P2V and V2V must be understood to make this possible.

1. Which cloud characteristic allows IT resources to dynamically meet changing IT workloads?
   A. Resource pooling
   B. Elasticity
   C. Metered usage
   D. Broad access

2. Developers in your organization need a quick, consistent method of creating cloud-based software testing environments with specific operating system and application software configurations. What should you configure?
   A. Operating system disk image
   B. Installation script
   C. Software as a Service
   D. Cloud templates

3. An on-premises database server needs to be migrated to the cloud as a virtual machine. What type of migration should be done?
   A. P2V
   B. V2P
   C. P2P
   D. V2V

4. A busy on-premises file server needs to be migrated to the cloud as a virtual machine. Which migration strategy should you employ?
   A. Online P2V
   B. Online V2P
   C. Offline P2V
   D. Offline V2P

5. Which standard allows virtual machine migration between vendors?

   A. VHD

   B. VHDX

   C. OVF

   D. VMDK

6. Which statement regarding virtual machine clones is correct?

   A. Changes made to the clone also affect the source virtual machine.

   B. Changes made to the clone do not affect the source virtual machine.

   C. Clones always share the same virtual disks as the source virtual machine.

   D. Clones use the same MAC address as the source virtual machine.

7. You are the virtualization administrator for a specific on-premises hypervisor host. You need to configure new software on a virtual machine. What should you do to ensure changes can be rolled back as quickly as possible?

   A. Take a virtual machine snapshot.

   B. Clone the virtual machine.

   C. Use file system tools to make a copy of the virtual machine.

   D. Replicate the virtual machine to the cloud.

8. A busy virtual machine's storage needs to be moved to a faster storage array. Which process should you employ?

   A. Virtual machine snapshot

   B. Virtual machine clone

   C. Storage migration

   D. Storage cloning

9. A high availability cluster of hypervisors allows virtual machine failover and migration with minimal to zero downtime. Which configuration makes this possible?

   A. Shared storage

   B. NIC teaming

   C. Virtual machine snapshots

   D. Dedicated heartbeat NIC

10. Which strategy ensures 24×7 IT support across time zones?

   A. Service level agreement

   B. Resource pooling

   C. International VPNs

   D. Follow the sun

11. In which type of computing environment does a single tenant lease equipment?
    A. Dedicated compute
    B. Solo compute
    C. Isolated compute
    D. Segmented compute

12. Which factor determines how long a P2V from on premises to the cloud will take?
    A. Network bandwidth
    B. Number of virtual disks
    C. Virtual switch configuration
    D. Number of virtual NICs

13. Your company is planning the virtualization of selected on-premises physical servers. Which criteria represents a good virtualization candidate?
    A. Small number of disk volumes
    B. Large number of disk volumes
    C. High average utilization
    D. Low average utilization

14. Which benefits are normally realized through virtualization? Choose two.
    A. Reduced software licensing costs
    B. Reduced rack space usage
    C. Reduced power consumption
    D. Increased performance

15. Which of the following statements is true?
    A. Cloud computing requires virtualization.
    B. Virtualization requires cloud computing.
    C. Cloud computing is always cheaper than on-premises computing.
    D. Public cloud computing is less secure than on-premises computing.

16. Which of the following benefits result from the use of public cloud computing? Choose two.
    A. Delegated permissions for resource provisioning
    B. Decreased cost over time
    C. Resiliency to network failure
    D. Tracking usage of IT resources

17. You have performed a P2V migration of an on-premises server named appserv1.acme.net to the public cloud. appserv1.acme.net is up and running on a cloud virtual network with other virtual machines that are reachable. Upon attempting to connect to appserv1.acme.net after the migration, you receive an error stating the server is not reachable. What is the most likely cause of the problem?
    A. Cloud virtual machines cannot use FQDNs.
    B. The cloud virtual network is not reachable from the Internet.

    C.   A DNS entry for appserv1.acme.net must be configured.

    D.   appserv1.acme.net is using IPv6.

18. Which Microsoft tool is used to prepare an operating system for placement on a different hardware platform?

    A.   Group Policy

    B.   Sysprep

    C.   System restore point

    D.   Performance Monitor

19. Your on-premises private cloud uses virtualization. The newest version of the current hypervisor will be available on new upgraded hardware. Which type of migration should you use to ensure existing virtual machines continue running on the new hypervisor?

    A.   P2V

    B.   V2P

    C.   V2V

    D.   P2P

20. After performing multiple P2V migrations of Windows and Linux on-premises servers to the public cloud, you notice that only the Linux servers are reachable over SSH. What should you do to ensure the Windows servers are reachable for remote administration?

    A.   Allow TCP port 3389 traffic into the cloud network.

    B.   Allow TCP port 22 traffic into the cloud network.

    C.   Allow TCP port 443 traffic into the cloud network.

    D.   Allow TCP port 389 traffic into the cloud network.

21. Which type of configuration allows multiple identical copies of a custom application to be tested at the same time?

    A.   Elasticity

    B.   Metered usage

    C.   Network isolation

    D.   Resource pooling

22. You are configuring cloud-based virtual machines in a virtual private cloud (VPC) network to support a web application that experiences periodic increased workloads. The application must respond to these peak workloads with increased compute ability. Which option in Figure 6-1 should you enable?

    A.   Launch into Auto Scaling group

    B.   Request Spot instances

    C.   Create new VPC

    D.   Create new subnet

Number of instances (i)	1	Launch into Auto Scaling Group (i)
Purchasing option (i)	☐ Request Spot instances	
Network (i)	vpc-74a7a10d | AWS Simple AD (default) ▼	C Create new VPC
Subnet (i)	No preference (default subnet in any Availability Zon ▼	Create new subnet
Auto-assign Public IP (i)	Use subnet setting (Enable) ▼	

FIGURE 6-1 Cloud virtual machine configuration settings

23. You are configuring cloud firewall inbound rules for newly migrated virtual machines. Which firewall setting in Figure 6-2 presents security risks?
    A. Port 22 traffic should never be allowed.
    B. Port 80 traffic should never be allowed.
    C. SSH traffic can be initiated from any location.
    D. HTTPS is configured with an incorrect port number.

Type (i)	Protocol (i)	Port Range (i)	Source (i)
HTTP	TCP	80	0.0.0.0/0
SSH	TCP	22	0.0.0.0/0
HTTPS	TCP	443	0.0.0.0/0

FIGURE 6-2 Cloud network inbound firewall rules

24. You are migrating a sensitive on-premises application to a public cloud provider. Data confidentiality must be provided, and disks must perform at the fastest possible speed. There must not be any data remnants when the virtual machine storage is removed. According to Figure 6-3, which of the following statements is correct?
    A. One of the requirements is satisfied.
    B. Two of the requirements are satisfied.
    C. Three of the requirements are satisfied.
    D. None of the requirements are satisfied.

Volume Type (i)	IOPS (i)	Throughput (MB/s) (i)	Delete on Termination (i)	Encrypted (i)
Magnetic ▼	N/A	N/A	☑	Not Encrypted

FIGURE 6-3 Storage configuration for a cloud virtual machine

25. You are configuring a cloud database instance as per Figure 6-4. Current workloads suggest 12GB of RAM is sufficient, but you anticipate increased usage in the coming weeks. The datasets are anticipated to consume 10GB of storage over the next year. Database access must be available at all times with minimal disk latency. Which setting should you change?

A. DB instance class

B. Create replica in different zone

C. Storage type

D. Allocated storage

FIGURE 6-4

Cloud database
instance settings

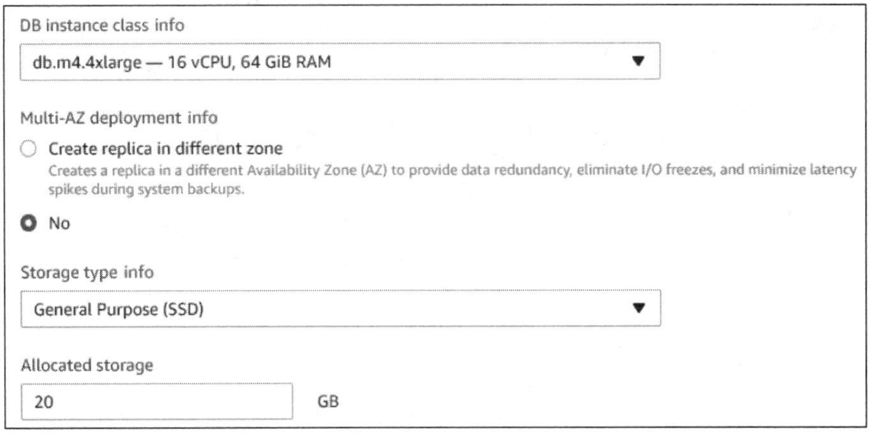

DB instance class info

db.m4.4xlarge — 16 vCPU, 64 GiB RAM ▼

Multi-AZ deployment info

○ **Create replica in different zone**
Creates a replica in a different Availability Zone (AZ) to provide data redundancy, eliminate I/O freezes, and minimize latency spikes during system backups.

● No

Storage type info

General Purpose (SSD) ▼

Allocated storage

20   GB

26. A workload you have already migrated to the cloud requires a reverse DNS record for the hosting virtual machine. You are creating a DNS record as per Figure 6-5. Which record type should you select?

A. CNAME

B. MX

C. PTR

D. SRV

FIGURE 6-5

Virtual machine
menu

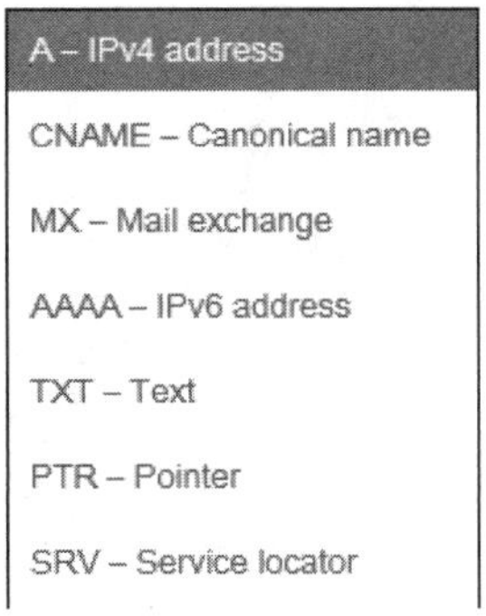

A – IPv4 address

CNAME – Canonical name

MX – Mail exchange

AAAA – IPv6 address

TXT – Text

PTR – Pointer

SRV – Service locator

QUICK ANSWER KEY

1.	B	**8.**	C	**15.**	A	**22.**	A
2.	D	**9.**	A	**16.**	A, D	**23.**	C
3.	A	**10.**	D	**17.**	C	**24.**	A
4.	C	**11.**	A	**18.**	B	**25.**	B
5.	C	**12.**	A	**19.**	C	**26.**	C
6.	B	**13.**	D	**20.**	A		
7.	A	**14.**	B, C	**21.**	C		

IN-DEPTH ANSWERS

1. Which cloud characteristic allows IT resources to dynamically meet changing IT workloads?
   A. Resource pooling
   B. Elasticity
   C. Metered usage
   D. Broad access

   ☑ **B.** Cloud elasticity allows for the rapid provisioning of resources to support dynamically changing IT workloads. An example of this is auto-scaling, where the additional virtual machine can be provisioned when an application's workload exceeds configured thresholds.
   ☒ **A, C,** and **D** are incorrect. Resource pooling groups all IT infrastructure together for use in a multitenant environment. Cloud computing charges are based on metered usage. Broad access provides accessibility to cloud resources over a network from anywhere.

2. Developers in your organization need a quick, consistent method of creating cloud-based software testing environments with specific operating system and application software configurations. What should you configure?
   A. Operating system disk image
   B. Installation script
   C. Software as a Service
   D. Cloud templates

   ☑ **D.** Cloud templates can facilitate and speed up the provisioning of cloud resources such as a single virtual machine or multiple virtual machine, databases, cloud virtual networks, and so on.
   ☒ **A, B,** and **C** are incorrect. Operating system disk imaging is useful on premises and not in the public cloud. Installation scripts are more complex than provisioning cloud resources using templates. Software as a Service (SaaS) provides end-user productivity software over a network where the provider hosts the service.

3. An on-premises database server needs to be migrated to the cloud as a virtual machine. What type of migration should be done?
   A. P2V
   B. V2P
   C. P2P
   D. V2V

☑ **A.** Physical-to-virtual (P2V) server migrations use an agent on a physical server that re-creates the server configuration in a virtual machine.

☒ **B, C,** and **D** are incorrect. Virtual-to-physical (V2P) migrations take a virtual machine server configuration and apply it to physical server hardware. Physical-to-physical (P2P) migrations use an agent to re-create a server's configuration on a target physical server. Virtual-to-virtual (V2V) migrations are used to transfer virtual machines between different hypervisors.

4. A busy on-premises file server needs to be migrated to the cloud as a virtual machine. Which migration strategy should you employ?
   A. Online P2V
   B. Online V2P
   C. Offline P2V
   D. Offline V2P

   ☑ **C.** Offline physical to virtual (P2V) is preferred with busy hosts to ensure data integrity.

   ☒ **A, B,** and **D** are incorrect. With online P2V, data could be corrupted or missed when migrating a very busy server that is in use. Virtual to physical (V2P) does not apply since the target must be a cloud virtual machine.

5. Which standard allows virtual machine migration between vendors?
   A. VHD
   B. VHDX
   C. OVF
   D. VMDK

   ☑ **C.** The Open Virtualization Format (OVF) allows virtual machines to be moved between various virtualization vendors using a standard format.

   ☒ **A, B,** and **D** are incorrect. VHD and VHDX are Microsoft Hyper-V–specific types of virtual hard disks. VMDK is a VMware-specific virtual hard disk file format.

6. Which statement regarding virtual machine clones is correct?
   A. Changes made to the clone also affect the source virtual machine.
   B. Changes made to the clone do not affect the source virtual machine.
   C. Clones always share the same virtual disks as the source virtual machine.
   D. Clones use the same MAC address as the source virtual machine.

   ☑ **B.** Virtual machine clones are copies of existing virtual machines, but changes to the copy are not pushed to the origin virtual machine.

   ☒ **A, C,** and **D** are incorrect. Changes to a cloned virtual machine do not have to share disk or MAC address configurations, and the changes remain only in the clone.

7. You are the virtualization administrator for a specific on-premises hypervisor host. You need to configure new software on a virtual machine. What should you do to ensure changes can be rolled back as quickly as possible?
   A. Take a virtual machine snapshot.
   B. Clone the virtual machine.

   C. Use file system tools to make a copy of the virtual machine.

   D. Replicate the virtual machine to the cloud.

   ☑   **A.** Virtual machine snapshots include a point-in-time copy of data in virtual disks as well as virtual machine configurations that can be reverted to quickly in the future if needed.

   ☒   **B, C,** and **D** are incorrect. Cloning, file system copying, and replicating to the cloud take more time than snapshotting a virtual machine.

8. A busy virtual machine's storage needs to be moved to a faster storage array. Which process should you employ?

   A. Virtual machine snapshot

   B. Virtual machine clone

   C. Storage migration

   D. Storage cloning

   ☑   **C.** Storage migration moves a virtual machine's virtual disks, configuration files, and snapshots to a new location.

   ☒   **A, B,** and **D** are incorrect. Virtual machine snapshots are a point-in-time copy of a virtual machine's state. Clones are complete copies of a virtual machine. Storage cloning is not a valid term in this context.

9. A high availability cluster of hypervisors allows virtual machine failover and migration with minimal to zero downtime. Which configuration makes this possible?

   A. Shared storage

   B. NIC teaming

   C. Virtual machine snapshots

   D. Dedicated heartbeat NIC

   ☑   **A.** Read-write shared storage used by a cluster provides the ability to migrate and failover virtual machines between hosts with little (failover) to no (migration) downtime.

   ☒   **B, C,** and **D** are incorrect. NIC teaming can improve the speed and resiliency for networking but does not relate to minimized downtime with virtual machine failover and migration. Virtual machine snapshots are a point-in-time copy of a virtual machine's state. A dedicated heartbeat NIC is used for cluster nodes to track each other's state.

10. Which strategy ensures 24×7 IT support across time zones?

   A. Service level agreement

   B. Resource pooling

   C. International VPNs

   D. Follow the sun

   ☑   **D.** The follow the sun (FTS) strategy ensures that IT shift workers in at least one time zone are available whenever a customer seeks help, thus providing 24×7 service.

   ☒   **A, B,** and **C** are incorrect. Service level agreements (SLAs) are contractual documents listing expected service and performance levels. Resource pooling groups all IT infrastructure together for use in a multitenant environment. Virtual private networks (VPNs) provide an encrypted network tunnel between two endpoints.

11. In which type of computing environment does a single tenant lease equipment?
    A. Dedicated compute
    B. Solo compute
    C. Isolated compute
    D. Segmented compute

    ☑ **A.** Some cloud providers offer the option of leasing dedicated equipment at a higher premium, but with more isolation and better performance.
    ☒ **B, C,** and **D** are incorrect. The listed terms are not valid.

12. Which factor determines how long a P2V from on premises to the cloud will take?
    A. Network bandwidth
    B. Number of virtual disks
    C. Virtual switch configuration
    D. Number of virtual NICs

    ☑ **A.** Network bandwidth, along with current network usage, determines how long migrating a physical on-premises server to the cloud will take.
    ☒ **B, C,** and **D** are incorrect. Disk and network configurations do not affect the amount of time required for P2V migrations.

13. Your company is planning the virtualization of selected on-premises physical servers. Which criteria represents a good virtualization candidate?
    A. Small number of disk volumes
    B. Large number of disk volumes
    C. High average utilization
    D. Low average utilization

    ☑ **D.** Physical servers with low average utilization are prime virtualization candidates for more efficient and cost-effective resource utilization.
    ☒ **A, B,** and **C** are incorrect. The number of disk volumes on a physical server is not sufficient criteria for determining whether it is a candidate for virtualization. Physical servers with high average utilization are not good candidates for server virtualization.

14. Which benefits are normally realized through virtualization? Choose two.
    A. Reduced software licensing costs
    B. Reduced rack space usage
    C. Reduced power consumption
    D. Increased performance

    ☑ **B** and **C.** Server virtualization reduces the number of physical server boxes, which in turn means less physical server rack space usage and less power consumption.
    ☒ **A** and **D** are incorrect. Server software licensing is normally based on physical or virtual CPUs, so there is no cost savings here. Server performance is not normally increased simply as a result of virtualization.

15. Which of the following statements is true?

   A. Cloud computing requires virtualization.

   B. Virtualization requires cloud computing.

   C. Cloud computing is always cheaper than on-premises computing.

   D. Public cloud computing is less secure than on-premises computing.

   ☑ **A.** Virtualization makes the rapid provisioning of compute resources possible in a cloud environment.

   ☒ **B, C,** and **D** are incorrect. Virtualization alone does not constitute a cloud environment, nor does it require a cloud computing environment. Since cloud computing fees normally occur monthly based on subscription and usage costs, it is not always cheaper than on-premises solutions over time. Most public cloud providers must undergo third-party security audits to receive accreditation, whereas most private firms do not undergo this security scrutiny.

16. Which of the following benefits result from the use of public cloud computing? Choose two.

   A. Delegated permissions for resource provisioning

   B. Decreased cost over time

   C. Resiliency to network failure

   D. Tracking usage of IT resources

   ☑ **A** and **D.** Cloud administrative permissions can be delegated, often through the use of groups or roles. Metered usage of IT resources is a beneficial cloud characteristic.

   ☒ **B** and **C** are incorrect. Cloud computing is not necessarily cheaper over the long term than on-premises computing. There is an increased network dependency to access public cloud resources.

17. You have performed a P2V migration of an on-premises server named appserv1.acme.net to the public cloud. appserv1.acme.net is up and running on a cloud virtual network with other virtual machines that are reachable. Upon attempting to connect to appserv1.acme.net after the migration, you receive an error stating the server is not reachable. What is the most likely cause of the problem?

   A. Cloud virtual machines cannot use FQDNs.

   B. The cloud virtual network is not reachable from the Internet.

   C. A DNS entry for appserv1.acme.net must be configured.

   D. appserv1.acme.net is using IPv6.

   ☑ **C.** appserv1.acme.net most likely does not have a DNS A record. The IP address should have also been tested.

   ☒ **A, B,** and **D** are incorrect. Cloud resources can use fully qualified domain names (FQDNs), which are generally easier to remember than IP addresses. The cloud virtual network is reachable since other virtual machines can be contacted. IPv6 would not prevent connectivity.

18. Which Microsoft tool is used to prepare an operating system for placement on a different hardware platform?

A. Group Policy

B. Sysprep

C. System restore point

D. Performance Monitor

☑ **B.** The System Preparation (Sysprep) tool removes unique identifiers such as computer name and hardware configurations so that an operating system image can be deployed to other computers.

☒ **A, C,** and **D** are incorrect. Group Policy configures Windows computers. System restore points allow a Windows client to revert to an earlier configuration. Performance Monitor can track metrics from various categories to view machine performance.

19. Your on-premises private cloud uses virtualization. The newest version of the current hypervisor will be available on new upgraded hardware. Which type of migration should you use to ensure existing virtual machines continue running on the new hypervisor?

A. P2V

B. V2P

C. V2V

D. P2P

☑ **C.** Virtual-to-virtual (V2V) server migrations are often used to move virtual machines to a different or upgraded hypervisor on another host.

☒ **A, B,** and **D** are incorrect. Physical-to-virtual (P2V) server migrations use an agent on a physical server that re-creates the server configuration in a virtual machine. Virtual-to-physical (V2P) migrations take a virtual machine server configuration and apply it to physical server hardware. Physical-to-physical (P2P) migrations use an agent to re-create a server's configuration on a target physical server.

20. After performing multiple P2V migrations of Windows and Linux on-premises servers to the public cloud, you notice that only the Linux servers are reachable over SSH. What should you do to ensure the Windows servers are reachable for remote administration?

A. Allow TCP port 3389 traffic into the cloud network.

B. Allow TCP port 22 traffic into the cloud network.

C. Allow TCP port 443 traffic into the cloud network.

D. Allow TCP port 389 traffic into the cloud network.

☑ **A.** Windows servers are normally remotely managed using Remote Desktop Protocol (RDP) over TCP port 3389.

☒ **B, C,** and **D** are incorrect. The listed ports are not normally used to remotely manage Windows computers.

21. Which type of configuration allows multiple identical copies of a custom application to be tested at the same time?

    A. Elasticity

    B. Metered usage

    C. Network isolation

    D. Resource pooling

    ☑ **C.** One benefit of cloud computing is the ease and speed with which isolated computing environments can be spun up for testing purposes.

    ☒ **A, B,** and **D** are incorrect. While the listed items are cloud computing characteristics, they are not directly related to concurrent application testing.

22. You are configuring cloud-based virtual machines in a virtual private cloud (VPC) network to support a web application that experiences periodic increased workloads. The application must respond to these peak workloads with increased compute ability. Which option in Figure 6-1 should you enable?

    A. Launch into Auto Scaling group

    B. Request Spot instances

    C. Create new VPC

    D. Create new subnet

FIGURE 6-1		
Cloud virtual machine configuration settings	**Number of instances** ⓘ `1` Launch into Auto Scaling Group ⓘ	
	Purchasing option ⓘ ☐ Request Spot instances	
	Network ⓘ `vpc-74a7a10d | AWS Simple AD (default)` ▼ ↻ Create new VPC	
	Subnet ⓘ `No preference (default subnet in any Availability Zon ▼` Create new subnet	
	Auto-assign Public IP ⓘ `Use subnet setting (Enable)` ▼	

    ☑ **A.** Auto-scaling can add additional virtual machines to handle increased application requests when configured thresholds are exceeded.

    ☒ **B, C,** and **D** are incorrect. Spot instances are extra available virtual machines provided at a reduced rate with the understanding they could be reclaimed at any time and thus made unavailable. A virtual private cloud (VPC) is a cloud virtual network. VPCs and subnets unto themselves will not improve application performance as auto-scaling will.

23. You are configuring cloud firewall inbound rules for newly migrated virtual machines. Which firewall setting in Figure 6-2 presents security risks?

    A. Port 22 traffic should never be allowed.

    B. Port 80 traffic should never be allowed.

    C. SSH traffic can be initiated from any location.

    D. HTTPS is configured with an incorrect port number.

FIGURE 6-2

Cloud network
inbound firewall
rules

Type ⓘ	Protocol ⓘ	Port Range ⓘ	Source ⓘ
HTTP	TCP	80	0.0.0.0/0
SSH	TCP	22	0.0.0.0/0
HTTPS	TCP	443	0.0.0.0/0

☑ **C.** A source of 0.0.0.0/0 means from anywhere. SSH administrative traffic should be limited to at least an IP subnet if not a specific IP address. Take care of NAT public IP addresses when configuring this type of settings.

☒ **A, B,** and **D** are incorrect. Port 22 and 80 traffic is often allowed into cloud virtual networks depending on the services being offered on that network. HTTPS does use port 443.

24. You are migrating a sensitive on-premises application to a public cloud provider. Data confidentiality must be provided, and disks must perform at the fastest possible speed. There must not be any data remnants when the virtual machine storage is removed. According to Figure 6-3, which of the following statements is correct?

A. One of the requirements is satisfied.

B. Two of the requirements are satisfied.

C. Three of the requirements are satisfied.

D. None of the requirements are satisfied.

FIGURE 6-3

Storage
configuration for
a cloud virtual
machine

Volume Type ⓘ	IOPS ⓘ	Throughput (MB/s) ⓘ	Delete on Termination ⓘ	Encrypted ⓘ
Magnetic ▼	N/A	N/A	☑	Not Encrypted

☑ **A.** One of the requirements is satisfied. Delete on Termination ensures the virtual disk volume is removed when the virtual machine is deleted.

☒ **B, C,** and **D** are incorrect. Magnetic disks are hard disk drives, which are slower than solid state drives (SSDs). Encryption is not enabled on the volume, therefore, data confidentiality is not being achieved.

25. You are configuring a cloud database instance as per Figure 6-4. Current workloads suggest 12GB of RAM is sufficient, but you anticipate increased usage in the coming weeks. The datasets are anticipated to consume 10GB of storage over the next year. Database access must be available at all times with minimal disk latency. Which setting should you change?

A. DB instance class

B. Create replica in different zone

C. Storage type

D. Allocated storage

FIGURE 6-4

Cloud database
instance settings

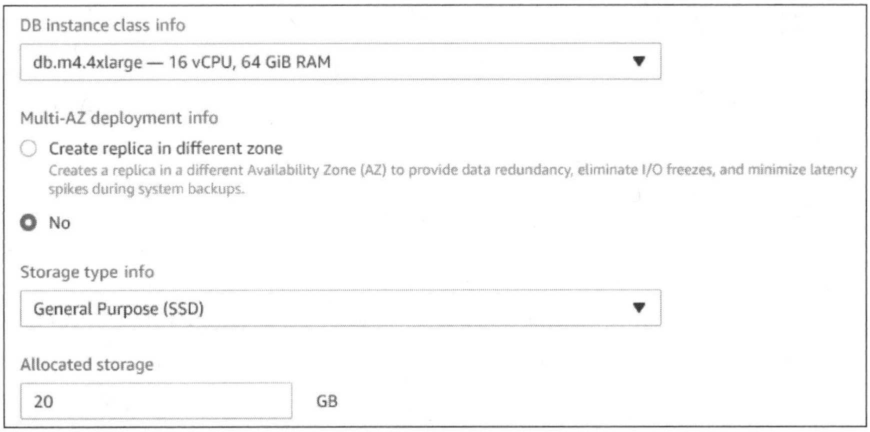

> DB instance class info
>
> | db.m4.4xlarge — 16 vCPU, 64 GiB RAM ▼ |
>
> Multi-AZ deployment info
>
> ○ Create replica in different zone
> Creates a replica in a different Availability Zone (AZ) to provide data redundancy, eliminate I/O freezes, and minimize latency spikes during system backups.
>
> ● No
>
> Storage type info
>
> | General Purpose (SSD) ▼ |
>
> Allocated storage
>
> | 20 | GB

☑ **B.** Replicating databases to different zones increases database high availability.

☒ **A, C,** and **D** are incorrect. The DB instance class determines the database power but not high availability, nor does the storage type or amount of storage.

26. A workload you have already migrated to the cloud requires a reverse DNS record for the hosting virtual machine. You are creating a DNS record as per Figure 6-5. Which record type should you select?

A. CNAME

B. MX

C. PTR

D. SRV

FIGURE 6-5

Virtual machine
menu

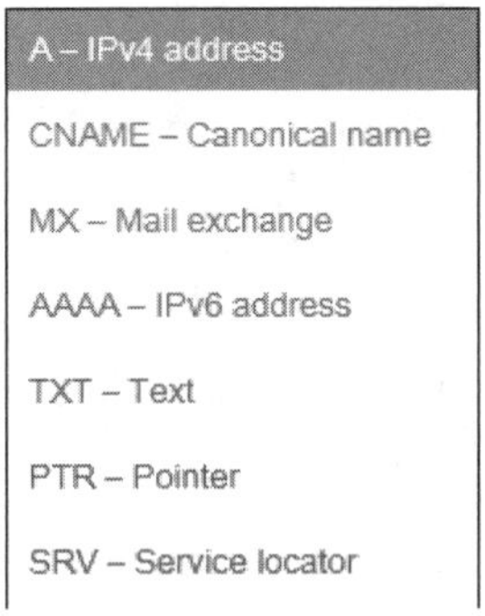

> A – IPv4 address
>
> CNAME – Canonical name
>
> MX – Mail exchange
>
> AAAA – IPv6 address
>
> TXT – Text
>
> PTR – Pointer
>
> SRV – Service locator

☑ **C.** PTR records are reverse DNS records. They are used to resolve IP addresses to names.

☒ **A, B,** and **D** are incorrect. CNAME records are aliases to other DNS records, MX are mail exchanger records for mail transfer between servers, and SRV are service location records used to locate network services such as Microsoft Active Directory.

Chapter 7

DevOps

CERTIFICATION OBJECTIVES

7.01   Resource Monitoring Techniques

7.02   Remote-Access Tools

7.03   Life Cycle Management

QUESTIONS

Cloud adoption means relying on remote IT resources to support business requirements. Monitoring is crucial to ensure business objectives are being met in a cost-effective and timely manner.

Remote access to Linux virtual machines normally uses SSH and remote access to Windows virtual machines uses RDP. Specifications, development, testing, deployment, and maintenance are application life cycle phases that apply to IT solutions on premises as well as in the cloud.

1. Your organization tracks internal IT resource usage by department for billing purposes. What type of cloud is this?
   A. Metered
   B. Private
   C. Departmental
   D. Charging

2. Which management and monitoring protocol uses "traps," otherwise called "notifications"?
   A. WMI
   B. WBEM
   C. IPMI
   D. SNMP

3. Which protocol does Microsoft System Center Configuration Manager (SCCM) use to gather hardware inventory?
   A. WMI
   B. WBEM
   C. IPMI
   D. SNMP

4. Which of the following are remote host management protocols? Choose two.
   A. WBEM
   B. SSH
   C. IPMI
   D. SMTP

5. Which of the following is an out-of-band management protocol?
   A. WMI
   B. WBEM
   C. IPMI
   D. SNMP

6. Which monitoring and reporting protocol uses port 514?
   A. WMI
   B. Syslog
   C. WBEM
   D. SNMP

7. You are using IPMI to remotely monitor a host whose operating system has crashed and is unresponsive. What type of items would you be monitoring?
   A. Running processes
   B. Halted processes
   C. BIOS settings
   D. Installed software

8. You need a central location to view log data gathered from 50 Linux servers. What should you configure?
   A. Syslog forwarding
   B. WMI forwarding
   C. IPMI forwarding
   D. SNMP forwarding

9. You need to determine if future cloud network performance values are acceptable. What should you do first?
   A. Enable syslog forwarding.
   B. Establish a performance baseline.
   C. Take virtual machine snapshots.
   D. Harden each virtual machine.

10. Which term is used to describe the automated execution of cloud actions based on performance metrics?
    A. Orchestration
    B. Logging
    C. Baselining
    D. Scripting

11. Which e-mail transfer protocol is commonly used to send notifications?
    A. POP3
    B. SNMP
    C. IMAP
    D. SMTP

12. Administrators in your organization complain that some cloud virtual machine log files are being deleted to free up disk space. You are responsible for cloud virtual machine maintenance. What should you do?
    A. Add disk space.
    B. Establish a log retention policy.
    C. Enable centralized log forwarding.
    D. Forward logs to an on-premises server.

13. Which factor is most likely to influence a data retention policy?
    A. Amount of available storage space
    B. Cost of cloud storage
    C. Regulations
    D. Technical expertise of cloud administrators

14. You need software that can associate network firewall activity with Windows and Linux server activity within the same time frame. What feature must the software support?
    A. Event correlation
    B. Log retention
    C. Log forwarding
    D. Event triggers

15. Your on-premises network has grown over the years to hundreds of devices. A VPN connection to a public cloud provider has extended the network into the cloud. You need a way to have device logs analyzed in real time against correlation rules to identify possible threats or problems. Which type of system should you invest in?
    A. SLA
    B. SIEM
    C. WMI
    D. IPMI

16. Which category does SIEM primarily relate to?
    A. Licensing
    B. Patching
    C. Scripting
    D. Security

17. An on-premises Microsoft Windows Server Core installation provides Hyper-V virtualization without a GUI. What should be used to remotely manage virtual machines at the command line?

    A. RDP

    B. SSH

    C. Telnet

    D. SNMP

18. Which key is used during SSH authentication for decryption?

    A. Public

    B. Private

    C. Symmetric

    D. Asymmetric

19. Which key is used to encrypt an SSH session?

    A. Public

    B. Private

    C. Symmetric

    D. Asymmetric

20. Which port is used for SSH administration?

    A. 22

    B. 80

    C. 389

    D. 3389

21. Which statement regarding SSH is correct?

    A. SSH is used only for Linux hypervisor remote administration.

    B. SSH is used only for virtual machine remote administration.

    C. SSH can be used to remotely manage hypervisors and virtual machines.

    D. SSH cannot be used to remotely manage Windows virtual machines.

22. Which of the following are examples of application life cycle management models? Choose two.

    A. WBEM

    B. ITIL

    C. MOF

    D. OSI

23. Which ITIL phase seeks flaws and fixes any that are found to make services more effective?

    A. Service strategy

    B. Continual service improvement

    C. Service transition

    D. Service operation

24. What is another name for the application life cycle?

    A. ITIL

    B. MOF

    C. OSI

    D. SDLC

25. At which application life cycle phase are breakpoints removed by developers?

    A. Deployment

    B. Specifications

    C. Testing

    D. Maintenance

26. At which application life cycle phase is the software installed and configured?

    A. Deployment

    B. Specifications

    C. Testing

    D. Maintenance

27. At which application life cycle phase is software performance tweaked?

    A. Deployment

    B. Specifications

    C. Testing

    D. Maintenance

28. You are working in a server room and need to connect your laptop directly to a hypervisor for management purposes. What should you plug your laptop into?

    A. RJ-45

    B. USB port

    C. SATA port

    D. Console port

29. Which of the following statements regarding the packet capture in Figure 7-1 is correct?

    A. The traffic originates from an SSH server.

    B. The SSH server IP address is 10.0.0.1.

    C. The SSH server IP address is 10.0.0.2.

    D. The credentials are sent in clear text.

FIGURE 7-1

Packet capture

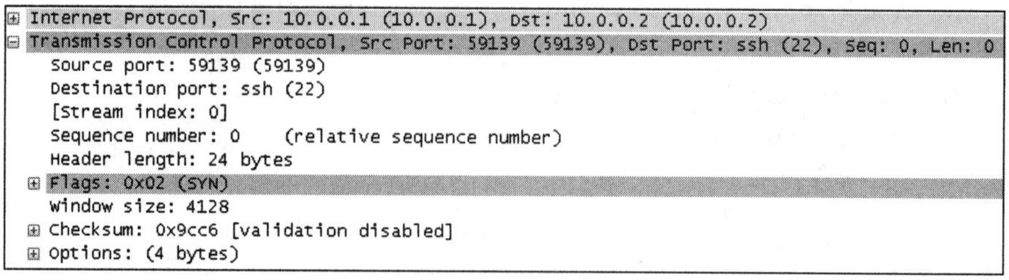

```
⊞ Internet Protocol, Src: 10.0.0.1 (10.0.0.1), Dst: 10.0.0.2 (10.0.0.2)
⊟ Transmission Control Protocol, Src Port: 59139 (59139), Dst Port: ssh (22), Seq: 0, Len: 0
    Source port: 59139 (59139)
    Destination port: ssh (22)
    [Stream index: 0]
    Sequence number: 0    (relative sequence number)
    Header length: 24 bytes
  ⊞ Flags: 0x02 (SYN)
    Window size: 4128
  ⊞ Checksum: 0x9cc6 [validation disabled]
  ⊞ Options: (4 bytes)
```

30. What type of allowed outbound traffic is configured in Figure 7-2?

    A. NTP

    B. SNMP

    C. SMTP

    D. Syslog

FIGURE 7-2	**Edit outbound rules**			
Cloud outbound firewall rules	**Type** ⓘ	**Protocol** ⓘ	**Port Range** ⓘ	**Destination** ⓘ
	Custom TCP F ▾	TCP	514	Custom ▾ 199.126.129.0/24

31. You manage a team of 12 cloud consultants whose smartphones do not use a mobile data plan. The consultants travel to customer locations and currently do not have Wi-Fi access on their smartphones. You need to ensure your cloud consultants receive alerts when crucial virtual machines go down regardless of their location. Which notification method should you configure?

    A. SNMP

    B. SMS

    C. SMTP

    D. HTTP

32. An existing on-premises application will no longer be used in your company's public cloud implementation. Instead, a functional cloud equivalent will be used. To which aspect of the application life cycle does this apply?

    A. Application upgrade

    B. Application retirement

    C. Application replacement

    D. Application migration

33. Historical log data for your users shows normal cloud storage usage increases by an average of 9 percent annually. Over the past year, however, usage has increased by 18 percent. How is this change best described?

    A. Deviation from baseline

    B. Metered usage

    C. Trend analysis

    D. Resource pooling

A
QUICK ANSWER KEY

1.	B	**10.**	A	**19.**	C	**28.**	D
2.	D	**11.**	D	**20.**	A	**29.**	C
3.	A	**12.**	B	**21.**	C	**30.**	D
4.	B, C	**13.**	C	**22.**	B, C	**31.**	B
5.	C	**14.**	A	**23.**	B	**32.**	C
6.	B	**15.**	B	**24.**	D	**33.**	A
7.	C	**16.**	D	**25.**	A		
8.	A	**17.**	A	**26.**	A		
9.	B	**18.**	B	**27.**	D		

IN-DEPTH ANSWERS

1. Your organization tracks internal IT resource usage by department for billing purposes. What type of cloud is this?
   A. Metered
   B. Private
   C. Departmental
   D. Charging

   ☑ **B.** A private cloud runs on equipment owned and operated by a single organization for the use of that same organization.

   ☒ **A, C,** and **D** are incorrect. Cloud subscribers pay monthly fees based on their metered usage of cloud resources, but metered is not a valid cloud type, nor are departmental and charging.

2. Which management and monitoring protocol uses "traps," otherwise called "notifications"?
   A. WMI
   B. WBEM
   C. IPMI
   D. SNMP

   ☑ **D.** Simple Network Management Protocol (SNMP) is a network device management and monitoring protocol that uses traps, or alerts, to send notifications to a centralized SNMP management console.

   ☒ **A, B,** and **C** are incorrect. Windows Management Instrumentation (WMI) is a protocol used to retrieve device hardware and software configuration details. Web-Based Enterprise Management (WBEM) uses Internet standards for the centralized management of dissimilar computing environments. Intelligent Platform Management Interface (IPMI) uses out-of-band management to remotely manage devices at the hardware level even if the software operating system is not functional.

3. Which protocol does Microsoft System Center Configuration Manager (SCCM) use to gather hardware inventory?
   A. WMI
   B. WBEM
   C. IPMI
   D. SNMP

☑ **A.** SCCM uses Windows Management Instrumentation (WMI) to gather software and hardware inventory.

☒ **B, C,** and **D** are incorrect. Web-Based Enterprise Management (WBEM) uses Internet standards for the centralized management of dissimilar computing environments. Intelligent Platform Management Interface (IPMI) uses out-of-band management to remotely manage devices at the hardware level even if the software operating system is not functional. Simple Network Management Protocol (SNMP) is a network device management and monitoring protocol that uses traps, or alerts, to send notifications to a centralized SNMP management console.

4. Which of the following are remote host management protocols? Choose two.

   A. WBEM
   B. SSH
   C. IPMI
   D. SMTP

☑ **B** and **C.** Secure Shell (SSH) is normally used to remotely manage Unix and Linux hosts as well as network devices. Intelligent Platform Management Interface (IPMI) uses out-of-band management to remotely manage devices at the hardware level even if the software operating system is not functional.

☒ **A** and **D** are incorrect. Web-Based Enterprise Management (WBEM) uses Internet standards for the centralized management of dissimilar computing environments. Simple Mail Transfer Protocol (SMTP) is used to transfer e-mail messages between SMTP e-mail servers.

5. Which of the following is an out-of-band management protocol?

   A. WMI
   B. WBEM
   C. IPMI
   D. SNMP

☑ **C.** Intelligent Platform Management Interface (IPMI) uses out-of-band management to remotely manage devices at the hardware level even if the software operating system is not functional.

☒ **A, B,** and **D** are incorrect. Windows Management Instrumentation (WMI) is a protocol used to retrieve device hardware and software configuration details. Web-Based Enterprise Management (WBEM) uses Internet standards for the centralized management of dissimilar computing environments. Simple Network Management Protocol (SNMP) is a network device management and monitoring protocol that uses traps, or alerts, to send notifications to a centralized SNMP management console.

6. Which monitoring and reporting protocol uses port 514?

   A. WMI
   B. Syslog
   C. WBEM
   D. SNMP

☑ **B.** Syslog has long been a Unix and Linux standard method of filtering and forwarding log data and is normally configured to use UDP or TCP port 514.

☒ **A, C,** and **D** are incorrect. Windows Management Instrumentation (WMI) is a protocol used to retrieve device hardware and software configuration details. Web-Based Enterprise Management (WBEM) uses Internet standards for the centralized management of dissimilar computing environments. Simple Network Management Protocol (SNMP) is a network device management and monitoring protocol that uses traps, or alerts, to send notifications to a centralized SNMP management console.

7. You are using IPMI to remotely monitor a host whose operating system has crashed and is unresponsive. What type of items would you be monitoring?

A. Running processes
B. Halted processes
C. BIOS settings
D. Installed software

☑ **C.** Intelligent Platform Management Interface (IPMI) does not rely on a functional operating system for remote management; instead it relies on device hardware for the management and monitoring of BIOS settings.

☒ **A, B,** and **D** are incorrect. Since the operating system is unresponsive, none of the listed items would be available through IPMI.

8. You need a central location to view log data gathered from 50 Linux servers. What should you configure?

A. Syslog forwarding
B. WMI forwarding
C. IPMI forwarding
D. SNMP forwarding

☑ **A.** Syslog has long been a Unix and Linux standard method of filtering and forwarding log data and is normally configured to use UDP or TCP port 514.

☒ **B, C,** and **D** are incorrect. WMI forwarding, IPMI forwarding, and SNMP forwarding are not industry-standard terms.

9. You need to determine if future cloud network performance values are acceptable. What should you do first?

A. Enable syslog forwarding.
B. Establish a performance baseline.
C. Take virtual machine snapshots.
D. Harden each virtual machine.

☑ **B.** Performance baselines determine normal usage activity and are compared to future performance metrics to identify abnormalities.

☒ **A, C,** and **D** are incorrect. Syslog forwarding, virtual machine snapshots, and the security hardening of a virtual machine are not directly related to cloud network performance.

10. Which term is used to describe the automated execution of cloud actions based on performance metrics?

    A. Orchestration

    B. Logging

    C. Baselining

    D. Scripting

    ☑ **A.** Orchestration automates tasks such as alert notifications and cloud resource deployments.

    ☒ **B, C,** and **D** are incorrect. Logging and baselines do not provide automation. While scripting can be used to automate tasks, it is not as closely related to cloud automation as orchestration, which can use scripts to aid in automation.

11. Which e-mail transfer protocol is commonly used to send notifications?

    A. POP3

    B. SNMP

    C. IMAP

    D. SMTP

    ☑ **D.** Simple Mail Transfer Protocol (SMTP) is the standard mail transfer protocol.

    ☒ **A, B,** and **C** are incorrect. Post Office Protocol 3 (POP3) and Internet Message Access Protocol (IMAP) are mail retrieval protocols, not mail transfer protocols. Simple Network Management Protocol (SNMP) is not related to e-mail.

12. Administrators in your organization complain that some cloud virtual machine log files are being deleted to free up disk space. You are responsible for cloud virtual machine maintenance. What should you do?

    A. Add disk space.

    B. Establish a log retention policy.

    C. Enable centralized log forwarding.

    D. Forward logs to an on-premises server.

    ☑ **B.** Log retention policies determine how log entries in log files are stored, where they are stored, and for how long. Laws and regulations can sometimes influence log retention policies.

    ☒ **A, C,** and **D** are incorrect. Adding more disk space and log forwarding do not address the inevitable issues of removing log entries and storage space consumption due to logs.

13. Which factor is most likely to influence a data retention policy?

    A. Amount of available storage space

    B. Cost of cloud storage

    C. Regulations

    D. Technical expertise of cloud administrators

☑   **C.** Regulations in certain industries can influence data retention policies.

☒   **A, B,** and **D** are incorrect. Available storage, cost, and technical cloud expertise are not as likely to influence data retention policies as regulations are.

14. You need software that can associate network firewall activity with Windows and Linux server activity within the same time frame. What feature must the software support?

A. Event correlation

B. Log retention

C. Log forwarding

D. Event triggers

☑   **A.** Associating activity from a multitude of network devices together, or event correlation, can provide a clearer view of what is happening on a network.

☒   **B, C,** and **D** are incorrect. The listed items do not cross-reference activity from multiple network device within the same time frame.

15. Your on-premises network has grown over the years to hundreds of devices. A VPN connection to a public cloud provider has extended the network into the cloud. You need a way to have device logs analyzed in real time against correlation rules to identify possible threats or problems. Which type of system should you invest in?

A. SLA

B. SIEM

C. WMI

D. IPMI

☑   **B.** Security information and event management (SIEM) solutions analyze device activity including logs in real time and compare this against correlation rule to identify security issues.

☒   **A, C,** and **D** are incorrect. Service level agreements (SLAs) are contracts between the provider and consumer of an IT service. Windows Management Instrumentation (WMI) is used to retrieve device hardware and software details. Intelligent Platform Management Interface (IPMI) uses out-of-band management to remotely manage devices at the hardware level even if the software operating system is not functional.

16. Which category does SIEM primarily relate to?

A. Licensing

B. Patching

C. Scripting

D. Security

☑   **D.** Security Information and Event Management (SIEM) solutions analyze device activity, including logs, in real time and compare this against correlation rules to identify security issues.

☒   **A, B,** and **C** are incorrect. Licensing, patching, and scripting are not the primary focus of SIEM systems.

17. An on-premises Microsoft Windows Server Core installation provides Hyper-V virtualization without a GUI. What should be used to remotely manage virtual machines at the command line?

    A. RDP

    B. SSH

    C. Telnet

    D. SNMP

    ☑ **A.** Remote Desktop Protocol (RDP) is normally used to remotely administer Windows machines, even if there is no GUI, in which case the administrator is given a remote command prompt screen.

    ☒ **B, C,** and **D** are incorrect. Secure Shell (SSH) is an encrypted remote admin tool normally used to manage routers, switches, and Unix and Linux machines. Telnet is the predecessor to SSH and transmits data in clear text. Simple Network Management Protocol (SNMP) is a network device management and monitoring protocol that uses traps, or alerts, to send notifications to a centralized SNMP management console.

18. Which key is used during SSH authentication for decryption?

    A. Public

    B. Private

    C. Symmetric

    D. Asymmetric

    ☑ **B.** The private key is used for decryption during SSH authentication.

    ☒ **A, C,** and **D** are incorrect. The listed keys are not used for decrypting during SSH authentication.

19. Which key is used to encrypt an SSH session?

    A. Public

    B. Private

    C. Symmetric

    D. Asymmetric

    ☑ **C.** After SSH authentication, a symmetric key is used to encrypt the transmissions.

    ☒ **A, B,** and **D** are incorrect. The listed keys are not used to protect SSH sessions after authentication.

20. Which port is used for SSH administration?

    A. 22

    B. 80

    C. 389

    D. 3389

    ☑ **A.** SSH traffic occurs over TCP port 22.

    ☒ **B, C,** and **D** are incorrect. The listed ports are not normally used for SSH transmissions. HTTP uses port 80, LDAP uses 389, and RDP uses 3389.

21. Which statement regarding SSH is correct?

    A. SSH is used only for Linux hypervisor remote administration.

    B. SSH is used only for virtual machine remote administration.

    C. SSH can be used to remotely manage hypervisors and virtual machines.

    D. SSH cannot be used to remotely manage Windows virtual machines.

    ☑ **C.** SSH can be used to remotely administrator any network device that runs an SSH daemon or service.

    ☒ **A, B,** and **D** are incorrect. SSH is not limited to hypervisors, virtual machines, or specific operating systems.

22. Which of the following are examples of application life cycle management models? Choose two.

    A. WBEM

    B. ITIL

    C. MOF

    D. OSI

    ☑ **B** and **C.** Information Technology Infrastructure Library (ITIL) and Microsoft Operations Framework (MOF) are application life cycle management models.

    ☒ **A** and **D** are incorrect. Web-Based Enterprise Management (WBEM) uses Internet standards for the centralized management of dissimilar computing environments. Open Systems Interconnect (OSI) is a conceptual seven-layer model used to map communications hardware and software.

23. Which ITIL phase seeks flaws and fixes any that are found to make services more effective?

    A. Service strategy

    B. Continual service improvement

    C. Service transition

    D. Service operation

    ☑ **B.** The continual service improvement phase of the Information Technology Infrastructure Library (ITIL) model identifies problems and then improves existing services and processes.

    ☒ **A, C,** and **D** are incorrect. The listed ITIL phases are not related to flaw identification used for service improvement.

24. What is another name for the application life cycle?

    A. ITIL

    B. MOF

    C. OSI

    D. SDLC

    ☑ **D.** Software development life cycle (SDLC) is synonymous with application life cycle.

    ☒ **A, B,** and **C** are incorrect. Information Technology Infrastructure Library (ITIL) and Microsoft Operations Framework (MOF) are application life cycle management models. Open Systems Interconnect (OSI) is a conceptual seven-layer model used to map communications hardware and software.

25. At which application life cycle phase are breakpoints removed by developers?

A. Deployment

B. Specifications

C. Testing

D. Maintenance

☑ **A.** One task that occurs during the deployment phase is the removal of debugging breakpoints.

☒ **B, C,** and **D** are incorrect. Breakpoint removal does not apply to the other listed phases.

26. At which application life cycle phase is the software installed and configured?

A. Deployment

B. Specifications

C. Testing

D. Maintenance

☑ **A.** Software installation and configuration occurs during the deployment phase.

☒ **B, C,** and **D** are incorrect. Software installation and configuration does not occur during the other listed phases.

27. At which application life cycle phase is software performance tweaked?

A. Deployment

B. Specifications

C. Testing

D. Maintenance

☑ **D.** Improving software performance occurs during the maintenance phase.

☒ **A, B,** and **C** are incorrect. Improving software performance does not occur during the other listed phases.

28. You are working in a server room and need to connect your laptop directly to a hypervisor for management purposes. What should you plug your laptop into?

A. RJ-45

B. USB port

C. SATA port

D. Console port

☑ **D.** Many devices, including hypervisor computers, allow a local direct connection via a console port, which might use a serial, parallel, or USB connection.

☒ **A, B,** and **C** are incorrect. RJ-45 connectors are for twisted pair cables; these as well as USB and SATA connections are not used to locally administer a hypervisor.

29. Which of the following statements regarding the packet capture in Figure 7-1 is correct?

A. The traffic originates from an SSH server.

B. The SSH server IP address is 10.0.0.1.

C. The SSH server IP address is 10.0.0.2.

D. The credentials are sent in clear text.

Packet capture

```
⊞ Internet Protocol, Src: 10.0.0.1 (10.0.0.1), Dst: 10.0.0.2 (10.0.0.2)
⊟ Transmission Control Protocol, Src Port: 59139 (59139), Dst Port: ssh (22), Seq: 0, Len: 0
    Source port: 59139 (59139)
    Destination port: ssh (22)
    [Stream index: 0]
    Sequence number: 0    (relative sequence number)
    Header length: 24 bytes
  ⊞ Flags: 0x02 (SYN)
    window size: 4128
  ⊞ Checksum: 0x9cc6 [validation disabled]
  ⊞ Options: (4 bytes)
```

☑ **C.** The SSH server IP address destination is 10.0.0.2, which corresponds to the destination SSH port of 22.

☒ **A, B,** and **D** are incorrect. The source port is not 22, and the source IP address is 10.0.0.1. Therefore, the traffic did not originate from an SSH server. SSH sessions are not transmitted in clear text.

30. What type of allowed outbound traffic is configured in Figure 7-2?

A. NTP

B. SNMP

C. SMTP

D. Syslog

Cloud outbound firewall rules

Edit outbound rules

Type ⓘ	Protocol ⓘ	Port Range ⓘ	Destination ⓘ	
Custom TCP F ▾	TCP	514	.	Custom ▾	199.126.129.0/24

☑ **D.** Syslog traffic normally uses either UDP or TCP port 514.

☒ **A, B,** and **C** are incorrect. NTP uses port 123, SNMP uses port 161, and SMTP uses port 25.

31. You manage a team of 12 cloud consultants whose smartphones do not use a mobile data plan. The consultants travel to customer locations and currently do not have Wi-Fi access on their smartphones. You need to ensure your cloud consultants receive alerts when crucial virtual machines go down regardless of their location. Which notification method should you configure?

A. SNMP

B. SMS

C. SMTP

D. HTTP

☑ **B.** Short Message Service (SMS) is text messaging, which still works without an Internet data connection.

☒ **A, C,** and **D** are incorrect. The other listed protocols require an Internet data connection.

32. An existing on-premises application will no longer be used in your company's public cloud implementation. Instead, a functional cloud equivalent will be used. To which aspect of the application life cycle does this apply?

    A. Application upgrade

    B. Application retirement

    C. Application replacement

    D. Application migration

    ☑ **C.** The existing on-premises application is being replaced with a functional equivalent.

    ☒ **A, B,** and **D** are incorrect. The existing on-premises application is not being upgraded or migrated. It is being retired, but replacement is a more accurate term in this scenario.

33. Historical log data for your users shows normal cloud storage usage increases by an average of 9 percent annually. Over the past year, however, usage has increased by 18 percent. How is this change best described?

    A. Deviation from baseline

    B. Metered usage

    C. Trend analysis

    D. Resource pooling

    ☑ **A.** Baseline deviations are items that stray from the norm.

    ☒ **B, C,** and **D** are incorrect. Cloud service usage is tracked (metered), and users pay a fee based on this. A trend analysis occurs over time to identify commonalities. Resource pooling is used by cloud providers to make IT services available to tenants.

Chapter 8

Performance Tuning

CERTIFICATION OBJECTIVES

8.01   Host and Guest Resource Allocation

8.02   Optimizing Performance

QUESTIONS

The efficient running of a virtual machine guest results not only from proper and well-thought-out virtual machine configurations, but also from the hypervisor's configuration settings.

Virtual machines must have the appropriate resources to function correctly while not using excessive resources that can be better used by other virtual machines. In some cases, adding more virtual machines (scaling out, horizontally) or removing virtual machines (scaling in) in response to application requests improves performance and reduces costs.

1. Which capacity setting ensures a guaranteed amount of resources for a hypervisor?
   A. Metered
   B. Reservations
   C. Quota
   D. Dynamic

2. Users in your company use a web portal in a private cloud to deploy new virtual machines. The underlying resource usage for all virtual machines is logged, but users are not prevented from creating new virtual machines. What type of configuration logs this type of data?
   A. Hard quota
   B. Reservation
   C. Limit
   D. Soft quota

3. Which Microsoft tool provides hypervisor and virtual machine management capabilities?
   A. SCCM
   B. SCVMM
   C. MSCM
   D. MSVMM

4. Which cloud option allows customers to use existing software licenses for new cloud deployments?
   A. BYOL
   B. BYOD
   C. SLA
   D. BYL

5. Which hypervisor component communicates to the hypervisor to reclaim memory inside a virtual machine guest?

A. Guest tools

B. USB controller

C. Dynamic memory

D. Balloon driver

6. Which term describes increasing the number of vCPUs for a virtual machine?

A. Scaling in

B. Scaling down

C. Scaling up

D. Scaling out

7. Your cloud-based web application has recently experienced usage spikes. Additional web servers are needed to handle these demands. What should you do?

A. Scale in

B. Scale down

C. Scale up

D. Scale out

8. Which configuration ensures continued SAN connectivity in the event of an HBA failure?

A. Multipathing

B. Clustering

C. Load balancing

D. Zoning

9. Which term describes the total number of routers and switches a packet passes through to reach its destination?

A. Default gateway

B. Network latency

C. Hop count

D. Network count

10. Which IP header field value is decremented each time the packet goes through a router?

A. Source IP address

B. Destination IP address

C. Version

D. TTL

11. You need to ensure VoIP traffic is sent over the network before other types of traffic. What should you configure?

A. SLA

B. QoS

C. Multipathing

D. TTL

12. Host DNS records for devices no longer on the network still exist in DNS. Which option should you enable to remove stale DNS entries?

A. Scavenging

B. Recursion

C. Forwarding

D. Aliasing

13. Which term describes child artifacts left behind by software that did not properly clean up after itself?

A. Data remnants

B. Paged blocks

C. Orphaned resources

D. Buffer overrun

14. Your company uses back-end virtual machines configured as web application servers. The servers are configured to allow connections on the standard HTTP port from a load balancer. Which configuration in Figure 8-1 is incorrect?

A. Port 80 should be port 88.

B. Port 88 should be 80.

C. Port 80 should be 443.

D. The instance port should be HTTPS.

FIGURE 8-1	Listener Configuration:			
	Load Balancer Protocol	**Load Balancer Port**	**Instance Protocol**	**Instance Port**
Load balancer configuration	HTTP ▾	80	HTTP ▾	88

15. A web server administrator has changed the listening port from 80 to 81 to increase security and restarted the web server daemon. External traffic must be able to reach the server. What is the next task that should be performed by the web server administrator?

A. Restart the web server.

B. Change the port back to 80.

C. Change the outdated firewall rule.

D. Add a malware exception.

16. Which PowerShell command retrieves log information from a remote computer named Charlee1?

    A. Retrieve-Log –ComputerName Charlee1

    B. Retrieve-EventLog –ComputerName Charlee1

    C. Get-Log –ComputerName Charlee1

    D. Get-EventLog –ComputerName Charlee1

17. Which statement about the following code snippet is correct?

```
$Logs = Get-EventLog -ComputerName $ComputerName -List | ForEach {$_.Log}
```

    A. $Logs is a reserved variable name and cannot be used.

    B. Get-EventLog should be Get-Log.

    C. $_ is a temporary placeholder variable.

    D. –ComputerName should be -ComputerNames.

18. What is wrong with the following PowerShell code?

```
$VMSet=Get-VMs
foreach ($vm in $VMSet)
{
if ($vm.ExtensionData.Runtime.ConnectionState -eq "orphaned") {$vm | Remove-VM}
}
```

    A. Get-VMs should be Get-VM.

    B. –eq should be =.

    C. foreach should be for-each.

    D. .ConnectionState is not a valid property.

19. Which term describes the timeframe where a CPU cannot perform computations because it is waiting for I/O operations?

    A. CPU cache time

    B. CPU wait time

    C. CPU latency

    D. CPU lag

20. You need to archive six virtual machines that were used for product development. The total consumed disk space is 3TB. What should you do to minimize consumed archival disk space?

    A. Compress the virtual machines.

    B. Ensure each virtual machine has only one vCPU.

    C. Ensure each virtual machine has only one vNIC.

    D. Store the archive on SSDs.

21. What does the following PowerShell code accomplish?

```
Search-ADAccount -AccountInactive -TimeSpan ([timespan]60d) -UsersOnly |
Set-ADUser -Enabled $false
```

   A. User accounts not having logged in for 60 days are deleted.
   B. User accounts not having logged in for 60 days are disabled.
   C. User accounts more than 60 days old are disabled.
   D. A syntax error is displayed.

22. Your company IT director asks you to check into running the company's public website in a public cloud provider environment. Uptime is of the utmost importance. Which document should you refer to?

   A. OSI
   B. ITIL
   C. MOF
   D. SLA

23. Your cloud load balancer has recently experienced excessive requests for a web application. What should you do to ensure the capacity exists to handle peak requests?

   A. Enable auto-scaling.
   B. Enable clustering.
   C. Configure multiple port numbers.
   D. Add additional IP addresses.

24. You plan to use a cloud provider CLI to automate monthly management tasks. What is the first thing you should do prior to running these tasks?

   A. Update the CLI.
   B. Enable billing alerts.
   C. Enable runbooks.
   D. Power off virtual machines.

25. A cloud SLA specifies that the maximum yearly downtime is approximately 6 minutes. Which term best describes this downtime?

   A. High availability
   B. RTO
   C. Load balancing
   D. RPO

26. Which DNS load balancing technique is shown in Figure 8-2?

   A. Duplicity
   B. Aliasing
   C. Round-robin
   D. CNAME

FIGURE 8-2

| www | Host (A) | 34.66.7.43 |
| www | Host (A) | 56.78.33.2 |

DNS record
configuration

27. To optimize costs, you need to ensure minimal virtual machine instances are used except during peak requests. Which option should you configure?

    A. Scaling up
    B. Scaling down
    C. Scaling out
    D. Scaling in

28. Which type of quota, when reached, prevents additional resource use?

    A. Soft
    B. Hard
    C. Outer
    D. Inner

29. You plan to use a Linux virtual machine guest to conduct wireless network penetration tests. The virtual NICs will not support this functionality. The hypervisor has a supported USB adapter plugged in. What should you do?

    A. Install and configure a physical Linux computer.
    B. Install an updated virtual NIC driver.
    C. Install an updated virtual USB driver.
    D. Enable USB pass-through.

30. Which configuration separates physical compute resources into groups for higher-level management?

    A. ACL
    B. Emulation
    C. USB pass-through
    D. Resource pools

31. Which of the following items normally have a large influence on cloud-based web application performance? Choose two.

    A. Data backups
    B. SSO
    C. Virtual machine settings
    D. Load balancing

32. Which of the following factors is most likely to improve the performance of a slow virtual machine?

    A. Additional vCPUs
    B. RAID 1
    C. Additional vNICs
    D. Reduced number of open firewall ports

33. You need to define limits for virtual machine disk resource utilization. What should you configure?
    A. RAID
    B. I/O throttling
    C. SSDs
    D. Magnetic hard disks

34. Adan has configured an isolated network infrastructure for a private cloud. After starting multiple hypervisors on the network for the first time, he notices unacceptable network latency for one specific hypervisor. What is the most likely cause of the problem?
    A. Speed or duplex mismatch
    B. Invalid IP address
    C. Incorrect subnet mask
    D. Missing default gateway

35. A web application is experiencing slow performance when running back-end database queries. Which configuration would most likely improve query performance?
    A. Optimized database read settings
    B. I/O throttling
    C. Tweaking write settings
    D. RAID 1

A QUICK ANSWER KEY

1. B	**10.** D	**19.** B	**28.** B
2. D	**11.** B	**20.** A	**29.** D
3. B	**12.** A	**21.** B	**30.** D
4. A	**13.** C	**22.** D	**31.** C, D
5. D	**14.** B	**23.** A	**32.** A
6. C	**15.** C	**24.** A	**33.** B
7. D	**16.** D	**25.** B	**34.** A
8. A	**17.** C	**26.** C	**35.** A
9. C	**18.** A	**27.** D	

IN-DEPTH ANSWERS

1. Which capacity setting ensures a guaranteed amount of resources for a hypervisor?
   A. Metered
   B. Reservations
   C. Quota
   D. Dynamic

   ☑ **B.** Reservations prevent virtual machines from consuming all available hardware resources.
   ☒ **A, C,** and **D** are incorrect. Metering tracks resources usage. Quotas either log excessive resource usage or prevent allocation of additional resources. Dynamic resource configuration applies to memory adjustments made to a virtual machine while it is running.

2. Users in your company use a web portal in a private cloud to deploy new virtual machines. The underlying resource usage for all virtual machines is logged, but users are not prevented from creating new virtual machines. What type of configuration logs this type of data?
   A. Hard quota
   B. Reservation
   C. Limit
   D. Soft quota

   ☑ **D.** Soft quotas will log the exceeding of configured resource utilization.
   ☒ **A, B,** and **C** are incorrect. Hard quotas actually prevent additional resource allocation. Reservations prevent virtual machines from consuming all available hardware resources. Limit is an ambiguous term as related to configuration.

3. Which Microsoft tool provides hypervisor and virtual machine management capabilities?
   A. SCCM
   B. SCVMM
   C. MSCM
   D. MSVMM

   ☑ **B.** System Center Virtual Machine Manager (SCVMM) provides hypervisor and virtual machine management capabilities.
   ☒ **A, C,** and **D** are incorrect. System Center Configuration Manager (SCCM) is a centralized configuration management tool. MSCM and MSVMM are not valid products in the context of hypervisor management.

4. Which cloud option allows customers to use existing software licenses for new cloud deployments?

  A. BYOL
  B. BYOD
  C. SLA
  D. BYL

  ☑ **A.** Bring your own license (BYOL) allows customers to use existing software licenses for new cloud deployments.

  ☒ **B, C,** and **D** are incorrect. Bring your own device (BYOD) allows personal mobile device usage for business. Service level agreements (SLAs) are contracts between IT service providers and consumers. BYL is not a valid term.

5. Which hypervisor component communicates to the hypervisor to reclaim memory inside a virtual machine guest?

  A. Guest tools
  B. USB controller
  C. Dynamic memory
  D. Balloon driver

  ☑ **D.** Memory ballooning through the balloon driver allows virtual machines not needing all of their allocated memory to share memory pages with the hypervisor.

  ☒ **A, B,** and **C** are incorrect. Guest tools provide virtual machines with additional capabilities such as synchronizing time with the hypervisor or improving mouse support for GUIs. USB controllers are not related to memory. Dynamic memory allows virtual machine memory settings to be modified by the administrator (and not the hypervisor) while the virtual machine is running.

6. Which term describes increasing the number of vCPUs for a virtual machine?

  A. Scaling in
  B. Scaling down
  C. Scaling up
  D. Scaling out

  ☑ **C.** Scaling up, or vertically, means adding more computing power to existing virtual machines.

  ☒ **A, B,** and **D** are incorrect. Scaling in reduces the number of virtual machines, scaling down decreases compute power, and scaling out adds virtual machines.

7. Your cloud-based web application has recently experienced usage spikes. Additional web servers are needed to handle these demands. What should you do?

  A. Scale in
  B. Scale down
  C. Scale up
  D. Scale out

  ☑ **D.** Scaling out adds additional virtual machines.

  ☒ **A, B,** and **C** are incorrect. Scaling in reduces the number of virtual machines. Scaling down decreases computing power. Scaling up, or vertically, means adding more computing power to existing virtual machines.

8. Which configuration ensures continued SAN connectivity in the event of an HBA failure?
   A. Multipathing
   B. Clustering
   C. Load balancing
   D. Zoning

   ☑ **A.** Providing multiple communication paths between a storage consumer and SAN components is called multipathing.
   ☒ **B, C,** and **D** are incorrect. Clustering and load balancing can provide high availability and performance improvements, but not for SANs. Zoning ensures shared storage is visible only to certain storage consumers.

9. Which term describes the total number of routers and switches a packet passes through to reach its destination?
   A. Default gateway
   B. Network latency
   C. Hop count
   D. Network count

   ☑ **C.** The hop count is the number of routers and switches a packet must cross on its way to the final destination.
   ☒ **A, B,** and **D** are incorrect. The default gateway, or router, provides a way out of a local area network. Network latency refers to an abnormal delay between the transmission and receipt of network traffic. A network count is the number of networks within a given scope.

10. Which IP header field value is decremented each time the packet goes through a router?
    A. Source IP address
    B. Destination IP address
    C. Version
    D. TTL

    ☑ **D.** Routers decrement the time-to-live (TTL) IP header field value as the packet traverses a router.
    ☒ **A, B,** and **C** are incorrect. The other listed IP header field values are not modified by routers.

11. You need to ensure VoIP traffic is sent over the network before other types of traffic. What should you configure?
    A. SLA
    B. QoS
    C. Multipathing
    D. TTL

    ☑ **B.** Quality of service (QoS) is a configuration that prioritizes specific types of network traffic.
    ☒ **A, C,** and **D** are incorrect. Service level agreements (SLAs) are contracts between IT service providers and consumers. Providing multiple communication paths between a storage consumer and SAN components is called multipathing. Routers decrement the time-to-live (TTL) IP header field value as the packet traverses a router.

12. Host DNS records for devices no longer on the network still exist in DNS. Which option should you enable to remove stale DNS entries?

    A. Scavenging
    B. Recursion
    C. Forwarding
    D. Aliasing

    ☑ **A.** DNS scavenging removes stale, or outdated, DNS records.
    ☒ **B, C,** and **D** are incorrect. DNS recursion occurs when a DNS server cannot resolve a request from its local DNS database, so it sends that request to other DNS servers. DNS forwarding simply sends DNS requests to specific DNS servers in a forwarding list. DNS aliasing occurs through the use of CNAME records.

13. Which term describes child artifacts left behind by software that did not properly clean up after itself?

    A. Data remnants
    B. Paged blocks
    C. Orphaned resources
    D. Buffer overrun

    ☑ **C.** Orphaned resources is a generic term that can apply to leftover software artifacts no longer tied to a parent configuration.
    ☒ **A, B,** and **D** are incorrect. Data remnants do not imply a parent-child relationship. Page blocks refer to memory swapping when physical RAM is unavailable. Buffer overruns are a memory vulnerability that can crash a system or expose sensitive memory contents.

14. Your company uses back-end virtual machines configured as web application servers. The servers are configured to allow connections on the standard HTTP port from a load balancer. Which configuration in Figure 8-1 is incorrect?

    A. Port 80 should be port 88.
    B. Port 88 should be 80.
    C. Port 80 should be 443.
    D. The instance port should be HTTPS.

FIGURE 8-1

Load balancer configuration

Listener Configuration:

Load Balancer Protocol	Load Balancer Port	Instance Protocol	Instance Port
HTTP ▼	80	HTTP ▼	88

☑ **B.** The standard HTTP port is 80, not 88.
☒ **A, C,** and **D** are incorrect. The listed items should not be changed; their configuration is correct.

15. A web server administrator has changed the listening port from 80 to 81 to increase security and restarted the web server daemon. External traffic must be able to reach the server. What is the next task that should be performed by the web server administrator?

    A. Restart the web server.
    B. Change the port back to 80.
    C. Change the outdated firewall rule.
    D. Add a malware exception.

    ☑ **C.** Changing a port number requires the old firewall rule to be changed to the new port number.
    ☒ **A, B,** and **D** are incorrect. The web server daemon was restarted; the server does not need to be restarted. The port does not need to be changed back to port 80. Malware exceptions do not apply in this case. They are normally used to exclude temporary folders that can trigger malware false positives.

16. Which PowerShell command retrieves log information from a remote computer named Charlee1?

    A. Retrieve-Log –ComputerName Charlee1
    B. Retrieve-EventLog –ComputerName Charlee1
    C. Get-Log –ComputerName Charlee1
    D. Get-EventLog –ComputerName Charlee1

    ☑ **D.** The correct PowerShell cmdlet is Get-Eventlog.
    ☒ **A, B,** and **C** are incorrect. The listed cmdlets are incorrect.

17. Which statement about the following code snippet is correct?

    ```
    $Logs = Get-EventLog -ComputerName $ComputerName -List | ForEach {$_.Log}
    ```

    A. $Logs is a reserved variable name and cannot be used.
    B. Get-EventLog should be Get-Log.
    C. $_ is a temporary placeholder variable.
    D. –ComputerName should be -ComputerNames.

    ☑ **C.** $_ is a built-in placeholder PowerShell variable used when processing an object collection.
    ☒ **A, B,** and **D** are incorrect. The listed items are incorrect.

18. What is wrong with the following PowerShell code?

    ```
    $VMSet=Get-VMs
    foreach ($vm in $VMSet)
    {
    if ($vm.ExtensionData.Runtime.ConnectionState -eq "orphaned") {$vm | Remove-VM}
    }
    ```

    A. Get-VMs should be Get-VM.
    B. –eq should be =.
    C. foreach should be for-each.
    D. .ConnectionState is not a valid property.

    ☑ **A.** Most PowerShell cmdlets are singular, not plural; Get-VM is correct.

    ☒ **B, C,** and **D** are incorrect. The listed "errors" are not actually correct.

19. Which term describes the timeframe where a CPU cannot perform computations because it is waiting for I/O operations?

    A. CPU cache time

    B. CPU wait time

    C. CPU latency

    D. CPU lag

    ☑ **B.** The timeframe where a CPU cannot perform computations because it is waiting for I/O operations is called CPU wait time.

    ☒ **A, C,** and **D** are incorrect. The listed terms do not describe waiting for the CPU to process requests.

20. You need to archive six virtual machines that were used for product development. The total consumed disk space is 3TB. What should you do to minimize consumed archival disk space?

    A. Compress the virtual machines.

    B. Ensure each virtual machine has only one vCPU.

    C. Ensure each virtual machine has only one vNIC.

    D. Store the archive on SSDs.

    ☑ **A.** Disk compression conserves disk space.

    ☒ **B, C,** and **D** are incorrect. The number of vCPUs and vNICs and the use of SSDs have no bearing on reducing disk space consumption.

21. What does the following PowerShell code accomplish?

```
Search-ADAccount -AccountInactive -TimeSpan ([timespan]60d) -UsersOnly |
Set-ADUser -Enabled $false
```

    A. User accounts not having logged in for 60 days are deleted.

    B. User accounts not having logged in for 60 days are disabled.

    C. User accounts more than 60 days old are disabled.

    D. A syntax error is displayed.

    ☑ **B.** The account of any user who has not logged in for 60 days is disabled.

    ☒ **A, C,** and **D** are incorrect. The listed items are incorrect and there are no syntax errors.

22. Your company IT director asks you to check into running the company's public website in a public cloud provider environment. Uptime is of the utmost importance. Which document should you refer to?

    A. OSI

    B. ITIL

    C. MOF

    D. SLA

☑ **D.** Service level agreements (SLAs) are contracts between IT service providers and consumers that can contain performance details such as uptime.

☒ **A, B,** and **C** are incorrect. Open Systems Interconnect (OSI) is a conceptual seven-layer model used to map communications hardware and software. Information Technology Infrastructure Library (ITIL) and Microsoft Operations Framework (MOF) are application life cycle management models.

23. Your cloud load balancer has recently experienced excessive requests for a web application. What should you do to ensure the capacity exists to handle peak requests?

    A. Enable auto-scaling.
    B. Enable clustering.
    C. Configure multiple port numbers.
    D. Add additional IP addresses.

    ☑ **A.** Auto-scaling configurations define settings related to when additional virtual machine instances should be started to handle increased requests.

    ☒ **B, C,** and **D** are incorrect. Clustering provides high availability but not dynamic resource allocation. Additional port numbers or IP addresses will not increase the ability to handle increased demands.

24. You plan to use a cloud provider CLI to automate monthly management tasks. What is the first thing you should do prior to running these tasks?

    A. Update the CLI.
    B. Enable billing alerts.
    C. Enable runbooks.
    D. Power off virtual machines.

    ☑ **A.** Always update components such as cloud provider command-line interface (CLI) tools before depending on them for monthly recurring tasks.

    ☒ **B, C,** and **D** are incorrect. Enabling billing alerts and powering off virtual machines are not related to automation. Runbooks are used in automation workflows but are not required when using a CLI.

25. A cloud SLA specifies that the maximum yearly downtime is approximately 6 minutes. Which term best describes this downtime?

    A. High availability
    B. RTO
    C. Load balancing
    D. RPO

    ☑ **B.** The recovery time objective (RTO) specifies the maximum tolerable amount of downtime.

    ☒ **A, C,** and **D** are incorrect. High availability ensures services remain running but does not specify an amount of acceptable downtime. Load balancing is used to improve application performance. The recovery point objective (RPO) reflects the maximum tolerable amount of data loss.

26. Which DNS load balancing technique is shown in Figure 8-2?

    A. Duplicity

    B. Aliasing

    C. Round-robin

    D. CNAME

FIGURE 8-2

DNS record
configuration

www	Host (A)	34.66.7.43
www	Host (A)	56.78.33.2

    ☑ **C.** DNS round-robin uses multiple DNS A or AAAA records with the same name but different IP addresses.

    ☒ **A, B,** and **D** are incorrect. Duplicity is not a valid term when discussing load balancing. DNS aliasing uses CNAME records that point to A or AAAA records.

27. To optimize costs, you need to ensure minimal virtual machine instances are used except during peak requests. Which option should you configure?

    A. Scaling up

    B. Scaling down

    C. Scaling out

    D. Scaling in

    ☑ **D.** Scaling in reduces the number of virtual machine instances.

    ☒ **A, B,** and **C** are incorrect. Scaling up, or vertically, means adding more compute power to existing virtual machines. Scaling down decreases compute power, and scaling out adds virtual machines.

28. Which type of quota, when reached, prevents additional resource use?

    A. Soft

    B. Hard

    C. Outer

    D. Inner

    ☑ **B.** Hard quotas prevent additional resource allocation when the quota limit is reached.

    ☒ **A, C,** and **D** are incorrect. Soft quotas do not prevent additional resource allocation but instead log the event information. Outer and inner are not valid quota types.

29. You plan to use a Linux virtual machine guest to conduct wireless network penetration tests. The virtual NICs will not support this functionality. The hypervisor has a supported USB adapter plugged in. What should you do?

    A. Install and configure a physical Linux computer.

    B. Install an updated virtual NIC driver.

    C. Install an updated virtual USB driver.

    D. Enable USB pass-through.

☑ **D.** USB pass-through allows a virtual machine to access physical USB devices plugged into the host.

☒ **A, B,** and **C** are incorrect. A physical server requires much more effort than simply enabling USB pass-through. Updated drivers will not solve the problem.

30. Which configuration separates physical compute resources into groups for higher-level management?
    A. ACL
    B. Emulation
    C. USB pass-through
    D. Resource pools

    ☑ **D.** Resource pools are groups of underlying resources managed as a single unit.

    ☒ **A, B,** and **C** are incorrect. Access control lists (ACLs) control resource access. Emulation and USB pass-through allow virtual machines to access hardware resources but they do not organize resources into groups.

31. Which of the following items normally have a large influence on cloud-based web application performance? Choose two.
    A. Data backups
    B. SSO
    C. Virtual machine settings
    D. Load balancing

    ☑ **C** and **D.** Virtual machine settings, such as the amount of memory, and using multiple virtual machines in a load balancing configuration can drastically improve application performance.

    ☒ **A** and **B** are incorrect. Data backups and Single Sign-On (SSO) are not related to application performance.

32. Which of the following factors is most likely to improve the performance of a slow virtual machine?
    A. Additional vCPUs
    B. RAID 1
    C. Additional vNICs
    D. Reduced number of open firewall ports

    ☑ **A.** Of the listed items, more vCPUs is the most likely to improve performance.

    ☒ **B, C,** and **D** are incorrect. RAID 1 (disk mirroring) increases fault tolerance but not performance. Additional vNICs and reduced open firewall ports will not improve performance.

33. You need to define limits for virtual machine disk resource utilization. What should you configure?
    A. RAID
    B. I/O throttling
    C. SSDs
    D. Magnetic hard disks

☑   **B.** I/O throttling prevents virtual machines from consuming all disk I/O cycles.

☒   **A, C,** and **D** are incorrect. RAID levels either provide fault tolerance, improve disk performance, or both—they do not set disk utilization limits. Solid state drives (SSDs) do not use moving parts as traditional magnetic hard disks do and they do not determine virtual machine disk limitations.

34. Adan has configured an isolated network infrastructure for a private cloud. After starting multiple hypervisors on the network for the first time, he notices unacceptable network latency for one specific hypervisor. What is the most likely cause of the problem?

A.   Speed or duplex mismatch

B.   Invalid IP address

C.   Incorrect subnet mask

D.   Missing default gateway

☑   **A.** If speed or duplex settings are mismatched between NICs and switches, it can result in network performance degradation.

☒   **B, C,** and **D** are incorrect. Incorrect or incomplete TCP/IP configurations are not as likely to cause network latency.

35. A web application is experiencing slow performance when running back-end database queries. Which configuration would most likely improve query performance?

A.   Optimized database read settings

B.   I/O throttling

C.   Tweaking write settings

D.   RAID 1

☑   **A.** Querying issues read requests against a database, thus optimizing read settings can help improve query performance.

☒   **B, C,** and **D** are incorrect. I/O throttling limits disk I/O consumption. Queries are read, and not write, intensive. RAID 1 (disk mirroring) does not increase performance. RAID 1 increases resiliency to disk failure.

Chapter 9
Systems Management

CERTIFICATION OBJECTIVES

9.01   Policies and Procedures

9.02   Systems Management Best Practices

9.03   Systems Maintenance

QUESTIONS

Organizations benefit from a structured and centralized approach to the deployment and management of their IT systems. Policies and standard operating procedures ensure that on-premises and cloud management tasks are performed consistently and efficiently.

Software patches such as hotfixes and service packs are built and tested by developers in staging environments before being made available to production environments. The deployment of these and other configuration settings can be automated using workflows.

1. Which organizational documentation ensures that tasks are performed consistently?
   A. Service level agreement
   B. Standard operating procedure
   C. Workflow
   D. Network diagram

2. During which ITIL phase are business requirements documented?
   A. Service strategy
   B. Service design
   C. Service transition
   D. Service operation

3. Which ITIL phase is related to support documentation such as service level agreements?
   A. Service strategy
   B. Service design
   C. Service transition
   D. Service operation

4. Which of the following can help technicians identify cloud performance issues?
   A. Service level agreement
   B. Firewall settings
   C. Additional virtual CPUs
   D. Key performance indicators

5. Your organization tracks private cloud usage by department for billing purposes. What type of model is this?

    A. Service level agreement

    B. Agile

    C. Waterfall

    D. Chargeback

6. Which type of document specifies the level of uptime that will be supported by the service provider?

    A. SLA

    B. KPI

    C. DRP

    D. BIA

7. You are configuring firewall rules as per Figure 9-1 to enable the gathering of device statistics over the network. Which protocol should you allow through the firewall?

    A. UDP 161

    B. TCP 161

    C. TCP 25

    D. TCP 8000

FIGURE 9-1

Firewall rule set

Type ⓘ	Protocol ⓘ	Port Range ⓘ
HTTP ▾	TCP	80
Custom TCP F ▾	TCP	8000
SMTP ▾	TCP	25
MYSQL/Auror ▾	TCP	3306
Custom TCP F ▾	TCP	161
Custom UDP I ▾	UDP	161

8. You are configuring the storage subsystem for an on-premises cloud hypervisor. Dependability is paramount for the server. Which phrase refers to the average amount of time before potential hard disk failures?

    A. MTTR

    B. MTBF

    C. RTO

    D. RPO

9. Which term describes the average time that it takes to repair a failed hardware component?

   A. MTTR

   B. MTBF

   C. RTO

   D. RPO

10. Which software development methodology has continuous software improvements being developed?

   A. Rolling updates

   B. Continuous updates

   C. Rolling deployment

   D. Continuous rollups

11. Developers use multiple cloud staging slots, or environments, for testing and production versions of an application. What type of testing model is this?

   A. Black-box

   B. Blue-box

   C. Blue-green

   D. Black-blue

12. Which of the following options ensures an effective failover cluster?

   A. Public IP address

   B. Shared storage

   C. Private IP address

   D. Hypervisors

13. You are configuring a failover cluster that will use SAN shared storage. What type of address should be added to a storage group on the shared disk array?

   A. FQDN

   B. MAC address

   C. IP address

   D. WWN

14. You are updating hypervisor cluster nodes one at a time. You have moved virtual machines running on Hypervisor1 to Hypervisor2. What should you do to place the virtual machines on the original cluster node?

   A. Failover

   B. Failback

   C. Scale in

   D. Storage migration

15. Which PowerShell command restarts a host?
    A. Service Restart
    B. Restart-Computer
    C. Restart-Server
    D. Restart Service

16. A new HBA has arrived for a physical cluster node server. You need to install the HBA while ensuring clustered apps continue to run. What is the first thing that you should do on the server?
    A. Enter maintenance mode.
    B. Perform a backup.
    C. Create a disk image.
    D. Create a system restore point.

17. Which strategy ensures adequate resources are available for future service provisioning?
    A. Storage provisioning
    B. Rapid elasticity
    C. Thin provisioning
    D. Capacity planning

18. What is required for code rollback to work?
    A. Disk image
    B. Virtual machine snapshot
    C. Code backup
    D. Deployment slot

19. You have created a runbook to orchestrate the maintenance of a cluster node. Which term best describes starting the runbook?
    A. Desired state configuration
    B. Workflow execution
    C. Script debugging
    D. Snapshotting

20. Before determining that performance levels are out of the norm, what is required?
    A. Key performance indicator
    B. Service level agreement
    C. Configuration item
    D. Baseline

21. An existing cloud virtual machine does not have the computing power to properly serve an application. What should you do?
    A. Scale out.
    B. Resize the virtual machine.
    C. Scale in.
    D. Redeploy the virtual machine.

22. A newly developed application is being tested under a large volume of client requests. What could increase application performance?

A. Replication

B. Data integrity

C. Load balancing

D. Scaling in

23. Which strategy uses a structured, centralized approach to applying IT modifications?

A. Load testing

B. Penetration testing

C. Change management

D. Workflow testing

24. You have deployed a custom web application to the cloud for testing. The IT security team plans to simulate malicious user attacks against the app. What type of testing is this?

A. Load

B. Stress

C. Penetration

D. Vulnerability

25. Your company uses SaaS office productivity tools from a public cloud provider. You need the latest updates applied to the tools. What should you do?

A. Use a runbook to install the updates.

B. Let the provider apply the updates.

C. Enter maintenance mode and install the updates manually.

D. Submit a support ticket to the cloud provider.

26. Refer to Figure 9-2. Which factor is the most likely to be influenced by this configuration?

A. Licensing

B. Performance

C. Security

D. Scaling

FIGURE 9-2	Load Balancer Protocol	Load Balancer Port	Instance Protocol	Instance Port
Load balancing configuration	HTTP ▼	80	HTTP ▼	84

27. Which type of patch addresses a single small issue?

  A. Service pack

  B. Hotfix

  C. Update dependency

  D. Rolling update

28. Users report stability issues with a custom web application deployed in a cloud virtual machine. Your team needs to address and test these concerns in a sandboxed environment. What is the next thing you should do to the virtual machine?

  A. Back it up.

  B. Apply patches.

  C. Clone it.

  D. Take a snapshot.

29. Jenny is responsible for a subset of cloud-based virtual machines. She needs a way of quickly viewing key performance indicators for the servers. What should Jenny do?

  A. Install and configure performance agents on all virtual machines.

  B. Configure custom alert notification.

  C. Create a custom dashboard.

  D. Establish a baseline.

30. Which item indicates a delay in service response time?

  A. MTTR

  B. MTBF

  C. RPO

  D. Latency

31. Your organizational security policies require a proxy server for cloud-initiated traffic destined for the Internet. What should you deploy?

  A. Virtual appliance

  B. Virtual machine

  C. Operating system image

  D. NAT

32. Which of the following is a storage component containing firmware that should be updated in an iSCSI environment?

  A. Network switch

  B. Router

  C. HBA

  D. VLAN

33. After a development team solves bugs within a web application, what should it do next?

    A. Deploy patches.

    B. Document the solution.

    C. Back up the virtual machine.

    D. Create a virtual machine snapshot.

34. You are reviewing charges from your public cloud provider. The past month indicates that cloud storage provisioning has increased 50 percent from the previous month. Which term best describes this scenario?

    A. Broad access

    B. Scaling up

    C. Elasticity

    D. Scaling out

35. Which term is closely related to chargeback?

    A. Showback

    B. Reverse cloud billing

    C. Metered billing

    D. Capital billing

A QUICK ANSWER KEY

1.	B	**10.**	A	**19.**	B	**28.**	C
2.	A	**11.**	C	**20.**	D	**29.**	C
3.	B	**12.**	B	**21.**	B	**30.**	D
4.	D	**13.**	D	**22.**	C	**31.**	A
5.	D	**14.**	B	**23.**	C	**32.**	C
6.	A	**15.**	B	**24.**	C	**33.**	B
7.	A	**16.**	A	**25.**	B	**34.**	C
8.	B	**17.**	D	**26.**	B	**35.**	A
9.	A	**18.**	C	**27.**	B		

IN-DEPTH ANSWERS

1. Which organizational documentation ensures that tasks are performed consistently?
   A. Service level agreement
   B. Standard operating procedure
   C. Workflow
   D. Network diagram

   ☑ **B.** Standard operating procedures (SOPs) ensure that tasks are performed efficiently and consistently.

   ☒ **A, C,** and **D** are incorrect. Service level agreements (SLAs) are contracts between service providers and consumers that detail expected service levels. Workflows are business processes that are organized into sets of discrete tasks from beginning to end. Network diagrams list the layout of network devices, connectivity to other networks, and addressing schemes in use.

2. During which ITIL phase are business requirements documented?
   A. Service strategy
   B. Service design
   C. Service transition
   D. Service operation

   ☑ **A.** The ITIL service strategy phase involves the documentation of business requirements.

   ☒ **B, C,** and **D** are incorrect. The service design phase involves technical solutions and support processes. The service transition phase deals with the implementation of service design components. The service operation phase ensures that SLAs are being honored and that services are being delivered efficiently.

3. Which ITIL phase is related to support documentation such as service level agreements?
   A. Service strategy
   B. Service design
   C. Service transition
   D. Service operation

☑ **B.** The service design phase involves technical solutions and support processes.

☒ **A, C,** and **D** are incorrect. The ITIL service strategy phase involves the documentation of business requirements. The service transition phase deals with the implementation of service design components. The service operation phase ensures that SLAs are being honored and that services are being delivered efficiently.

4. Which of the following can help technicians identify cloud performance issues?

   A. Service level agreement
   B. Firewall settings
   C. Additional virtual CPUs
   D. Key performance indicators

☑ **D.** Key performance indicators (KPIs) in IT services allow the identification of performance problems.

☒ **A, B,** and **C** are incorrect. Service level agreements (SLAs) are contracts between service providers and consumers that detail expected service levels. Firewall settings and vCPUs are not related to the identification of performance problems.

5. Your organization tracks private cloud usage by department for billing purposes. What type of model is this?

   A. Service level agreement
   B. Agile
   C. Waterfall
   D. Chargeback

☑ **D.** Chargeback models track usage and bill based on that usage.

☒ **A, B,** and **C** are incorrect. Service level agreements (SLAs) are contracts between service providers and consumers that detail expected service levels. Agile and waterfall are software development methodologies.

6. Which type of document specifies the level of uptime that will be supported by the service provider?

   A. SLA
   B. KPI
   C. DRP
   D. BIA

☑ **A.** Service level agreements (SLAs) are contracts between service providers and consumers that detail expected service levels.

☒ **B, C,** and **D** are incorrect. Key performance indicators (KPIs) in IT services allow the identification of performance problems. A disaster recovery plan (DRP) outlines what is to be done to recover a specific system in the event of a disaster. The business impact analysis (BIA) identifies asset threats and their impact on business processes.

7. You are configuring firewall rules as per Figure 9-1 to enable the gathering of device statistics over the network. Which protocol should you allow through the firewall?

A. UDP 161

B. TCP 161

C. TCP 25

D. TCP 8000

FIGURE 9-1

Firewall rule set

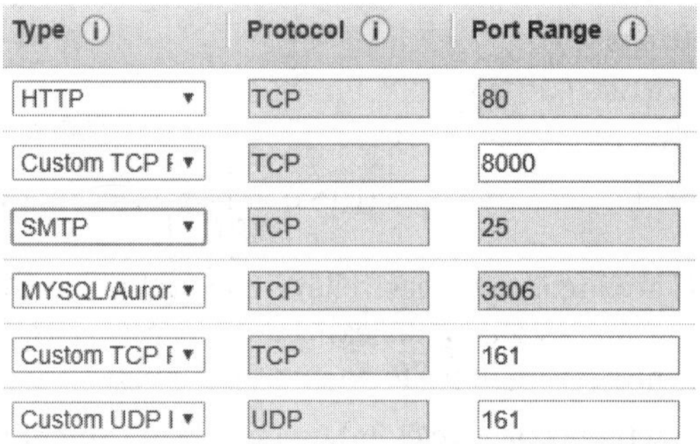

Type ⓘ	Protocol ⓘ	Port Range ⓘ
HTTP ▾	TCP	80
Custom TCP F ▾	TCP	8000
SMTP ▾	TCP	25
MYSQL/Auror ▾	TCP	3306
Custom TCP F ▾	TCP	161
Custom UDP I ▾	UDP	161

☑ **A.** Simple Network Management Protocol uses UDP port 161 to gather configuration settings and usage statistics from network devices.

☒ **B, C,** and **D** are incorrect. SNMP does not use TCP 161, SMTP uses port 25, and TCP port 8000 is not reserved for a specific network service.

8. You are configuring the storage subsystem for an on-premises cloud hypervisor. Dependability is paramount for the server. Which phrase refers to the average amount of time before potential hard disk failures?

A. MTTR

B. MTBF

C. RTO

D. RPO

☑ **B.** The mean time between failures (MTBF) measurement refers to the average amount of time that will pass before a component fails.

☒ **A, C,** and **D** are incorrect. The mean time to repair (MTTR) is the average time that it takes to repair a failed hardware component. Recovery time objective (RTO) is the maximum tolerable amount of downtime, and recovery point objective (RPO) is the maximum tolerable amount of data loss.

9. Which term describes the average time that it takes to repair a failed hardware component?

A. MTTR

B. MTBF

C. RTO

D. RPO

☑   **A.** The mean time to repair (MTTR) is the average time that it takes to repair a failed hardware component.

☒   **B, C,** and **D** are incorrect. The mean time between failures (MTBF) measurement refers to the average amount of time that will pass before a component fails. Recovery time objective (RTO) is the maximum tolerable amount of downtime, and recovery point objective (RPO) is the maximum tolerable amount of data loss.

10. Which software development methodology has continuous software improvements being developed?

   A. Rolling updates
   B. Continuous updates
   C. Rolling deployment
   D. Continuous rollups

☑   **A.** Rolling updates refer to continuous integration of software improvements through small updates.

☒   **B, C,** and **D** are incorrect. The listed items are not industry-standard terms in this context.

11. Developers use multiple cloud staging slots, or environments, for testing and production versions of an application. What type of testing model is this?

   A. Black-box
   B. Blue-box
   C. Blue-green
   D. Black-blue

☑   **C.** Blue-green environments are used for staging changes to an app or system. Blue refers to the production version of the app and green is the testing environment.

☒   **A, B,** and **D** are incorrect. Black-box testing refers to security testing where the testers have no knowledge of internal configuration details. Blue-box and black-blue are not valid testing methods.

12. Which of the following options ensures an effective failover cluster?

   A. Public IP address
   B. Shared storage
   C. Private IP address
   D. Hypervisors

☑   **B.** Shared storage provides a central data store for clustered services that is visible to all cluster nodes.

☒   **A, C,** and **D** are incorrect. IP addressing and whether or not hypervisors are involved are not directly related to effective failover cluster configurations.

13. You are configuring a failover cluster that will use SAN shared storage. What type of address should be added to a storage group on the shared disk array?

    A. FQDN
    B. MAC address
    C. IP address
    D. WWN

    ☑ **D.** The World Wide Name (WWN) should be added; it is a unique identifier used by a host to register with a SAN.
    ☒ **A, B,** and **C** are incorrect. Fully qualified domain names (FQDNs) are DNS names. MAC addresses are physical NIC addresses. IP addresses are software addresses. These identifiers are not used when configuring a SAN storage group.

14. You are updating hypervisor cluster nodes one at a time. You have moved virtual machines running on Hypervisor1 to Hypervisor2. What should you do to place the virtual machines on the original cluster node?

    A. Failover
    B. Failback
    C. Scale in
    D. Storage migration

    ☑ **B.** A failback returns a failover clustered service to the original host.
    ☒ **A, C,** and **D** are incorrect. Failover occurs when a clustered service runs on another cluster node due to an original cluster node failure. Scaling in refers to reducing the number of virtual machine instances supporting an application. Storage migration moves virtual machine storage to a new location, in some cases, with zero downtime.

15. Which PowerShell command restarts a host?

    A. Service Restart
    B. Restart-Computer
    C. Restart-Server
    D. Restart Service

    ☑ **B.** Restart-Computer restarts a host.
    ☒ **A, C,** and **D** are incorrect. The listed items are not standard PowerShell cmdlets.

16. A new HBA has arrived for a physical cluster node server. You need to install the HBA while ensuring clustered apps continue to run. What is the first thing that you should do on the server?

    A. Enter maintenance mode.
    B. Perform a backup.
    C. Create a disk image.
    D. Create a system restore point.

☑ **A.** Entering maintenance mode allows the host to be drained of clustered services and brought down gracefully so that the host bus adapter (HBA) can be installed.

☒ **B, C,** and **D** are incorrect. Server backups and disk imaging do not ensure that clustered apps continue to run. System restore points work only on Windows client stations, not servers.

17. Which strategy ensures adequate resources are available for future service provisioning?

A. Storage provisioning

B. Rapid elasticity

C. Thin provisioning

D. Capacity planning

☑ **D.** Planning for future IT service consumption is called capacity planning.

☒ **A, B,** and **C** are incorrect. Storage provisioning is the allocation of more storage space, but it is not a future planning strategy. Rapid elasticity is a cloud computing characteristic that allows resources to be quickly provisioned and deprovisioned. Thin provisioning allows the creation of multiple disk volumes whose total space exceeds available physical space; the volumes grow dynamically over time.

18. What is required for code rollback to work?

A. Disk image

B. Virtual machine snapshot

C. Code backup

D. Deployment slot

☑ **C.** Software code must be backed up so that rollback, or going back to a previous code version, is possible.

☒ **A, B,** and **D** are incorrect. The listed items do not specifically allow code rollbacks.

19. You have created a runbook to orchestrate the maintenance of a cluster node. Which term best describes starting the runbook?

A. Desired state configuration

B. Workflow execution

C. Script debugging

D. Snapshotting

☑ **B.** Runbooks allow for the orchestration of IT service management workflows.

☒ **A, C,** and **D** are incorrect. While the list items are related to configuration management, automation, and recovery, they do not reflect starting a runbook.

20. Before determining that performance levels are out of the norm, what is required?

   A. Key performance indicator

   B. Service level agreement

   C. Configuration item

   D. Baseline

   ☑ **D.** A baseline is a measure of metrics under normal activity. Baselines are required to identify deviations or abnormal activity related to security or performance.

   ☒ **A, B,** and **C** are incorrect. Key performance indicators (KPIs) in IT services allow the identification of performance problems. Service level agreements (SLAs) are contracts between service providers and consumers that detail expected service levels. Configuration items (CIs) are components of an overall management system and could include things such as licensing documents, software, and so on.

21. An existing cloud virtual machine does not have the computing power to properly serve an application. What should you do?

   A. Scale out.

   B. Resize the virtual machine.

   C. Scale in.

   D. Redeploy the virtual machine.

   ☑ **B.** Resizing refers to adjusting the underlying virtual machine power, such as adding more vCPUs, faster and more storage, more RAM, and so on.

   ☒ **A, C,** and **D** are incorrect. Scaling out adds virtual machine instances to support an application. Scaling in reduces the number of virtual machine instances that support an application. Redeploying a virtual machine will not increase its computing power.

22. A newly developed application is being tested under a large volume of client requests. What could increase application performance?

   A. Replication

   B. Data integrity

   C. Load balancing

   D. Scaling in

   ☑ **C.** Load balancers forward incoming client requests to the least busy and responsive backend server in order to increase application performance.

   ☒ **A, B,** and **D** are incorrect. In some cases, replication increases performance by placing data near users, but that is not stated in this scenario. Data integrity ensures the trustworthiness of data and has nothing to do with performance other than to possibly slow things down slightly. Scaling in reduces the number of virtual machine instances supporting an application.

23. Which strategy uses a structured, centralized approach to applying IT modifications?

   A. Load testing

   B. Penetration testing

   C. Change management

   D. Workflow testing

☑ **C.** Change management refers to structured and centralized approvals and deployments of IT system changes.

☒ **A, B,** and **D** are incorrect. The listed testing methods are not structured and centralized IT modification strategies.

24. You have deployed a custom web application to the cloud for testing. The IT security team plans to simulate malicious user attacks against the app. What type of testing is this?

A. Load
B. Stress
C. Penetration
D. Vulnerability

☑ **C.** Penetration testing actively exploits detected host and network vulnerabilities to test system resiliency to attacks.

☒ **A, B,** and **D** are incorrect. Load testing applies a simulation of normal usage to determine app security, stability, and performance. Stress testing differs from load testing in that an abnormally large volume of usage is applied to an app. Vulnerability testing searches for but does not exploit weaknesses.

25. Your company uses SaaS office productivity tools from a public cloud provider. You need the latest updates applied to the tools. What should you do?

A. Use a runbook to install the updates.
B. Let the provider apply the updates.
C. Enter maintenance mode and install the updates manually.
D. Submit a support ticket to the cloud provider.

☑ **B.** The cloud provider is responsible for applying updates to Software as a Service solutions.

☒ **A, C,** and **D** are incorrect. The listed items are incorrect; the cloud provider must apply updates in this scenario.

26. Refer to Figure 9-2. Which factor is the most likely to be influenced by this configuration?

A. Licensing
B. Performance
C. Security
D. Scaling

FIGURE 9-2	Load Balancer Protocol	Load Balancer Port	Instance Protocol	Instance Port
Load balancing configuration	HTTP ▼	80	HTTP ▼	84

☑ **B.** Load balancing improves application performance.

☒ **A, C,** and **D** are incorrect. The listed items would not influence load balancing as much as performance does.

27. Which type of patch addresses a single small issue?
    A. Service pack
    B. Hotfix
    C. Update dependency
    D. Rolling update

    ☑ **B.** A hotfix is a patch that addresses a single specific issue.
    ☒ **A, C,** and **D** are incorrect. Service packs contain many fixes. Update dependency refers to a previous update version that may need to be installed before a current update can be applied. Rolling updates refer to the continuous software improvement cycle.

28. Users report stability issues with a custom web application deployed in a cloud virtual machine. Your team needs to address and test these concerns in a sandboxed environment. What is the next thing you should do to the virtual machine?
    A. Back it up.
    B. Apply patches.
    C. Clone it.
    D. Take a snapshot.

    ☑ **C.** Cloning a virtual machine is a quick way to have an exact copy so that testing can be done without affecting the production environment.
    ☒ **A, B,** and **D** are incorrect. While backups and snapshots can be used to later create a sandbox environment, cloning is much quicker. Applying patches does not address the need for a sandboxed environment.

29. Jenny is responsible for a subset of cloud-based virtual machines. She needs a way of quickly viewing key performance indicators for the servers. What should Jenny do?
    A. Install and configure performance agents on all virtual machines.
    B. Configure custom alert notification.
    C. Create a custom dashboard.
    D. Establish a baseline.

    ☑ **C.** Many on-premises and cloud management tools allow the creation of custom visual dashboards that include items of specific interest for monitoring purposes.
    ☒ **A, B,** and **D** are incorrect. The listed items do not provide Jenny with a way of quickly viewing KPIs.

30. Which item indicates a delay in service response time?
    A. MTTR
    B. MTBF
    C. RPO
    D. Latency

☑   **D.** Latency, such as related to a network, reflects a delay in the use of an IT service.

☒   **A, B,** and **C** are incorrect. The mean time to repair (MTTR) is the average time that it takes to repair a failed hardware component. The mean time between failures (MTBF) measurement refers to the average amount of time that will pass before a component fails. Recovery point objective (RPO) is the maximum tolerable amount of data loss.

31.   Your organizational security policies require a proxy server for cloud-initiated traffic destined for the Internet. What should you deploy?

A.   Virtual appliance

B.   Virtual machine

C.   Operating system image

D.   NAT

☑   **A.** Virtual appliances are specialized virtual machines configured to perform a specific task.

☒   **B, C,** and **D** are incorrect. The term virtual machine is general compared to the term virtual appliance. Operating system images do not get deployed to the cloud. Network address translation allows internal clients using private IP addresses to access Internet content while at the same time blocking Internet-initiated connections.

32.   Which of the following is a storage component containing firmware that should be updated in an iSCSI environment?

A.   Network switch

B.   Router

C.   HBA

D.   VLAN

☑   **C.** The host bus adapter (HBA) is a storage card placed in a server to provide access to local or shared network storage, depending on the type of HBA. Its firmware needs to be kept up to date.

☒   **A, B,** and **D** are incorrect. The listed items are not storage components.

33.   After a development team solves bugs within a web application, what should it do next?

A.   Deploy patches.

B.   Document the solution.

C.   Back up the virtual machine.

D.   Create a virtual machine snapshot.

☑   **B.** Documentation is required immediately when problems are solved.

☒   **A, C,** and **D** are incorrect. While new patches should be deployed and backups or snapshots should be taken, documentation related to the fix must be produced first.

34. You are reviewing charges from your public cloud provider. The past month indicates that cloud storage provisioning has increased 50 percent from the previous month. Which term best describes this scenario?

A. Broad access

B. Scaling up

C. Elasticity

D. Scaling out

☑   **C.** Elasticity refers to the quick and easy provisioning and deprovisioning of IT resources such as cloud storage.

☒   **A, B,** and **D** are incorrect. Broad access allows access to cloud resources from anywhere, using any device over a network. Scaling up increases underlying virtual machine power by adding vCPUs, RAM, and so on. Scaling out adds virtual machine instances to support an application.

35. Which term is closely related to chargeback?

A. Showback

B. Reverse cloud billing

C. Metered billing

D. Capital billing

☑   **A.** Chargeback is closely related to showback. Chargeback refers to tracing usage and billing based on that usage, often to a department within an organization whereas showback tracks usage for purposes other than billing.

☒   **B, C,** and **D** are incorrect. The listed items are not synonymous with a chargeback.

Chapter 10

Security in the Cloud

CERTIFICATION OBJECTIVES

10.01   Data Security

10.02   Network Security

10.02   Access Control

QUESTIONS

Today's cloud computing environments use a variety of security mechanisms to protect sensitive data, and regulatory compliance sometimes necessitates their use.

Sensitive stored and transmitted data is protected with encryption and digital signatures. Access control methods limit IT resource usage through a variety of models including MAC and RBAC. Resource access can be streamlined using solutions such as identity federation and SSO.

1. Encryption provides which service?
    A. Data integrity
    B. Authentication
    C. Confidentiality
    D. Hashing

2. Digital signatures provide which services? Choose two.
    A. Data integrity
    B. Authentication
    C. Confidentiality
    D. Non-repudiation

3. Which of the following is another term for PKI certificate?
    A. Public certificate
    B. Private certificate
    C. X.509 certificate
    D. Symmetric certificate

4. Which of the following is NOT stored in a PKI certificate?
    A. Public key
    B. Private key
    C. Symmetric key
    D. Expiration date

5. A large corporation has a single PKI administrator. What should be done to ensure the PKI administrator is not overwhelmed?

   A.   Add other admins to the CA trust chain.

   B.   Create subordinate CAs, delegate to other admins.

   C.   Reduce certificate expiration time.

   D.   Create another CA, delegate to other admins.

6. What is encrypted plaintext called?

   A.   Ciphertext

   B.   Cryptext

   C.   Keyedtext

   D.   Securetext

7. Which type of encryption uses the same key for encryption and decryption?

   A.   Public key

   B.   Private key

   C.   Asymmetric

   D.   Symmetric

8. Which type of encryption scheme uses mathematically related keys?

   A.   Public key

   B.   Private key

   C.   Asymmetric

   D.   Symmetric

9. You are encrypting an e-mail addressed to your colleague Roman. Which key is used to encrypt?

   A.   Public

   B.   Private

   C.   Asymmetric

   D.   Symmetric

10. You need to decrypt an e-mail message sent to your mail account. Which key is required to decrypt the message?

   A.   Public

   B.   Private

   C.   Asymmetric

   D.   Symmetric

11. Which statement regarding symmetric encryption is correct?

   A.   It uses two mathematically related keys.

   B.   The key should be made available to everybody.

   C.   It does not scale well.

   D.   It scales well.

12. Which key is used to create a digital signature?
    A. Public
    B. Private
    C. Asymmetric
    D. Symmetric

13. You are enabling identity federation with a partner organization. Trust is established between the two organizations through digitally signed tokens that result from successful user authentication. Which key is used to verify the digital signatures?
    A. Public
    B. Private
    C. Asymmetric
    D. Symmetric

14. Your company uses IPSec to secure IP traffic in a cloud virtual network named East1Net. A new cloud virtual machine named Web1 is deployed into East1Net along with a second virtual machine named Db1 that will host a MySQL database. Web1 will host a new custom web application to communicate with MySQL. You need to ensure communication between Web1 and Web2. What should you do?
    A. Nothing.
    B. Acquire a PKI certificate for Web1.
    C. Acquire a PKI certificate for Web2.
    D. Enable HTTPS on Web1.

15. You are deploying a new cloud virtual machine. In the last step of deployment, you are shown the message in Figure 10-1. Which of the following terms describes the scheme being used?
    A. SSO
    B. Digital signature
    C. Public key
    D. Asymmetric

FIGURE 10-1

Key pair
dialog box

Choose an existing key pair	▼
Select a key pair	
LinuxKeyPair	▼

☑ I acknowledge that I have access to the selected private key file (LinuxKeyPair.pem), and that without this file, I won't be able to log into my instance.

16. Your organization has adopted public cloud computing and is in the process of migrating on-premises IT services. Which solution can extend an on-premises network into the public cloud?
    A. SSL
    B. TLS
    C. Tunneling
    D. Encryption

17. Which of the following is considered a secure protocol or protocol pair for tunneling?

    A. GRE

    B. SNMP

    C. PPTP

    D. L2TP/IPSec

18. Which of the following ciphers are symmetric? Choose two.

    A. 3DES

    B. RSA

    C. DSA

    D. AES

19. Which statements regarding block and stream ciphers are correct? Choose two.

    A. Block ciphers work well with consistent packet sizes.

    B. Stream ciphers are generally faster than block ciphers.

    C. Block ciphers are generally faster than stream ciphers.

    D. Stream ciphers work well with consistent packet sizes.

20. You need a security appliance that can detect abnormal activity on the network and send administrative alerts when it is detected. What should you implement?

    A. HIPS

    B. NIPS

    C. HIDS

    D. NIDS

21. In which access control model does the operating system determine who has access to a resource?

    A. RBAC

    B. DAC

    C. ADUC

    D. MAC

22. Which access control model uses resource labeling for granular access control?

    A. RBAC

    B. DAC

    C. ADUC

    D. MAC

23. Your company uses Amazon Web Services (AWS) as a public cloud provider. Using the AWS CLI, how can you associate role-based administrative policies to groups?

    A. aws iam link-group-policy

    B. aws iam attach-group-policy

    C. aws iam set-group-policy

    D. aws iam associate-group-policy

24. Which access control model places permission configuration in the hands of the data owner?

A. RBAC

B. DAC

C. ADUC

D. MAC

25. Your company plans to implement multifactor authentication for office desktops. Which of the following could be used?

A. Username, password

B. E-mail address, password, father's middle name

C. E-mail address, password1, password2

D. Smartcard, PIN

26. A user, Pete, complains that his smartphone no longer authenticates to the company VPN when he is traveling for work. The company issues a unique PKI certificate to each smartphone for VPN access. What is the most likely cause of Pete's problem?

A. The certificate is corrupt.

B. The SIM card configuration is incorrect.

C. The PKI certificate configuration is incorrect.

D. The certificate has expired.

27. You are the e-mail administrator for your organization. Currently, a cloud-based e-mail solution is being used. Users must be able to encrypt e-mail messages to one another. What should you do?

A. Make user public keys available to everybody.

B. Make user private keys available to everybody.

C. Make user public keys available for decryption.

D. Make user private keys available for encryption.

28. Your firewall ensures that incoming and outgoing packets are a part of an established session. Which feature does your firewall support?

A. Stateful packet inspection

B. Packet filtering

C. Stateless packet inspection

D. Proxying

29. Which of the following exposes programmatic functionality to developers?

A. Driver

B. Source code

C. API

D. Script

30. Which mechanism can detect whether a network packet has been tampered with?

  A.   Digital signature

  B.   Encryption

  C.   Tunneling

  D.   NAT

31. You need to harden Linux cloud-based virtual machines. What should you do? Choose two.

  A.   Disable unnecessary services.

  B.   Deactivate default accounts.

  C.   Change the IP address.

  D.   Change the hostname.

32. Which cloud service model provides the most flexibility in assigning cloud resource permissions?

  A.   IaaS

  B.   SaaS

  C.   SECaaS

  D.   PaaS

33. Which solution requires users to sign in only once to access multiple resources?

  A.   Federation

  B.   SSO

  C.   Tunneling

  D.   Multifactor authentication

34. Which of the following terms are related to mandatory access control (MAC)? Choose two.

  A.   Resource labeling

  B.   Data classification

  C.   Data owner

  D.   User groups

35. You are planning user authentication between your on-premises network and the public cloud. User identities must exist only once. What should you configure?

  A.   SSO

  B.   Federation

  C.   Multifactor authentication

  D.   MAC

A QUICK ANSWER KEY

1.	C	**10.**	B	**19.**	A, B	**28.**	A
2.	A, B	**11.**	C	**20.**	D	**29.**	C
3.	C	**12.**	B	**21.**	D	**30.**	A
4.	C	**13.**	A	**22.**	D	**31.**	A, B
5.	B	**14.**	A	**23.**	B	**32.**	A
6.	A	**15.**	D	**24.**	B	**33.**	B
7.	D	**16.**	C	**25.**	D	**34.**	A, B
8.	C	**17.**	D	**26.**	D	**35.**	B
9.	A	**18.**	A, D	**27.**	A		

A
IN-DEPTH ANSWERS

1. Encryption provides which service?
   A. Data integrity
   B. Authentication
   C. Confidentiality
   D. Hashing

   ☑ **C.** Encryption provides data confidentiality.
   ☒ **A, B,** and **D** are incorrect. Data integrity ensures that data has not been tampered with. Authentication ensures that a user is who they say they are. Hashing is one method of implementing data integrity; a change will result in a new, different hash from the original.

2. Digital signatures provide which services? Choose two.
   A. Data integrity
   B. Authentication
   C. Confidentiality
   D. Non-repudiation

   ☑ **A** and **B.** Authentication ensures that a user is who they say they are. Data integrity ensures that data has not been tampered with. Both of these are provided with digital signatures.
   ☒ **C** and **D** are incorrect. Confidentiality is achieved through encryption. Non-repudiation uses a private key for signing data such that the signer cannot deny having sent the message because they are the only one with access to the private key.

3. Which of the following is another term for PKI certificate?
   A. Public certificate
   B. Private certificate
   C. X.509 certificate
   D. Symmetric certificate

   ☑ **C.** PKI certificates are sometimes also called X.509 certificates.
   ☒ **A, B,** and **D** are incorrect. PKI certificates contain many items, including public and private keys. Symmetric certificate is not a valid term.

4.   Which of the following is NOT stored in a PKI certificate?
     A.   Public key
     B.   Private key
     C.   Symmetric key
     D.   Expiration date

     ☑   **C.** Symmetric keys are not stored in PKI certificates; public and private key pairs are.
     ☒   **A, B,** and **D** are incorrect. Public and private keys and a certificate expiration date are all contained within a PKI certificate.

5.   A large corporation has a single PKI administrator. What should be done to ensure the PKI administrator is not overwhelmed?
     A.   Add other admins to the CA trust chain.
     B.   Create subordinate CAs, delegate to other admins.
     C.   Reduce certificate expiration time.
     D.   Create another CA, delegate to other admins.

     ☑   **B.** Subordinate certificate authorities (CAs) are created from the top-level CA and can issue certificates. This is often done for PKI delegation to different geographic regions or departments.
     ☒   **A, C,** and **D** are incorrect. The listed items would not reduce the workload from the single PKI administrator. Using subordinate CAs makes more sense than creating new CAs within a single organization.

6.   What is encrypted plaintext called?
     A.   Ciphertext
     B.   Cryptext
     C.   Keyedtext
     D.   Securetext

     ☑   **A.** After plaintext is processed by an encryption algorithm, the result is ciphertext.
     ☒   **B, C,** and **D** are incorrect. The listed terms are invalid in this context.

7.   Which type of encryption uses the same key for encryption and decryption?
     A.   Public key
     B.   Private key
     C.   Asymmetric
     D.   Symmetric

     ☑   **D.** Symmetric encryption uses the same key for encryption and decryption.
     ☒   **A, B,** and **C** are incorrect. Public and private key pairs (different keys) are used for asymmetric encryption.

8. Which type of encryption scheme uses mathematically related keys?

    A. Public key

    B. Private key

    C. Asymmetric

    D. Symmetric

    ☑ **C.** Public and private key pairs (different keys) are used for asymmetric encryption.

    ☒ **A, B,** and **D** are incorrect. Public and private keys are not encryption schemes. Symmetric encryption uses the same key to encrypt and decrypt.

9. You are encrypting an e-mail addressed to your colleague Roman. Which key is used to encrypt?

    A. Public

    B. Private

    C. Asymmetric

    D. Symmetric

    ☑ **A.** Encrypting a message requires the public key of the recipient.

    ☒ **B, C,** and **D** are incorrect. The private key is used to decrypt a message. Asymmetric and symmetric are not specific enough to answer the question.

10. You need to decrypt an e-mail message sent to your mail account. Which key is required to decrypt the message?

    A. Public

    B. Private

    C. Asymmetric

    D. Symmetric

    ☑ **B.** The private key is used to decrypt a message that was encrypted with the mathematically related public key.

    ☒ **A, C,** and **D** are incorrect. Encrypting a message requires the public key of the recipient. Public and private key pairs (different keys) are used for asymmetric encryption. Symmetric encryption uses the same key to encrypt and decrypt.

11. Which statement regarding symmetric encryption is correct?

    A. It uses two mathematically related keys.

    B. The key should be made available to everybody.

    C. It does not scale well.

    D. It scales well.

    ☑ **C.** The problem with symmetric keys is how to securely distribute them.

    ☒ **A, B,** and **D** are incorrect. Symmetric encryption uses the same key to encrypt and decrypt. Since one key is used, it should not be made available to everybody.

12. Which key is used to create a digital signature?

A. Public

B. Private

C. Asymmetric

D. Symmetric

☑ **B.** Digital signature creation requires a private key.

☒ **A, C,** and **D** are incorrect. Public keys verify digital signatures, and they can also encrypt messages. Asymmetric and symmetric are not specific enough to answer the question.

13. You are enabling identity federation with a partner organization. Trust is established between the two organizations through digitally signed tokens that result from successful user authentication. Which key is used to verify the digital signatures?

A. Public

B. Private

C. Asymmetric

D. Symmetric

☑ **A.** Public keys verify digital signatures that were created with the mathematically related private key.

☒ **B, C,** and **D** are incorrect. The listed items are not used to verify digital signatures.

14. Your company uses IPSec to secure IP traffic in a cloud virtual network named East1Net. A new cloud virtual machine named Web1 is deployed into East1Net along with a second virtual machine named Db1 that will host a MySQL database. Web1 will host a new custom web application to communicate with MySQL. You need to ensure communication between Web1 and Web2. What should you do?

A. Nothing.

B. Acquire a PKI certificate for Web1.

C. Acquire a PKI certificate for Web2.

D. Enable HTTPS on Web1.

☑ **A.** Nothing needs to be done. IPSec is configured to secure IP traffic in the cloud network already.

☒ **B, C,** and **D** are incorrect. PKI certificates would be required to secure client connections from the Internet, but IPSec is already being used on the cloud network.

15. You are deploying a new cloud virtual machine. In the last step of deployment, you are shown the message in Figure 10-1. Which of the following terms describes the scheme being used?

A. SSO

B. Digital signature

C. Public key

D. Asymmetric

> Choose an existing key pair ▼
> **Select a key pair**
> LinuxKeyPair ▼
> ☑ I acknowledge that I have access to the selected private key file (LinuxKeyPair.pem), and that without this file, I won't be able to log into my instance.

☑ **D.** Because there is a reference to a private key from a pair, asymmetric encryption is implied.

☒ **A, B,** and **C** are incorrect. The listed encryption terms do not describe the scenario. Single sign-on (SSO) prevents users from having to keep entering the same credentials when accessing multiple resources. Digital signatures prove the authenticity of a message. Public keys encrypt data and verify digital signatures.

16. Your organization has adopted public cloud computing and is in the process of migrating on-premises IT services. Which solution can extend an on-premises network into the public cloud?

    A. SSL
    B. TLS
    C. Tunneling
    D. Encryption

    ☑ **C.** A virtual private network (VPN) tunnel can securely link an on-premises network to a public cloud network.

    ☒ **A, B,** and **D** are incorrect. Secure Sockets Layer (SSL) and its successor, Transport Layer Security (TLS), secure network communications using a PKI certificates. Encryption provides confidentiality.

17. Which of the following is considered a secure protocol or protocol pair for tunneling?

    A. GRE
    B. SNMP
    C. PPTP
    D. L2TP/IPSec

    ☑ **D.** Layer 2 Tunnel Protocol with IP Security is considered more secure than the other listed items.

    ☒ **A, B,** and **C** are incorrect. Generic Routing Encapsulation (GRE) does not provide encryption. Simple Network Management Protocol (SNMP) is not used for network tunneling; it is used to gather statistics and configuration data from network devices. Point-to-Point Tunneling Protocol (PPTP) is no longer considered a secure tunneling option.

18. Which of the following ciphers are symmetric? Choose two.

    A. 3DES
    B. RSA
    C. DSA
    D. AES

☑ **A and D.** Triple Digital Encryption Standard (3DES) and the newer Advanced Encryption Standard (AES) ciphers are both symmetric.

☒ **B and C** are incorrect. Rivest, Shamir, Adleman (RSA) and Digital Signature Algorithm (DSA) are asymmetric ciphers.

19. Which statements regarding block and stream ciphers are correct? Choose two.
    A. Block ciphers work well with consistent packet sizes.
    B. Stream ciphers are generally faster than block ciphers.
    C. Block ciphers are generally faster than stream ciphers.
    D. Stream ciphers work well with consistent packet sizes.

    ☑ **A and B.** Block ciphers are designed to process "blocks" of a consistent size efficiently. Stream ciphers are designed to process variable-length transmissions and are considered faster than block ciphers.

    ☒ **C and D** are incorrect. The listed statements are incorrect.

20. You need a security appliance that can detect abnormal activity on the network and send administrative alerts when it is detected. What should you implement?
    A. HIPS
    B. NIPS
    C. HIDS
    D. NIDS

    ☑ **D.** A network-based intrusion detection system (NIDS) detects abnormal network activity and can log or send alerts.

    ☒ **A, B,** and **C** are incorrect. Host-based and network-based intrusion prevention systems can log and alert but also prevent suspicious activity from continuing, which is not listed as a requirement. A host-based intrusion detection system is not appropriate because it cannot detect abnormal activity on the network.

21. In which access control model does the operating system determine who has access to a resource?
    A. RBAC
    B. DAC
    C. ADUC
    D. MAC

    ☑ **D.** With mandatory access control (MAC), resources are labeled, security clearances are assigned, and the operating system determines whether access is granted or not.

    ☒ **A, B,** and **C** are incorrect. Role-based access control (RBAC) uses roles or groups to assign permissions. The data owner determines resource access through access control lists (ACLs) with discretionary access control (DAC). ADUC is not an access control model.

22. Which access control model uses resource labeling for granular access control?

 A. RBAC

 B. DAC

 C. ADUC

 D. MAC

☑ **D.** With mandatory access control (MAC), resources are labeled, security clearances are assigned, and the operating system determines whether access is granted or not.

☒ **A, B,** and **C** are incorrect. Role-based access control (RBAC) uses roles or groups to assign permissions. The data owner determines resource access through access control lists (ACLs) with discretionary access control (DAC). ADUC is not an access control model.

23. Your company uses Amazon Web Services (AWS) as a public cloud provider. Using the AWS CLI, how can you associate role-based administrative policies to groups?

 A. aws iam link-group-policy

 B. aws iam attach-group-policy

 C. aws iam set-group-policy

 D. aws iam associate-group-policy

☑ **B.** With the AWS CLI, the aws iam attach-group-policy command is used to associate policies with groups.

☒ **A, C,** and **D** are incorrect. The syntax for the listed items is incorrect.

24. Which access control model places permission configuration in the hands of the data owner?

 A. RBAC

 B. DAC

 C. ADUC

 D. MAC

☑ **B.** The data owner determines resource access through access control lists (ACLs) with discretionary access control (DAC).

☒ **A, C,** and **D** are incorrect. Role-based access control (RBAC) uses roles or groups to assign permissions. ADUC is not an access control model. With mandatory access control (MAC), resources are labeled, security clearances are assigned, and the operating system determines whether access is granted or not.

25. Your company plans to implement multifactor authentication for office desktops. Which of the following could be used?

 A. Username, password

 B. E-mail address, password, father's middle name

 C. E-mail address, password1, password2

 D. Smartcard, PIN

☑ **D.** A smartcard (something you have) and a PIN (something you know) constitute multifactor authentication.

☒ **A, B,** and **C** are incorrect. The listed items fall only under a single category; something you know.

26. A user, Pete, complains that his smartphone no longer authenticates to the company VPN when he is traveling for work. The company issues a unique PKI certificate to each smartphone for VPN access. What is the most likely cause of Pete's problem?

    A. The certificate is corrupt.

    B. The SIM card configuration is incorrect.

    C. The PKI certificate configuration is incorrect.

    D. The certificate has expired.

    ☑ **D.** An expired PKI certificate means it can no longer be used for security purposes.

    ☒ **A, B,** and **C** are incorrect. Certificates rarely become corrupt; this is not likely. The SIM card and PKI configuration worked previously, so these are not likely.

27. You are the e-mail administrator for your organization. Currently, a cloud-based e-mail solution is being used. Users must be able to encrypt e-mail messages to one another. What should you do?

    A. Make user public keys available to everybody.

    B. Make user private keys available to everybody.

    C. Make user public keys available for decryption.

    D. Make user private keys available for encryption.

    ☑ **A.** Public keys are safe to distribute to everybody.

    ☒ **B, C,** and **D** are incorrect. Private keys must be accessible only to the owner. Public keys encrypt, not decrypt. Private keys decrypt, not encrypt.

28. Your firewall ensures that incoming and outgoing packets are a part of an established session. Which feature does your firewall support?

    A. Stateful packet inspection

    B. Packet filtering

    C. Stateless packet inspection

    D. Proxying

    ☑ **A.** Stateful packet inspection verifies that individual packets are part of an established session.

    ☒ **B, C,** and **D** are incorrect. The listed firewall solutions do not address the requirement of established sessions.

29. Which of the following exposes programmatic functionality to developers?

    A. Driver

    B. Source code

    C. API

    D. Script

    ☑ **C.** An application programming interface (API) exposes programmatic functionality to developers.

    ☒ **A, B,** and **D** are incorrect. A driver is software that enables hardware to work. Source code is used to compile software. A script allows for the automation of repetitive tasks.

30. Which mechanism can detect whether a network packet has been tampered with?

    A.   Digital signature

    B.   Encryption

    C.   Tunneling

    D.   NAT

    ☑   **A.** Digital signatures determine whether a transmission has been altered. They also verify that the sender is who they say they are.

    ☒   **B, C,** and **D** are incorrect. Encryption provides confidentiality, not integrity. Tunneling is commonly used for VPN secure connectivity between two endpoints. Network address translation (NAT) allows a single public IP address to be used by multiple hosts using internal private IP addresses.

31. You need to harden Linux cloud-based virtual machines. What should you do? Choose two.

    A.   Disable unnecessary services.

    B.   Deactivate default accounts.

    C.   Change the IP address.

    D.   Change the hostname.

    ☑   **A** and **B.** Reducing the attack surface (hardening) means removing items not being used and changing default settings.

    ☒   **C** and **D** are incorrect. Changing the IP address or hostname does not enhance security.

32. Which cloud service model provides the most flexibility in assigning cloud resource permissions?

    A.   IaaS

    B.   SaaS

    C.   SECaaS

    D.   PaaS

    ☑   **A.** Infrastructure as a Service (IaaS) places the responsibility of installation, configuration, and management on the cloud consumer.

    ☒   **B, C,** and **D** are incorrect. Software as a Service (SaaS), Security as a Service (SECaaS) and Platform as a Service (PaaS) do not allow as much control when assigning permission as IaaS does.

33. Which solution requires users to sign in only once to access multiple resources?

    A.   Federation

    B.   SSO

    C.   Tunneling

    D.   Multifactor authentication

    ☑   **B.** Single sign-on allows users to sign on once and then access many network resources without entering credentials again.

    ☒   **A, C,** and **D** are incorrect. Federation uses a single identify provider across organization boundaries. Tunneling is commonly used for VPN secure connectivity between two endpoints. Multifactor authentication requires two or more categories of authentication to be used together, such as something you have and something you know.

34. Which of the following terms are related to mandatory access control (MAC)? Choose two.

A. Resource labeling

B. Data classification

C. Data owner

D. User groups

☑ **A and B.** With mandatory access control (MAC), resources are labeled, which is also called data classification. Security clearances are then assigned, and the operating system determines whether access is granted or not.

☒ **C and D** are incorrect. Data owner is related to discretionary access control (DAC), and user groups are related to role-based access control (RBAC).

35. You are planning user authentication between your on-premises network and the public cloud. User identities must exist only once. What should you configure?

A. SSO

B. Federation

C. Multifactor authentication

D. MAC

☑ **B.** Federation uses a single identity provider across organization boundaries.

☒ **A, C,** and **D** are incorrect. Single sign-on allows users to sign on once and then access many network resources without entering credentials again. Multifactor authentication requires two or more categories of authentication to be used together such as something you have and something you know. With mandatory access control (MAC), resources are labeled, security clearances are assigned, and the operating system determines whether access is granted or not.

Chapter 11

Security Best Practices

CERTIFICATION OBJECTIVES

11.01   Cloud Security Engineering

11.02   Security Governance and Strategy

11.03   Vulnerability Management

QUESTIONS

Malicious users and malware often target public cloud providers because they host many tenants sharing pooled resources. However, most public cloud providers achieve third-party security accreditations, which is a prerequisite to doing business with larger enterprises.

Cloud consumers still have plenty of security issues to contend with, including host and network hardening as well as proper user account and data governance. Periodic security testing is key to maintaining a strong security posture.

1. Which type of testing identifies weaknesses but does not exploit them?
   A. Penetration testing
   B. Vulnerability testing
   C. Regression testing
   D. Load testing

2. Which type of testing identifies weaknesses and actively exploits them?
   A. Penetration testing
   B. Vulnerability testing
   C. Regression testing
   D. Load testing

3. Due to regulatory compliance, your organization's security policies require firewall rules on all cloud networks. You need to allow inbound Windows and Linux management traffic. Which ports must be opened in the firewall?
   A. 389, 636
   B. 3389, 25
   C. 3389, 22
   D. 389, 22

4. Which of the following actions violates the principle of least privilege?
   A. Unchanged default passwords
   B. Unpatched router firmware
   C. Granting read and write permissions to a shared network folder
   D. Adding a regular Windows user account to the Administrators group

5. Sensitive cloud virtual machines are grouped together on a cloud network called HQApp. Two public websites will be deployed. One of the websites will require access to resources on the HQApp network. What strategy should be employed?

    A. VLANs

    B. Scale out

    C. Demilitarized zone

    D. Scale up

6. Which firewall configuration item controls access to network resources?

    A. DMZ

    B. Access list

    C. Port list

    D. Cipher

7. Which of the following solutions can shut down detected malicious traffic to prevent further damage?

    A. IDS

    B. DMZ

    C. IPS

    D. NAT

8. You receive an alert notification that one of your cloud servers has been receiving excessive amounts of network traffic from hosts with different IP addresses for the past hour. What type of attack is most likely taking place?

    A. SQL injection

    B. DDoS

    C. DoS

    D. Rainbow table

9. Your website has experienced numerous DoS attacks over the past month. What should you do to mitigate future attacks? Choose two.

    A. Block port 80.

    B. Enable a web application firewall.

    C. Reduce web server session timeout values.

    D. Block port 443.

10. Laura is a Linux server administrator. Your company runs an HR payroll system on the Linux servers. At a recent IT meeting, Laura suggested being granted permissions to clear Linux server logs as their size reaches a specific size. Which security principle is violated if Laura is given the ability to clear Linux server logs?

    A. Principle of least privilege

    B. Attack surface reduction

    C. Job rotation

    D. Separation of duties

11. A user sends jokes to a large number of users through the organization's cloud mail system. What type of policy violation is this?

    A. Audit

    B. Acceptable use

    C. Backup

    D. BYOD

12. You are negotiating SLA support details with a public cloud provider. Which type of policy should you consult during negotiations?

    A. Audit

    B. Acceptable use

    C. Backup

    D. Incident response

13. Which type of policy dictates that user accounts be temporarily disabled after too many incorrect login attempts?

    A. IDS

    B. IPS

    C. Lockout

    D. Password complexity

14. Which of the following are industry-specific regulatory frameworks? Choose two.

    A. MOF

    B. SOX

    C. PCI DSS

    D. ITIL

15. Which industry standard is used to rank IT security weaknesses?

    A. PCI DSS

    B. National Institute of Standards and Technology

    C. SOX

    D. Common Vulnerabilities and Exposures

16. Which three phases constitute the vulnerability scanning process?

    A. Intelligence gathering, assessment, validation

    B. Assessment, intelligence gathering, validation

    C. Validation, assessment, intelligence gathering

    D. Assessment, validation, intelligence gathering

17. Your network has recently experienced a spike in spam activity where user stations have been used as SMTP relay hosts. Which of the following partial configurations should be used?

A. Set-NetFirewallProfile –DefaultInboundAction Block –DefaultOutboundAction Allow

B. Set-NetFirewallProfile –DefaultInboundAction Allow –DefaultOutboundAction Allow

C. Set-NetFirewallProfile –DefaultInboundAction Block –DefaultOutboundAction Block

D. Set-NetFirewallProfile –DefaultInboundAction Disable –DefaultOutboundAction Disable

18. You are using PowerShell to configure a host-based firewall on a Windows server. RDP administrative traffic must be allowed to reach the host. Which command should you issue?

A. New-NetFirewallRule –DisplayName "RDP Allowed" –Direction Inbound –Protocol TCP –LocalPort 2382 –Action allow

B. New-NetFirewallRule –DisplayName "RDP Allowed" –Direction Inbound –Protocol TCP –LocalPort 2382 –Action deny

C. New-NetFirewallRule –DisplayName "RDP Allowed" –Direction Inbound –Protocol TCP –LocalPort 3389 –Action allow

D. New-NetFirewallRule –DisplayName "RDP Allowed" –Direction Inbound –Protocol TCP –LocalPort 389 –Action allow

19. Which command resets the Windows Firewall to default settings?

A. advfirewall reset

B. set advfirewall default

C. netsh advfirewall reset

D. netsh advfirewall default

20. Your organizational data loss prevention policy has recently been amended to include virtual machine management. Which VMware setting should be configured to remain compliant with organization security policies?

A. disallow = console.vm.copy

B. keyword = isolation.tool.copy.disable

C. keyword = encrypt.vmdk

D. disallow = password.plaintext

21. You need to automate file system permission management. Which Windows command should you use?

A. dir

B. cipher

C. certutil

D. cacls

22. Which command shows permissions for a file named budget_eastregion.xls?
    A. cacls j:/budget_eastregion.xls
    B. acls j:/budget_eastregion.xls
    C. cacls –show j:/budget_eastregion.xls
    D. cacls –acl j:/budget_eastregion.xls

23. Which cacls command-line switch allows changing new user file permissions without changing other user permissions?
    A. /E
    B. /F
    C. /S
    D. /K

24. Which type of testing is executed with no knowledge of how systems have been implemented?
    A. Black-box
    B. White-box
    C. Gray-box
    D. Blue-box

25. Which type of testing is executed by developers who wrote the code?
    A. Black-box
    B. White-box
    C. Gray-box
    D. Blue-box

26. Penetration testers have performed reconnaissance on a target through web scraping, where publicly accessible information has been compiled. What type of testing is this?
    A. Black-box
    B. White-box
    C. Gray-box
    D. Blue-box

27. Which of the following is commonly performed as part of a vulnerability assessment?
    A. Executing known firmware exploits
    B. Software license reconciliation
    C. Determining server uptime
    D. Port scanning

28. Which type of testing is depicted in Figure 11-1?
    A. Penetration testing
    B. Vulnerability testing
    C. Regression testing
    D. Load testing

FIGURE 11-1

Port scan results

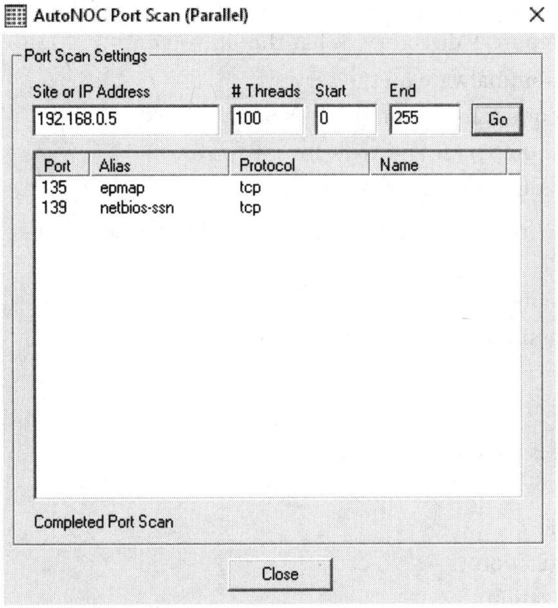

29. Port scanning falls under which vulnerability testing phase?

A. Intelligence gathering

B. Validation

C. Penetration testing

D. Assessment

30. What type of testing involves user deception?

A. Regression

B. Penetration

C. Social engineering

D. Vulnerability

31. Which type of testing best simulates external malicious users?

A. Gray-box

B. Blue-box

C. Black-box

D. White-box

32. IT administrators within the organization are conducting penetration tests against the organization's cloud IT systems. What type of testing is this?

A. Gray-box

B. Blue-box

C. Black-box

D. White-box

33. Your development server antimalware solution generates false positives when developers compile code in a temporary directory. What should you do?

    A. Disable antimalware on the server.

    B. Forbid code compilation on the server.

    C. Upgrade the server antimalware software.

    D. Add the directory as a scanning exception.

34. Which of the following is the most likely to determine whether quick or slow cloud storage is used for files?

    A. Permissions

    B. Data classification

    C. File size

    D. File owner

35. Which term is most closely associated with ACLs?

    A. SSO

    B. Federation

    C. Authentication

    D. Authorization

36. Which term best describes Figure 11-2?

    A. Single-factor authentication

    B. Federation

    C. Multifactor authentication

    D. Authorization

FIGURE 11-2

Sign-in message

37. Louisette is an accountant and has been granted access to Office 365 cloud services. Her account is configured as depicted in Figure 11-3. Which statements best reflect Louisette's Office 365 configuration? Choose two.

  A. The principle of least privilege has been violated.

  B. The customized administrator role should be assigned.

  C. The user role should be assigned.

  D. SSO needs to be enabled.

FIGURE 11-3

Office 365 user
management

User (no administrator access)

This user won't have permissions to the Office 365 admin center or any admin tasks.

Global administrator

This user will have access to all features in the admin center and can perform all tasks in the Office 365 admin center.

Customized administrator

You can assign this user one or many roles so they can manage specific areas of Office 365.

38. Refer to Figure 11-4. Which functionality could be adversely affected?

  A. Local account login, access to cloud services

  B. Cloud account login, access to cloud services

  C. Local account login, access to local resources

  D. Cloud account login, access to local resources

FIGURE 11-4

Office 365
directory
synchronization

Integration with local Active Directory

Company Name	
Domains verified	3
Domains not verified	1
Directory sync enabled	true
Last directory sync	Warning: last synced more than 3 days ago Troubleshoot
Password sync enabled	true

39. What is being shown in Figure 11-5?

    A.   SSO

    B.   Federation

    C.   Data classification

    D.   ACL

FIGURE 11-5

File system properties dialog box

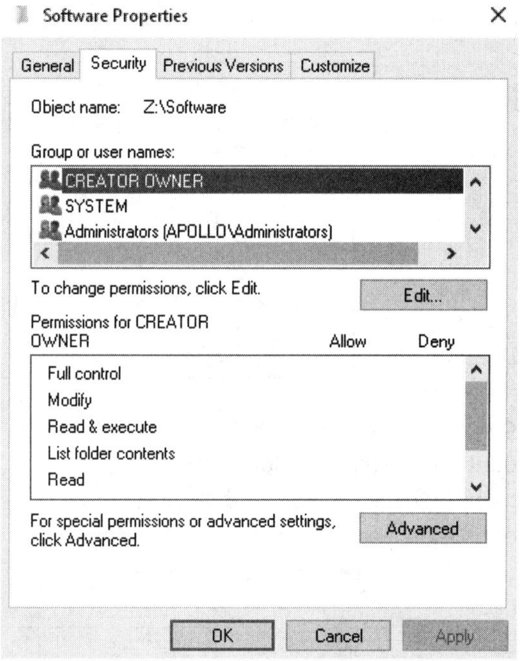

40. What is being depicted in Figure 11-6?

    A.   SSO

    B.   Federation

    C.   Resource labeling

    D.   ACL

FIGURE 11-6

Windows File
Server Resource
Manager

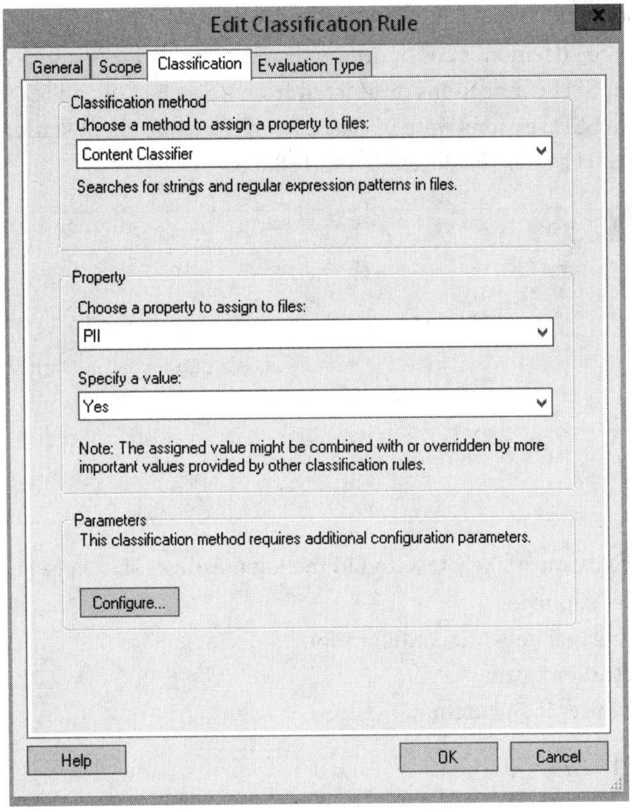

Edit Classification Rule

General | Scope | Classification | Evaluation Type

Classification method
Choose a method to assign a property to files:

Content Classifier

Searches for strings and regular expression patterns in files.

Property
Choose a property to assign to files:

PII

Specify a value:

Yes

Note: The assigned value might be combined with or overridden by more
important values provided by other classification rules.

Parameters
This classification method requires additional configuration parameters.

Configure...

Help   OK   Cancel

41. A script automating the monthly rotating of web server logs has been copied to all cloud Unix
virtual machines. You have configured Unix script file permissions (r-read, w-write, x-execute) as
shown in Figure 11-7. Which statement is correct about this scenario?

  A. script1.sh can run as planned.
  B. Scripts can run as planned.
  C. script1.sh will not run as planned.
  D. Scripts will not run as planned.

FIGURE 11-7

Unix file system
listing

```
[root@freebsdhost2 /scripts]# ls -l
total 0
-rw-r--r--  1 root  wheel  0 Nov 29 08:24 script1.sh
```

42. Which statement regarding Figure 11-8 is correct?

  A. The SSH daemon is configured to listen on port 54279 and 55002.

  B. Client SSH connections originated from ports 54279 and 55002.

  C. Client SSH sessions were initiated from the same client station.

  D. The SSH server IP address is 192.168.0.6.

FIGURE 11-8	
| Unix authentication log contents | ```
[root@freebsdhost2 /scripts]# tail /var/log/auth.log
Nov 27 08:12:05 freebsdhost2 login: pam_authenticate(): conversation failure
Nov 27 08:12:07 freebsdhost2 login: 2 LOGIN FAILURES ON pts/0
Nov 27 08:12:07 freebsdhost2 login: 2 LOGIN FAILURES ON pts/0, Pa$$w0rd
Nov 27 08:12:10 freebsdhost2 login: pam_acct_mgmt(): authentication error
Nov 27 08:12:19 freebsdhost2 login: in prompt_tty(): caught signal 2
Nov 27 08:12:19 freebsdhost2 login: pam_authenticate(): conversation failure
Nov 27 08:12:24 freebsdhost2 login: 2 LOGIN FAILURES ON pts/0
Nov 27 08:12:24 freebsdhost2 login: 2 LOGIN FAILURES ON pts/0, ROOT
Nov 27 08:12:44 freebsdhost2 sshd[4959]: Accepted keyboard-interactive/pam f
 root from 192.168.0.6 port 54279 ssh2
Nov 29 08:24:11 freebsdhost2 sshd[11788]: Accepted keyboard-interactive/pam
r root from 192.168.0.5 port 55002 ssh2
``` |

43. What activity most likely resulted in the log messages shown in Figure 11-9?

  A. Packet capturing

  B. New virtual network configuration

  C. Penetration testing

  D. Failed user login attempt

FIGURE 11-9	
| Unix log contents | ```
uhid1 on uhub0
uhid1: <VMware> on usbus0
em0: promiscuous mode enabled
``` |

44. Refer to Figure 11-10. You have hired a summer student to create a web application on the Unix platform. Which user management option should you configure?

  A. pw usermod –p

  B. pw usermod –e

  C. Pw usermod –p

  D. Pw usermod –e

FIGURE 11-10	
| Unix log contents | ```
usage: pw usermod [uid|name] [switches]
        -V etcdir       alternate /etc location
        -R rootdir      alternate root directory
        -C config       configuration file
        -q              quiet operation
        -F              force add if no user
        -n name         login name
        -u uid          user id
        -c comment      user name/comment
        -d directory    home directory
        -e date         account expiry date
        -p date         password expiry date
``` |
```

45. Which type of attack is depicted in Figure 11-11?

    A. DoS

    B. DDoS

    C. Phishing

    D. Ping flood

FIGURE 11-11

E-mail message

Re: [Statement Update Service] : We Information Your Apple ID Was Login In Another Device

AS Apple Support <news@email.avast.com>

    ↰ ◼ ▣ ↩ Reply | ∨

Wed 10-18, 6:22 PM
You ≫

46. You have run the netstat –p tcp command on an accounting department Windows desktop to view TCP port usage. Which item is of concern in the output shown in Figure 11-12?

    A. HTTPS is being used.

    B. All connection states are established.

    C. A web server is running.

    D. A DDoS is being executed.

FIGURE 11-12

Workstation
netstat
command output

```
Proto  Local Address          Foreign Address            State
TCP    192.168.0.5:80         52.162.166.27:55122        ESTABLISHED
TCP    192.168.0.5:55123      52.162.166.27:https        ESTABLISHED
TCP    192.168.0.5:55127      qk-in-f188:https           ESTABLISHED
TCP    192.168.0.5:55128      edge-star-shv-01-yyz1:https  ESTABLISHED
```

A QUICK ANSWER KEY

1.	B	**13.**	C	**25.**	B	**37.**	A, C
2.	A	**14.**	B, C	**26.**	C	**38.**	A
3.	C	**15.**	D	**27.**	D	**39.**	D
4.	D	**16.**	A	**28.**	B	**40.**	C
5.	C	**17.**	C	**29.**	D	**41.**	C
6.	B	**18.**	C	**30.**	C	**42.**	B
7.	C	**19.**	C	**31.**	C	**43.**	A
8.	B	**20.**	B	**32.**	D	**44.**	B
9.	B, C	**21.**	D	**33.**	D	**45.**	C
10.	D	**22.**	A	**34.**	B	**46.**	C
11.	B	**23.**	A	**35.**	D		
12.	D	**24.**	A	**36.**	C		

A IN-DEPTH ANSWERS

1. Which type of testing identifies weaknesses but does not exploit them?
   A. Penetration testing
   B. Vulnerability testing
   C. Regression testing
   D. Load testing

   ☑ **B.** Vulnerability testing passively identifies weaknesses.
   ☒ **A, C,** and **D** are incorrect. Penetration testing attempts to exploit detected vulnerabilities and could cause IT service disruptions. Regression testing is used to ensure new changes have not compromised previously working functionality. Load testing is used to verify whether a system is secure and stable under normal activity conditions.

2. Which type of testing identifies weaknesses and actively exploits them?
   A. Penetration testing
   B. Vulnerability testing
   C. Regression testing
   D. Load testing

   ☑ **A.** Penetration testing attempts to exploit detected vulnerabilities and could cause IT service disruptions.
   ☒ **B, C,** and **D** are incorrect. Vulnerability testing passively identifies weaknesses. Regression testing is used to ensure new changes have not compromised previously working functionality. Load testing is used to verify whether a system is secure and stable under normal activity conditions.

3. Due to regulatory compliance, your organization's security policies require firewall rules on all cloud networks. You need to allow inbound Windows and Linux management traffic. Which ports must be opened in the firewall?
   A. 389, 636
   B. 3389, 25
   C. 3389, 22
   D. 389, 22

   ☑ **C.** Remote Desktop Protocol (RDP) is normally used to administer Windows hosts over TCP port 3389, and Secure Shell (SSH) is normally used to administer Linux hosts over TCP port 22.
   ☒ **A, B,** and **D** are incorrect. The listed ports are not for RDP and SSH.

4. Which of the following actions violates the principle of least privilege?

- A. Unchanged default passwords
- B. Unpatched router firmware
- C. Granting read and write permissions to a shared network folder
- D. Adding a regular Windows user account to the Administrators group

☑ **D.** The Windows Administrators group provides many more permissions than needed by regular users.

☒ **A, B,** and **C** are incorrect. Patching and changing default settings apply to hardening. Granting folder permissions is scenario-specific and cannot be generalized.

5. Sensitive cloud virtual machines are grouped together on a cloud network called HQApp. Two public websites will be deployed. One of the websites will require access to resources on the HQApp network. What strategy should be employed?

- A. VLANs
- B. Scale out
- C. Demilitarized zone
- D. Scale up

☑ **C.** A demilitarized zone (DMZ) separates an internal network from a public network. Publicly accessible services are normally placed on the DMZ, which also uses firewalls to control inbound and outbound traffic to the DMZ and internal network.

☒ **A, B,** and **D** are incorrect. Virtual local area networks (VLANs) are configured at the network switch level for traffic isolation purposes. Scaling out adds virtual machine instances to support an application. Scaling up increases the power of an existing virtual machine.

6. Which firewall configuration item controls access to network resources?

- A. DMZ
- B. Access list
- C. Port list
- D. Cipher

☑ **B.** Resource access is controlled at the firewall level with access lists.

☒ **A, C,** and **D** are incorrect. The listed terms are not considered firewall configuration items.

7. Which of the following solutions can shut down detected malicious traffic to prevent further damage?

- A. IDS
- B. DMZ
- C. IPS
- D. NAT

☑ **C.** In addition to detecting host and network anomalies, intrusion prevention systems (IPSs) can be configured to stop malicious activity.

☒ **A, B,** and **D** are incorrect. Intrusion detection systems (IDSs) can be configured to detect and report suspicious computing activities. Demilitarized zones (DMZs) separate an internal network from a public network. Publicly accessible services are normally placed on the DMZ, which also uses firewalls to control inbound and outbound traffic to the DMZ and internal network. Network address translation (NAT) allows Internet access through a single public IP address for internal clients configured with private IP addresses.

8. You receive an alert notification that one of your cloud servers has been receiving excessive amounts of network traffic from hosts with different IP addresses for the past hour. What type of attack is most likely taking place?

   A. SQL injection
   B. DDoS
   C. DoS
   D. Rainbow table

   ☑ **B.** Distributed denial of service (DDoS) attacks originate from two or more infected systems with the common intent of flooding a legitimate host or network with useless traffic, thus preventing legitimate access.

   ☒ **A, C,** and **D** are incorrect. SQL injection attacks target improper web form or URL validation, which results in malicious user database query statements to be executed. Denial of service (DoS) attacks can originate from a single host. Rainbow table attacks compare pre-computed password hashes against a stolen password hash list.

9. Your website has experienced numerous DoS attacks over the past month. What should you do to mitigate future attacks? Choose two.

   A. Block port 80.
   B. Enable a web application firewall.
   C. Reduce web server session timeout values.
   D. Block port 443.

   ☑ **B** and **C.** Web application firewalls (WAFs) are designed to mitigate against web app attacks. A smaller web session timeout value mitigates against a multitude of fake requests that consume server resources.

   ☒ **A** and **D** are incorrect. Blocking ports 80 and 443 also blocks legitimate traffic.

10. Laura is a Linux server administrator. Your company runs an HR payroll system on the Linux servers. At a recent IT meeting, Laura suggested being granted permissions to clear Linux server logs as their size reaches a specific size. Which security principle is violated if Laura is given the ability to clear Linux server logs?

    A. Principle of least privilege
    B. Attack surface reduction
    C. Job rotation
    D. Separation of duties

    ☑ **D.** Separation of duties ensures that intricately related processes are not under the control of a single individual.

    ☒ **A, B,** and **C** are incorrect. The listed items are not as specific to the scenario as separation of duties is.

11.   A user sends jokes to a large number of users through the organization's cloud mail system. What type of policy violation is this?

   A.   Audit

   B.   Acceptable use

   C.   Backup

   D.   BYOD

   ☑   **B.** Acceptable use policies dictate the proper usage of organizational tools.

   ☒   **A, C,** and **D** are incorrect. Audit policies dictate what and who should be audited, and to which degree. Backup policies specify backup types, locations, and frequency. Bring your own device (BYOD) policy allows the use of personal computing devices on an organization's network.

12.   You are negotiating SLA support details with a public cloud provider. Which type of policy should you consult during negotiations?

   A.   Audit

   B.   Acceptable use

   C.   Backup

   D.   Incident response

   ☑   **D.** The incident response policy focuses on dealing with problems including support arrangements and contact lists.

   ☒   **A, B,** and **C** are incorrect. The listed policies do not focus on support details in the event of a problem.

13.   Which type of policy dictates that user accounts be temporarily disabled after too many incorrect login attempts?

   A.   IDS

   B.   IPS

   C.   Lockout

   D.   Password complexity

   ☑   **C.** Account lockout policies temporarily disable user accounts after a configured number of incorrect login attempts, in the interest of preventing password attacks.

   ☒   **A, B,** and **D** are incorrect. Intrusion detection and intrusion prevention (IDS and IPS) and password policies are not as specific as account lockout in this scenario.

14.   Which of the following are industry-specific regulatory frameworks? Choose two.

   A.   MOF

   B.   SOX

   C.   PCI DSS

   D.   ITIL

☑ **B** and **C.** Sarbanes-Oxley (SOX) and Payment Card Industry Data Security Standard (PCI DSS) are regulatory frameworks that promote security, transparency, and accountability.

☒ **A** and **D** are incorrect. Microsoft Operations Framework (MOF) and Information Technology Infrastructure Library (ITIL) are frameworks used to efficiently deliver IT services and are not specifically tied to industry regulations.

15. Which industry standard is used to rank IT security weaknesses?

    A. PCI DSS
    B. National Institute of Standards and Technology
    C. SOX
    D. Common Vulnerabilities and Exposures

    ☑ **D.** Common Vulnerabilities and Exposures (CVEs) is an IT industry-standard method of ranking security threats.

    ☒ **A, B,** and **C** are incorrect. Sarbanes-Oxley (SOX) and Payment Card Industry Data Security Standard (PCI DSS) are regulatory frameworks that promote security, transparency, and accountability. NIST provides documentation for a large variety of electronics and technologies, including IT security recommendations.

16. Which three phases constitute the vulnerability scanning process?

    A. Intelligence gathering, assessment, validation
    B. Assessment, intelligence gathering, validation
    C. Validation, assessment, intelligence gathering
    D. Assessment, validation, intelligence gathering

    ☑ **A.** The correct sequence for vulnerability scanning is intelligence gathering, assessment, validation.

    ☒ **B, C,** and **D** are incorrect. The listed vulnerability scanning phases are not in the correct order.

17. Your network has recently experienced a spike in spam activity where user stations have been used as SMTP relay hosts. Which of the following partial configurations should be used?

    A. Set-NetFirewallProfile –DefaultInboundAction Block –DefaultOutboundAction Allow
    B. Set-NetFirewallProfile –DefaultInboundAction Allow –DefaultOutboundAction Allow
    C. Set-NetFirewallProfile –DefaultInboundAction Block –DefaultOutboundAction Block
    D. Set-NetFirewallProfile –DefaultInboundAction Disable –DefaultOutboundAction Disable

    ☑ **C.** –DefaultOutboundAction Block is the correct syntax. Start by blocking all, then add specific allowances for required traffic only.

    ☒ **A, B,** and **D** are incorrect. The correct firewall ruleset approach is to start by blocking all traffic, then add exceptions as needed.

18. You are using PowerShell to configure a host-based firewall on a Windows server. RDP administrative traffic must be allowed to reach the host. Which command should you issue?

    A. New-NetFirewallRule –DisplayName "RDP Allowed" –Direction Inbound –Protocol TCP –LocalPort 2382 –Action allow

    B. New-NetFirewallRule –DisplayName "RDP Allowed" –Direction Inbound –Protocol TCP –LocalPort 2382 –Action deny

    C. New-NetFirewallRule –DisplayName "RDP Allowed" –Direction Inbound –Protocol TCP –LocalPort 3389 –Action allow

    D. New-NetFirewallRule –DisplayName "RDP Allowed" –Direction Inbound –Protocol TCP –LocalPort 389 –Action allow

    ☑ **C.** Remote Desktop Protocol (RDP) uses TCP port 3389.

    ☒ **A, B,** and **D** are incorrect. The listed port numbers are incorrect.

19. Which command resets the Windows Firewall to default settings?

    A. advfirewall reset

    B. set advfirewall default

    C. netsh advfirewall reset

    D. netsh advfirewall default

    ☑ **C.** The netsh advfirewall reset command sets the Windows Firewall to default settings.

    ☒ **A, B,** and **D** are incorrect. The listed syntax is incorrect.

20. Your organizational data loss prevention policy has recently been amended to include virtual machine management. Which VMware setting should be configured to remain compliant with organization security policies?

    A. disallow = console.vm.copy

    B. keyword = isolation.tool.copy.disable

    C. keyword = encrypt.vmdk

    D. disallow = password.plaintext

    ☑ **B.** isolation.tool.copy.disable is related to data loss prevention by preventing data (such as passwords) from being copied to a guest virtual machine from a remote management console.

    ☒ **A, C,** and **D** are incorrect. The provided syntax is incorrect.

21. You need to automate file system permission management. Which Windows command should you use?

    A. dir

    B. cipher

    C. certutil

    D. cacls

    ☑ **D.** The Windows cacls command can be used for command-line file system permissions management.

    ☒ **A, B,** and **C** are incorrect. The listed commands, while valid, are not related to file system permissions management.

22. Which command shows permissions for a file named budget_eastregion.xls?

    A. cacls j:/budget_eastregion.xls

    B. acls j:/budget_eastregion.xls

    C. cacls –show j:/budget_eastregion.xls

    D. cacls –acl j:/budget_eastregion.xls

    ☑ **A.** A filename following the cacls command shows the permissions configured for that file.

    ☒ **B, C,** and **D** are incorrect. The provided syntax is incorrect.

23. Which cacls command-line switch allows changing new user file permissions without changing other user permissions?

    A. /E

    B. /F

    C. /S

    D. /K

    ☑ **A.** The /E cacls command-line switch allows new user permissions management without altering existing user permissions.

    ☒ **B, C,** and **D** are incorrect. The listed cacls command-line switches do not retain existing file permissions.

24. Which type of testing is executed with no knowledge of how systems have been implemented?

    A. Black-box

    B. White-box

    C. Gray-box

    D. Blue-box

    ☑ **A.** With black-box testing, testers have no knowledge of an IT ecosystem's configuration settings.

    ☒ **B, C,** and **D** are incorrect. With white-box testing, testers have intimate knowledge of an IT system's implementation details. Gray-box testers have limited knowledge of an IT system such as DNS names, IP addresses, and so on. Blue-box testing is not a valid testing type.

25. Which type of testing is executed by developers who wrote the code?

    A. Black-box

    B. White-box

    C. Gray-box

    D. Blue-box

    ☑ **B.** With white-box testing, testers have intimate knowledge of an IT system's implementation details.

    ☒ **A, C,** and **D** are incorrect. With black-box testing, testers have no knowledge of an IT ecosystem's configuration settings. Gray-box testers have limited knowledge of an IT system such as DNS names, IP addresses, and so on. Blue-box testing is not a valid testing type.

26. Penetration testers have performed reconnaissance on a target through web scraping, where publicly accessible information has been compiled. What type of testing is this?

A. Black-box

B. White-box

C. Gray-box

D. Blue-box

☑ **C.** Gray-box testers have limited knowledge of an IT system such as DNS names, IP addresses, and so on.

☒ **A, B,** and **D** are incorrect. With black-box testing, testers have no knowledge of an IT ecosystem's configuration settings. With white-box testing, testers have intimate knowledge of an IT system's implementation details. Blue-box testing is not a valid testing type.

27. Which of the following is commonly performed as part of a vulnerability assessment?

A. Executing known firmware exploits

B. Software license reconciliation

C. Determining server uptime

D. Port scanning

☑ **D.** Port scanning can reveal vulnerabilities in the form of unnecessary network services listening for connections.

☒ **A, B,** and **C** are incorrect. The execution of exploits is part of penetration testing. Software license reconciliation and server uptime statistics are not as directly related to vulnerability scanning as port scanning is.

28. Which type of testing is depicted in Figure 11-1?

A. Penetration testing

B. Vulnerability testing

C. Regression testing

D. Load testing

FIGURE 11-1

Port scan results

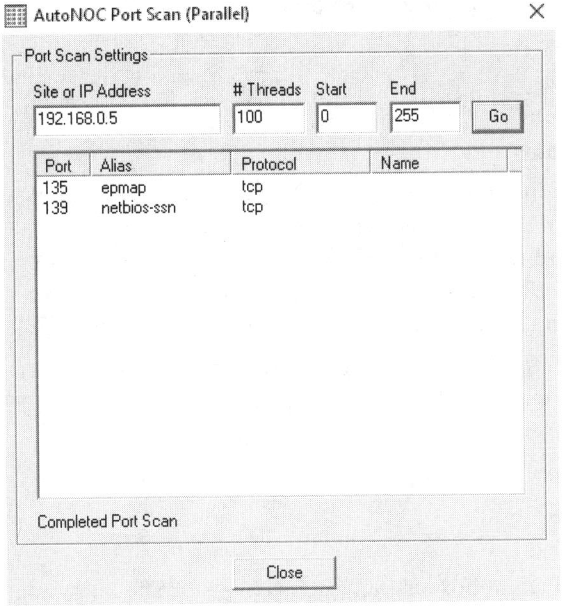

	AutoNOC Port Scan (Parallel)				×

Port Scan Settings

Site or IP Address	# Threads	Start	End	
192.168.0.5	100	0	255	Go

Port	Alias	Protocol	Name
135	epmap	tcp	
139	netbios-ssn	tcp	

Completed Port Scan

Close

☑   **B.** Part of a vulnerability assessment is port scanning.

☒   **A, C,** and **D** are incorrect. Penetration testing attempts to exploit detected vulnerabilities and could cause IT service disruptions. Regression testing is used to ensure new changes have not compromised previously working functionality. Load testing is used to verify whether a system is secure and stable under normal activity conditions.

29.   Port scanning falls under which vulnerability testing phase?

A.   Intelligence gathering

B.   Validation

C.   Penetration testing

D.   Assessment

☑   **D.** The assessment phase of vulnerability scanning includes activities such as port scanning.

☒   **A, B,** and **C** are incorrect. The listed phases and activities are not tied to port scanning and the vulnerability phase it applies to.

30.   What type of testing involves user deception?

A.   Regression

B.   Penetration

C.   Social engineering

D.   Vulnerability

☑   **C.** Social engineering uses trickery to get users to disclose sensitive information.

☒   **A, B,** and **D** are incorrect. Regression testing is used to ensure new changes have not compromised previously working functionality. Penetration testing attempts to exploit detected vulnerabilities and could cause IT service disruptions. Vulnerability testing seeks weaknesses.

31. Which type of testing best simulates external malicious users?

    A. Gray-box

    B. Blue-box

    C. Black-box

    D. White-box

    ☑ **C.** Black-box testers have no knowledge of a system and its implementation details, much as external malicious users would not.

    ☒ **A, B,** and **D** are incorrect. Gray-box testers have limited knowledge of an IT system such as DNS names, IP addresses, and so on. Blue-box testing is not a valid testing type. With white-box testing, testers have intimate knowledge of an IT system's implementation details.

32. IT administrators within the organization are conducting penetration tests against the organization's cloud IT systems. What type of testing is this?

    A. Gray-box

    B. Blue-box

    C. Black-box

    D. White-box

    ☑ **D.** With white-box testing, testers have intimate knowledge of an IT system's implementation details.

    ☒ **A, B,** and **C** are incorrect. Gray-box testers have limited knowledge of an IT system such as DNS names, IP addresses, and so on. Blue-box testing is not a valid testing type. Black-box testers have no knowledge a system and its implementation details, much as external malicious users would not.

33. Your development server antimalware solution generates false positives when developers compile code in a temporary directory. What should you do?

    A. Disable antimalware on the server.

    B. Forbid code compilation on the server.

    C. Upgrade the server antimalware software.

    D. Add the directory as a scanning exception.

    ☑ **D.** Antimalware exceptions can reduce false positives.

    ☒ **A, B,** and **C** are incorrect. Antimalware solutions should not be disabled, and most are software, so they do not have firmware that requires updates. Adding an antimalware scanning exception makes much more sense than forbidding software compilation on a development server.

34. Which of the following is the most likely to determine whether quick or slow cloud storage is used for files?

    A. Permissions

    B. Data classification

    C. File size

    D. File owner

☑ **B.** Data classification adds file system metadata such as sensitivity level, department, region, project, and so on. This metadata can be used to determine frequently accessed or sensitive data that should be stored in a certain manner or stored on certain types of storage.

☒ **A, C,** and **D** are incorrect. The listed items are not as likely to be used to determine how data is stored in the cloud.

35. Which term is most closely associated with ACLs?

A. SSO

B. Federation

C. Authentication

D. Authorization

☑ **D.** Access control lists (ACLs) control authorized access to resources such as files, websites, and so on.

☒ **A, B,** and **C** are incorrect. While single sign-on (SSO) allows resource access without re-entering credentials, it is not as specific as the term authorization. Federation and authentication consist of a single identity store to prove identities; authorization occurs only after successful authentication.

36. Which term best describes Figure 11-2?

A. Single-factor authentication

B. Federation

C. Multifactor authentication

D. Authorization

FIGURE 11-2

Sign-in message

☑ **C.** The figure depicts a sign-in screen where a phone is being called as an additional authentication factor.

☒ **A, B,** and **D** are incorrect. The listed items are incorrect since multifactor authentication is taking place.

37. Louisette is an accountant and has been granted access to Office 365 cloud services. Her account is configured as depicted in Figure 11-3. Which statements best reflect Louisette's Office 365 configuration? Choose two.

A. The principle of least privilege has been violated.

B. The customized administrator role should be assigned.

C. The user role should be assigned.

D. SSO needs to be enabled.

FIGURE 11-3

Office 365 user
management

○ User (no administrator access)

This user won't have permissions to the Office 365 admin center or any admin tasks.

◉ Global administrator

This user will have access to all features in the admin center and can perform all tasks in the Office 365 admin center.

○ Customized administrator

You can assign this user one or many roles so they can manage specific areas of Office 365.

☑ **A and C.** Accountants do not need global administrative rights in a cloud computing environment, they require only regular user access. Granting too many permissions violated the principle of least privilege.

☒ **B and D** are incorrect. Accountants do not need delegated cloud administrative privileges of any kind.

38. Refer to Figure 11-4. Which functionality could be adversely affected?

A. Local account login, access to cloud services

B. Cloud account login, access to cloud services

C. Local account login, access to local resources

D. Cloud account login, access to local resources

FIGURE 11-4

Office 365
directory
synchronization

Integration with local Active Directory	
Company Name	
Domains verified	3
Domains not verified	1
Directory sync enabled	true
Last directory sync	Warning: last synced more than 3 days ago Troubleshoot
Password sync enabled	true

☑ **A.** Because cloud synchronization with an on-premises local Active Directory environment has failed for three days, changes to Active Directory users are not in the cloud, thus access to cloud services could be unavailable.

☒ **B, C,** and **D** are incorrect. Accounts created in the cloud can be used to authenticate and then access cloud services. Local login and resource access are not affected.

39. What is being shown in Figure 11-5?

A. SSO

B. Federation

C. Data classification

D. ACL

FIGURE 11-5

File system properties dialog box

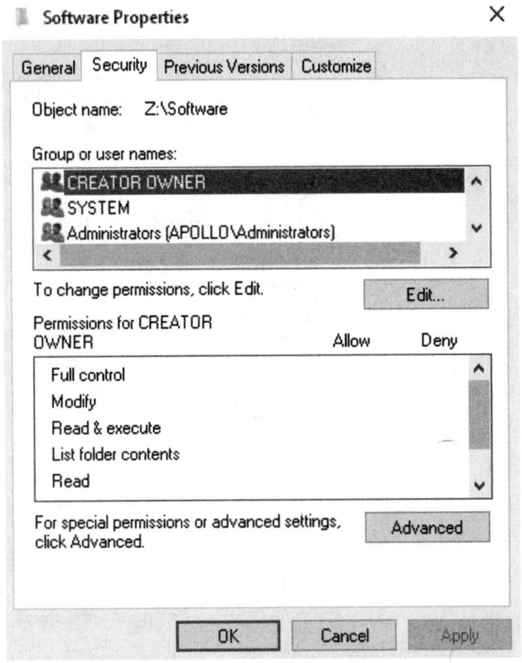

> **Software Properties** ✕
>
> General | **Security** | Previous Versions | Customize
>
> Object name: Z:\Software
>
> Group or user names:
>
> 👥 CREATOR OWNER ⌃
> 👥 SYSTEM
> 👥 Administrators (APOLLO\Administrators) ⌄
> ‹ ›
>
> To change permissions, click Edit. [Edit...]
>
> Permissions for CREATOR OWNER Allow Deny
>
> Full control ⌃
> Modify
> Read & execute —
> List folder contents
> Read ⌄
>
> For special permissions or advanced settings, click Advanced. [Advanced]
>
> [OK] [Cancel] [Apply]

☑ **D.** Figure 11-5 shows a file system access control list (ACL) on a Windows computer.

☒ **A, B,** and **C** are incorrect. Single sign-on (SSO), federation, and access control list (ACL) are not shown in Figure 11-5.

40. What is being depicted in Figure 11-6?

    A. SSO

    B. Federation

    C. Resource labeling

    D. ACL

FIGURE 11-6

Windows File
Server Resource
Manager

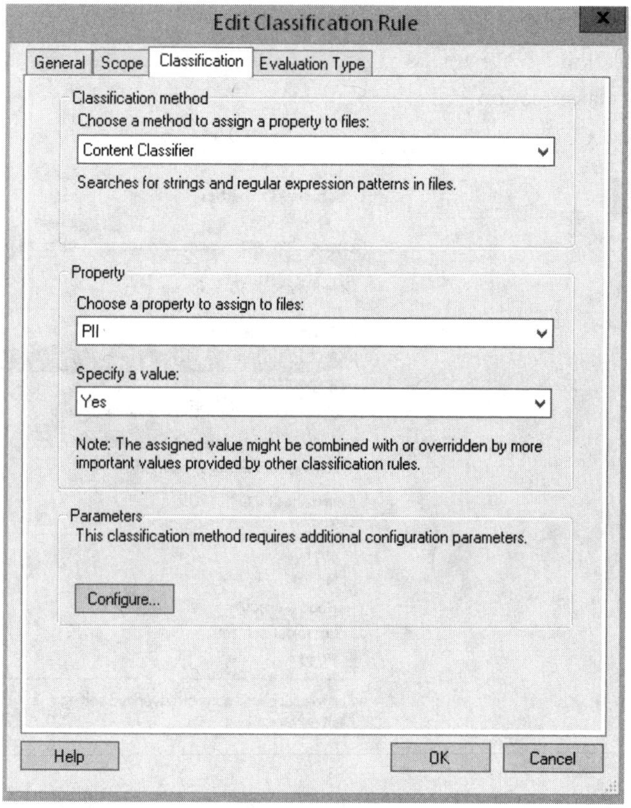

☑ **C.** Figure 11-6 depicts a configuration for labeling sensitive files.

☒ **A, B,** and **D** are incorrect. Single sign-on (SSO), federation, and access control list (ACL) are not shown in Figure 11-6.

41. A script automating the monthly rotating of web server logs has been copied to all cloud Unix virtual machines. You have configured Unix script file permissions (r-read, w-write, x-execute) as shown in Figure 11-7. Which statement is correct about this scenario?

    A. script1.sh can run as planned.

    B. Scripts can run as planned.

    C. script1.sh will not run as planned.

    D. Scripts will not run as planned.

FIGURE 11-7

Unix file system
listing

```
[root@freebsdhost2 /scripts]# ls -l
total 0
-rw-r--r--  1 root  wheel  0 Nov 29 08:24 script1.sh
```

☑ **C.** script1.sh will never run because nobody has execute (x) permissions to the file.
☒ **A, B,** and **D** are incorrect. The script will not run; read (r) and execute (x) permissions are required. Directories (scripts) are not collections of executable commands run together.

42. Which statement regarding Figure 11-8 is correct?
   A. The SSH daemon is configured to listen on port 54279 and 55002.
   B. Client SSH connections originated from ports 54279 and 55002.
   C. Client SSH sessions were initiated from the same client station.
   D. The SSH server IP address is 192.168.0.6.

FIGURE 11-8

Unix
authentication
log contents

```
[root@freebsdhost2 /scripts]# tail /var/log/auth.log
Nov 27 08:12:05 freebsdhost2 login: pam_authenticate(): conversation failure
Nov 27 08:12:07 freebsdhost2 login: 2 LOGIN FAILURES ON pts/0
Nov 27 08:12:07 freebsdhost2 login: 2 LOGIN FAILURES ON pts/0, Pa$$w0rd
Nov 27 08:12:10 freebsdhost2 login: pam_acct_mgmt(): authentication error
Nov 27 08:12:19 freebsdhost2 login: in prompt_tty(): caught signal 2
Nov 27 08:12:19 freebsdhost2 login: pam_authenticate(): conversation failure
Nov 27 08:12:24 freebsdhost2 login: 2 LOGIN FAILURES ON pts/0
Nov 27 08:12:24 freebsdhost2 login: 2 LOGIN FAILURES ON pts/0, ROOT
Nov 27 08:12:44 freebsdhost2 sshd[4959]: Accepted keyboard-interactive/pam f
 root from 192.168.0.6 port 54279 ssh2
Nov 29 08:24:11 freebsdhost2 sshd[11788]: Accepted keyboard-interactive/pam
r root from 192.168.0.5 port 55002 ssh2
```

☑ **B.** Clients talk to SSH hosts on port 22, but SSH hosts talk back to clients on higher-level ports such as 54279 and 55002.
☒ **A, C,** and **D** are incorrect. SSH daemons normally listen on TCP port 22; 54279 and 55002 are accepted SSH connections from clients. The listed SSH sessions have different IP addresses. 192.168.0.5 and 192.168.0.6 are client IP addresses.

43. What activity most likely resulted in the log messages shown in Figure 11-9?
   A. Packet capturing
   B. New virtual network configuration
   C. Penetration testing
   D. Failed user login attempt

FIGURE 11-9

Unix log contents

```
uhid1 on uhub0
uhid1: <VMware> on usbus0
em0: promiscuous mode enabled
```

☑ **A.** Packet capturing most likely took place. A network interface (em0) must be placed into promiscuous mode before the capture of potentially all network traffic.
☒ **B, C,** and **D** are incorrect. The listed items are in no way implied in Figure 11-9.

44. Refer to Figure 11-10. You have hired a summer student to create a web application on the Unix platform. Which user management option should you configure?

A. pw usermod –p

B. pw usermod –e

C. Pw usermod –p

D. Pw usermod –e

```
usage: pw usermod [uid|name] [switches]
        -V etcdir        alternate /etc location
        -R rootdir       alternate root directory
        -C config        configuration file
        -q               quiet operation
        -F               force add if no user
        -n name          login name
        -u uid           user id
        -c comment       user name/comment
        -d directory     home directory
        -e date          account expiry date
        -p date          password expiry date
```

☑ **B.** When creating summer student accounts, set the account expiry immediately, in this case using the Unix pw usermod –e command.

☒ **A, C,** and **D** are incorrect. Expire the entire account, not just the password. Unix is case sensitive; Pw is invalid, while pw is valid.

45. Which type of attack is depicted in Figure 11-11?

A. DoS

B. DDoS

C. Phishing

D. Ping flood

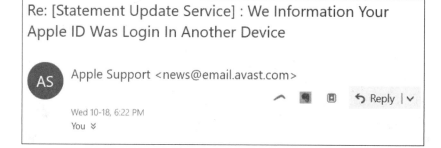

Re: [Statement Update Service] : We Information Your Apple ID Was Login In Another Device

AS Apple Support <news@email.avast.com>

Wed 10-18, 6:22 PM
You ⌄

☑ **C.** The poor grammar and e-mail address are dead giveaways to the illegitimacy of this message.

☒ **A, B,** and **D** are incorrect. Figure 11-11 does not depict denial of service (DoS), distributed denial of service (DDoS), or a ping flood.

46. You have run the netstat –p tcp command on an accounting department Windows desktop to view TCP port usage. Which item is of concern in the output shown in Figure 11-12?

A. HTTPS is being used.

B. All connection states are established.

C. A web server is running.

D. A DDoS is being executed.

| **FIGURE 11-12** | ```
Proto  Local Address        Foreign Address               State
TCP    192.168.0.5:80       52.162.166.27:55122           ESTABLISHED
TCP    192.168.0.5:55123    52.162.166.27:https           ESTABLISHED
TCP    192.168.0.5:55127    qk-in-f188:https              ESTABLISHED
TCP    192.168.0.5:55128    edge-star-shv-01-yyz1:https   ESTABLISHED
``` |

Workstation netstat command output

☑ **C.** Web servers normally listen on TCP port 80 (listed as 80 in Figure 11-12). It is uncommon for accountant desktops to be running web servers.

☒ **A, B,** and **D** are incorrect. If HTTPS were being used, port 443 would be listed. There is nothing wrong with established TCP sessions. A distributed denial of service (DDoS) is not occurring.
```

Chapter 12

Business Continuity and Disaster Recovery

CERTIFICATION OBJECTIVES

12.01   Business Continuity Methods

12.02   Disaster Recovery Methods

12.03   Backup and Recovery

QUESTIONS

Planning for failure may sound counterintuitive, but it is the key to business survival in the event of a disaster. Policies are created to provide structure in the efficient recovery of failed systems.

Fault tolerance removes single points of failure while maintaining an acceptable level of performance. Alternate sites provide a way of continuing business operations across geographic distances. Data is protected with backups, snapshots, cloning, and so on.

1. A company has concluded based on past website downtime events that two hours is as long as its website can be down before the company suffers irreparably. What does this timeframe apply to?
    A. SLA
    B. RPO
    C. RTO
    D. MOF

2. Incremental cloud database backups occur three times daily. What is the RPO?
    A. One hour
    B. Three hours
    C. Five days
    D. Eight hours

3. Your on-premises virtual machine mail server is in the process of being migrated to the cloud, but some users are still using it. You need to restore the virtual machine to a previous state and then restore messages. What should you do prior to the restoration?
    A. Take a virtual machine snapshot.
    B. Notify affected users prior to the restoration.
    C. Clone the virtual machine.
    D. Notify affected users during the restoration.

4. Which statement regarding the RPO is correct?
    A. The RPO is the maximum tolerable downtime of a business process.
    B. A single RPO applies to all data.
    C. The RPO is the minimum tolerable downtime of a business process.
    D. Different types of data could require different RPOs.

5. Which of the following puts the business continuity plan guidelines into motion?
   A. Business impact analysis
   B. Business continuity management
   C. Disaster recovery plan
   D. Incident response plan

6. Which of the following are related to fault tolerance? Choose two.
   A. NIC teaming
   B. NIC TCP offload
   C. RAID 0
   D. RAID 1

7. Which type of document states how service providers will compensate service consumers if specific conditions are not met?
   A. BCP
   B. DRP
   C. BIA
   D. SLA

8. Which monitoring technique uses hard disk metrics to predict hard disk imminent failure?
   A. SMART
   B. MTTR
   C. MTBF
   D. KPI

9. Your cloud-based website is hosted in a cloud provider data center in California. Website visitors in Europe are experiencing delays when loading web pages and downloading files. You need to reduce network latency for European users. What should you configure?
   A. Load balancing
   B. Failover zone
   C. Data deduplication
   D. A content delivery network

10. What type of replication notifies an application that data has been written before replica servers verify data has been committed to disk?
    A. Asynchronous
    B. Master-slave
    C. Synchronous
    D. Peer-to-peer

11. You are the IT director for a law enforcement agency. The agency IT system must remain running at all times. An alternate location to house mission-critical servers, data, and personnel has been acquired. What else is needed for this hot site?

    A. Load balancing

    B. Replication

    C. Failover clustering

    D. Virtualization

12. Which type of alternative business site is the cheapest?

    A. Warm

    B. Hot

    C. Cold

    D. Lukewarm

13. Which type of alternative business site is the most expensive?

    A. Warm

    B. Hot

    C. Cold

    D. Lukewarm

14. Which recovery factor has the largest influence on the selection of the type of alternate site?

    A. RPO

    B. RTO

    C. SLA

    D. DRP

15. Refer to Figure 12-1. Users in a different location complain that both web servers are not responding. After verifying that the servers are running and then testing connectivity from client stations, you determine that users are configured with a default gateway of 192.168.0.1 and are connecting to www.app1.com, which resolves to 10.1.1.1. Why are users unable to connect to the website?

    A. The default gateway is incorrect.

    B. The FQDN is invalid.

    C. www.app1.com should resolve to 10.1.1.2.

    D. www.app1.com should resolve to 199.126.129.67.

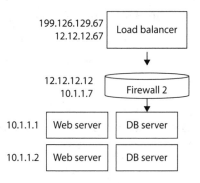

FIGURE 12-1

Network diagram

16. Refer to Figure 12-1. You are configuring Firewall 2. The web servers use standard HTTP ports. What traffic must Firewall 2 allow?
    A. Inbound from 12.12.12.67 destined for 10.1.1.1, 10.1.1.2 TCP port 80
    B. Inbound from 199.126.129.67 destined for 10.1.1.1, 10.1.1.2 TCP port 80
    C. Inbound from 12.12.12.67 destined for 10.1.1.1, 10.1.1.2 TCP port 3389
    D. Inbound from 199.126.129.67 destined for 10.1.1.1, 10.1.1.2 TCP port 3389

17. Refer to Figure 12-1. Which statement regarding the network diagram is correct?
    A. The internal interface for Firewall 2 is configured on an incorrect subnet.
    B. The load balancer external interface IP address is a private IP address.
    C. The web server IP addresses must be private IP addresses.
    D. Firewall 2 must allow outbound HTTP traffic using ports above 1024.

18. Refer to Figure 12-1. Which statement regarding the load balancer is correct?
    A. The load balancer must have connectivity to the web servers.
    B. The load balancer does not need connectivity to the web servers.
    C. The load balancer listening port must match the internal web server listening port.
    D. The load balancer will not detect if a web server is down.

19. Your company is migrating on-premises services to the public cloud. In the interim, you need a way to use existing backup solutions while backing up data to the public cloud. Which on-premises backup functionality is required?
    A. Write verify
    B. Tape encryption
    C. VTL emulation
    D. Tunneling

20. The archive bit for files modified since the last backup will be set to which value?
    A. b
    B. m
    C. 0
    D. 1

21. The archive bit for unmodified files that have been backed up will be set to which value?
    A. b
    B. m
    C. 0
    D. 1

22. A virtual machine file server's virtual hard disks are corrupt and cannot be repaired. Which type of tape backup will take the least amount of time to restore?
    A. Snapshot
    B. Incremental
    C. Differential
    D. Full

23. A virtual machine file server's virtual hard disks are corrupt and cannot be repaired. Which type of tape backup takes the most amount of time to restore?
    A. Snapshot
    B. Incremental
    C. Differential
    D. Full

24. Which type of backup contains only those files modified since the last full backup?
    A. Snapshot
    B. Incremental
    C. Differential
    D. Full

25. Which type of backup does not modify the archive bit?
    A. Snapshot
    B. Incremental
    C. Differential
    D. Full

26. While creating a DRP, you are concerned with how long the restoration of data files will take. You conclude the restoration cannot exceed three hours. What is another way of stating this?
    A. RPO = 3 hours
    B. Backup = 3 hours
    C. RTO = 3 hours
    D. Restore = 3 hours

27. What is the purpose of a backup catalog?
    A. It is an index of the data on backup media.
    B. It contains decryption keys.
    C. It contains software licenses.
    D. It lists backup sources available on the network.

28. Which term is best associated with data backups?

    A. Performance

    B. Integrity

    C. Availability

    D. Confidentiality

29. Your network link to the public cloud is 80 percent utilized by other services. On-premises files must be replicated to the public cloud while minimizing bandwidth usage. What type of replication method should you use?

    A. Asynchronous

    B. Synchronous

    C. Block-level backup

    D. Content delivery network

30. Which type of snapshot technology has the least computational requirements?

    A. Copy-on-write

    B. Deduplication

    C. Compression

    D. Redirect-on-write

31. What is another name for a cloud backup?

    A. Snapshot

    B. Clone

    C. Online backup

    D. Offline backup

32. You need to ensure that critical on-premises virtual machines are immediately available in the event of a regional disaster. What should you configure?

    A. Cloud failover

    B. Failover cluster

    C. Hourly backups

    D. Virtual machine clones

33. Due to a short RTO of five minutes, you need to ensure a mission-critical website is available in the event of a regional disaster. What should you configure?

    A. Mirrored site

    B. Staged site

    C. Container site

    D. Zone site

34. A custom application draws insights from big data analytics. Due to the large volume of data transmitted between application components, you need to minimize computational and network latency. Which pair of options should you consider?

    A. Distributed processing, jumbo frames

    B. Jumbo frames, NIC teaming

    C. Clustering, edge sites

    D. Scaling in, edge sites

35. You need to ensure that server backups have a minimal impact on user productivity. When should you schedule backups to occur?

    A. During maintenance windows

    B. 12 A.M.–5 A.M.

    C. During failback windows

    D. 6 P.M.–12 A.M.

36. Which action could have resulted in the state of the file depicted in Figure 12-2?

    A. A change was made to the file.

    B. Block-level snapshots were enabled.

    C. A full backup was just performed.

    D. An incremental backup was just performed.

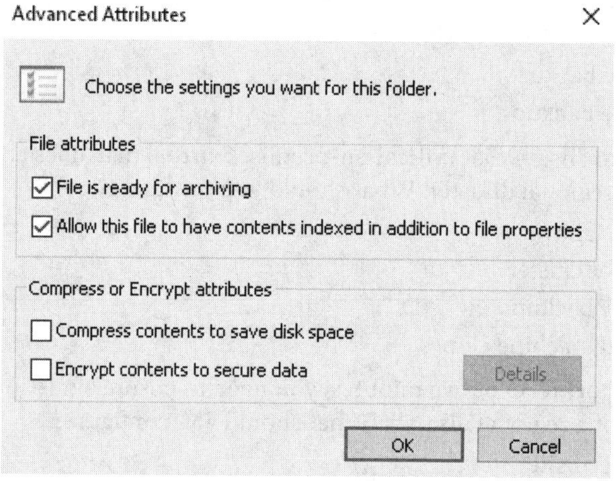

FIGURE 12-2

Windows file properties

37. Which benefits are realized by using a content delivery network? Choose two.

    A. Enhanced security

    B. Dynamic website content

    C. Increased performance

    D. Data availability

38. What can be done to adhere to the RPO?

    A. Enable deduplication.

    B. Increase backup storage capacity.

    C. Increase backup frequency.

    D. Use SSD storage.

39. How is the DRP different from the BCP?

    A. The DRP is specific to a system.

    B. The BCP is specific to a system.

    C. The DRP is related to business continuity.

    D. The BCP is related business continuity.

40. Which of the following items can reduce the RTO? Choose two.

    A. Runbooks

    B. Increased network bandwidth

    C. Decreased network bandwidth

    D. Content delivery networks

41. Which communication method is used for inter-node cluster communication?

    A. Shared storage

    B. LUN

    C. iSCSI

    D. Heartbeat

42. What do cluster nodes use to conclude that a member is no longer available?

    A. Heartbeat

    B. Ping

    C. Tracert

    D. DNS TTL

43. Which type of alternative disaster recovery site contains equipment but lacks up-to-date data?

    A. Cold site

    B. Warm site

    C. Hot site

    D. Lukewarm site

44. Which type of redundancy allows nodes to reside on different sides of a WAN?

    A. WAN clustering

    B. Geo-clustering

    C. Disparate clustering

    D. Long-haul clustering

45. Which of the following is a common SAN redundancy configuration?

A. Failover clustering

B. Regional replication

C. Multipathing

D. RAID 0

46. You are about to apply a new batch of updates to a Linux virtual machine. What should you do before performing this task?

A. Take a snapshot.

B. Create a clone.

C. Enable RAID 0.

D. Enable RAID 1.

A QUICK ANSWER KEY

1. C
2. D
3. B
4. D
5. B
6. A, D
7. D
8. A
9. D
10. A
11. B
12. C

13. B
14. B
15. D
16. A
17. D
18. A
19. C
20. D
21. C
22. D
23. B
24. C

25. C
26. C
27. A
28. C
29. C
30. D
31. C
32. A
33. A
34. A
35. A
36. A

37. C, D
38. C
39. A
40. A, B
41. D
42. A
43. B
44. B
45. C
46. A

A
IN-DEPTH ANSWERS

1. A company has concluded based on past website downtime events that two hours is as long as its website can be down before the company suffers irreparably. What does this timeframe apply to?
   A. SLA
   B. RPO
   C. RTO
   D. MOF

   ☑ **C.** The recovery time objective (RTO) is the maximum amount of tolerable downtime.
   ☒ **A, B,** and **D** are incorrect. Service level agreements (SLAs) are contracts between service providers and consumers concerning expected levels of service. The recovery point objective (RPO) is the maximum tolerable amount of data loss. The Microsoft Operations Framework (MOF) is a service delivery framework.

2. Incremental cloud database backups occur three times daily. What is the RPO?
   A. One hour
   B. Three hours
   C. Five days
   D. Eight hours

   ☑ **D.** The recovery point objective (RPO) in this case is eight hours; three times daily.
   ☒ **A, B,** and **C** are incorrect. The listed values are incorrect.

3. Your on-premises virtual machine mail server is in the process of being migrated to the cloud, but some users are still using it. You need to restore the virtual machine to a previous state and then restore messages. What should you do prior to the restoration?
   A. Take a virtual machine snapshot.
   B. Notify affected users prior to the restoration.
   C. Clone the virtual machine.
   D. Notify affected users during the restoration.

   ☑ **B.** Affected stakeholders must always be notified before changes are made.
   ☒ **A, C,** and **D** are incorrect. A snapshot is not required before taking a snapshot. Cloning a virtual machine does not make sense before taking a snapshot. Users must be notified prior to the change, not during the change.

4. Which statement regarding the RPO is correct?

  A. The RPO is the maximum tolerable downtime of a business process.

  B. A single RPO applies to all data.

  C. The RPO is the minimum tolerable downtime of a business process.

  D. Different types of data could require different RPOs.

  ☑ **D.** The recovery point objective (RPO) is the maximum amount of tolerable data loss, such as four hours' worth. Mission-critical data that changes often would have a smaller RPO than less critical static data.

  ☒ **A, B,** and **C** are incorrect. The recovery point objective (RPO) is not related to the amount of downtime; it is related to the amount of data loss.

5. Which of the following puts the business continuity plan guidelines into motion?

  A. Business impact analysis

  B. Business continuity management

  C. Disaster recovery plan

  D. Incident response plan

  ☑ **B.** Business continuity management (BCM) puts business continuity plan guidelines into action.

  ☒ **A, C,** and **D** are incorrect. A business impact analysis (BIA) analyzes the impact of threats against assets. Disaster recovery plans (DRPs) are specific to the restoration of a system. Incident response plans outline reactionary details for negative events.

6. Which of the following are related to fault tolerance? Choose two.

  A. NIC teaming

  B. NIC TCP offload

  C. RAID 0

  D. RAID 1

  ☑ **A** and **D.** NIC teaming groups two or more network interface cards (NICs) together for the purpose of redundancy or aggregated bandwidth. RAID 1 (disk mirroring) commits each data write to two disks for redundancy.

  ☒ **B** and **C** are incorrect. TCP offload transfers CPU processing for TCP/IP to the NIC. RAID 0 (disk striping) uses a group of disks to handle reads and writes, which increases performance.

7. Which type of document states how service providers will compensate service consumers if specific conditions are not met?

  A. BCP

  B. DRP

  C. BIA

  D. SLA

☑ **D.** Service level agreements (SLAs) are contracts between service providers and consumers concerning expected levels of service.

☒ **A, B,** and **C** are incorrect. The business continuity plan (BCP) prioritizes assets and business processes that must remain running. Disaster recovery plans (DRPs) are specific to the restoration of a system. A business impact analysis (BIA) analyzes the impact of threats against assets.

8. Which monitoring technique uses hard disk metrics to predict hard disk imminent failure?

A. SMART

B. MTTR

C. MTBF

D. KPI

☑ **A.** Self-monitoring, analysis, and reporting technology (SMART) uses disk metrics to predict disk failures.

☒ **B, C,** and **D** are incorrect. Mean time to repair (MTTR) is the average time that it takes to repair a failed hardware component. Mean time between failures (MTBF) is the average time a device will function before it fails. Key performance indicators (KPI) are metrics that are monitored to determine progress.

9. Your cloud-based website is hosted in a cloud provider data center in California. Website visitors in Europe are experiencing delays when loading web pages and downloading files. You need to reduce network latency for European users. What should you configure?

A. Load balancing

B. Failover zone

C. Data deduplication

D. A content delivery network

☑ **D.** A content delivery network (CDN) replicates data from a central location to geographical endpoints in order to reduce network latency for end users.

☒ **A, B,** and **C** are incorrect. Load balancing distributes application processing across multiple backend servers. Failover zones isolate clustered applications from other clustered applications. Data deduplication conserves disk space by avoiding the storage of duplicate disk blocks.

10. What type of replication notifies an application that data has been written before replica servers verify data has been committed to disk?

A. Asynchronous

B. Master-slave

C. Synchronous

D. Peer-to-peer

☑ **A.** Asynchronous replication does not wait for data to be committed to replicas before returning a completed message.

☒ **B, C,** and **D** are incorrect. Master-slave and peer-to-peer are general terms that apply to high-performance cluster node types, replication topologies, and so on. Synchronous replication reports to applications that data is written only after it has been committed to all replicas.

11. You are the IT director for a law enforcement agency. The agency IT system must remain running at all times. An alternate location to house mission-critical servers, data, and personnel has been acquired. What else is needed for this hot site?
    A. Load balancing
    B. Replication
    C. Failover clustering
    D. Virtualization

    ☑ **B.** Hot alternate sites require an up-to-date copy of current data, which is possible only through replication.

    ☒ **A, C,** and **D** are incorrect. Load balancing distributes application processing across multiple backend servers. Failover clustering uses multiple cluster nodes to serve an application for redundancy. Virtualization allows multiple virtual machine operating systems to run concurrently on shared hardware managed by a hypervisor.

12. Which type of alternative business site is the cheapest?
    A. Warm
    B. Hot
    C. Cold
    D. Lukewarm

    ☑ **C.** Cold alternative sites are cheapest since they are not fully equipped and contain no data.

    ☒ **A, B,** and **D** are incorrect. Warm sites are equipped but do not contain up-to-date data. Hot sites are fully equipped and contain up-to-date data. Lukewarm is not an alternate site type.

13. Which type of alternative business site is the most expensive?
    A. Warm
    B. Hot
    C. Cold
    D. Lukewarm

    ☑ **B.** Hot sites are fully equipped and contain up-to-date data and therefore are the most expensive type of alternative site.

    ☒ **A, C,** and **D** are incorrect. Warm sites are equipped but do not contain up-to-date data. Cold alternative sites are cheapest since they are not fully equipped and contain no data. Lukewarm is not an alternate site type.

14. Which recovery factor has the largest influence on the selection of the type of alternate site?
    A. RPO
    B. RTO
    C. SLA
    D. DRP

☑ **B.** The recovery time objective (RTO) is the maximum amount of tolerable downtime.

☒ **A, C,** and **D** are incorrect. The recovery point objective (RPO) is the maximum tolerable amount of data loss. Service level agreements (SLAs) are contracts between service providers and consumers concerning expected levels of service. Disaster recovery plans (DRPs) are specific to the restoration of a system.

15. Refer to Figure 12-1. Users in a different location complain that both web servers are not responding. After verifying that the servers are running and then testing connectivity from client stations, you determine that users are configured with a default gateway of 192.168.0.1 and are connecting to www.app1.com, which resolves to 10.1.1.1. Why are users unable to connect to the website?

    A. The default gateway is incorrect.
    B. The FQDN is invalid.
    C. www.app1.com should resolve to 10.1.1.2.
    D. www.app1.com should resolve to 199.126.129.67.

FIGURE 12-1

Network diagram

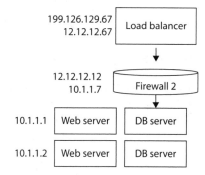

☑ **D.** www.app1.com currently resolves to 10.1.1.1, which is behind the load balancer. www.app1.com needs to resolve the load balancer external IP address of 199.126.129.67.

☒ **A, B,** and **C** are incorrect. There is no concrete way of verifying whether the default gateway is correct or not. The FQDN www.app1.com is valid.

16. Refer to Figure 12-1. You are configuring Firewall 2. The web servers use standard HTTP ports. What traffic must Firewall 2 allow?

    A. Inbound from 12.12.12.67 destined for 10.1.1.1, 10.1.1.2 TCP port 80
    B. Inbound from 199.126.129.67 destined for 10.1.1.1, 10.1.1.2 TCP port 80
    C. Inbound from 12.12.12.67 destined for 10.1.1.1, 10.1.1.2 TCP port 3389
    D. Inbound from 199.126.129.67 destined for 10.1.1.1, 10.1.1.2 TCP port 3389

☑ **A.** The load balancer internal IP address of 12.12.12.67 needs connectivity to port 80 on both backend web servers.

☒ **B, C,** and **D** are incorrect. The internal, and not external, load balancer IP address must have access to backend servers. Port 3389 is used for the Remote Desktop Protocol (RDP), not web servers.

17. Refer to Figure 12-1. Which statement regarding the network diagram is correct?

    A. The internal interface for Firewall 2 is configured on an incorrect subnet.

    B. The load balancer external interface IP address is a private IP address.

    C. The web server IP addresses must be private IP addresses.

    D. Firewall 2 must allow outbound HTTP traffic using ports above 1024.

    ☑ **D.** Clients connect to web servers on port 80 or 443 (HTTP or HTTPS) and the servers talk back to clients on higher-numbered ports above 1024.

    ☒ **A, B,** and **C** are incorrect. Without a subnet mask, it is impossible to determine valid IP addresses on subnets. The load balancer external IP address is already a public IP address, and the web servers already have private IP addresses.

18. Refer to Figure 12-1. Which statement regarding the load balancer is correct?

    A. The load balancer must have connectivity to the web servers.

    B. The load balancer does not need connectivity to the web servers.

    C. The load balancer listening port must match the internal web server listening port.

    D. The load balancer will not detect if a web server is down.

    ☑ **A.** Load balancers must have connectivity to backend web servers for load balancing to work.

    ☒ **B, C,** and **D** are incorrect. Load balancers must talk to backend servers and can detect unresponsive servers, but the ports do not have to match.

19. Your company is migrating on-premises services to the public cloud. In the interim, you need a way to use existing backup solutions while backing up data to the public cloud. Which on-premises backup functionality is required?

    A. Write verify

    B. Tape encryption

    C. VTL emulation

    D. Tunneling

    ☑ **C.** Virtual tape library (VTL) emulation exposes storage in a format understood by backup software.

    ☒ **A, B,** and **D** are incorrect. Write verify ensures that backed-up data is not corrupt. Tape encryption provides data confidentiality. Tunneling is not related to data backup.

20. The archive bit for files modified since the last backup will be set to which value?

    A. b

    B. m

    C. 0

    D. 1

    ☑ **D.** When a file is modified, it needs to be archived (backed up), so the archive bit is turned on to a value of 1.

    ☒ **A, B,** and **C** are incorrect. b and m are not valid file attributes. 0 normally means the file has been backed up and has not since been modified.

21. The archive bit for unmodified files that have been backed up will be set to which value?
    A. b
    B. m
    C. 0
    D. 1

    ☑ **C.** 0 normally means the file has been backed up and has not since been modified.
    ☒ **A, B,** and **D** are incorrect. b and m are not valid file attributes. When a file is modified, it needs to be archived (backed up), so the archive bit is turned on to a value of 1.

22. A virtual machine file server's virtual hard disks are corrupt and cannot be repaired. Which type of tape backup will take the least amount of time to restore?
    A. Snapshot
    B. Incremental
    C. Differential
    D. Full

    D. Full backups require a single backup set, or volume, to restore instead of switching out multiple backup tapes.
    ☒ **A, B,** and **C** are incorrect. Snapshots provide a point-in-time picture of the state of a virtual machine or disk volume. Incremental backups include files modified since the last full or incremental backup. Differential backups include files modified since the last full backup.

23. A virtual machine file server's virtual hard disks are corrupt and cannot be repaired. Which type of tape backup takes the most amount of time to restore?
    A. Snapshot
    B. Incremental
    C. Differential
    D. Full

    ☑ **B.** Incremental backups are the longest to restore since multiple backup tapes must be switched out to complete the restore.
    ☒ **A, C,** and **D** are incorrect. Snapshots provide a point-in-time picture of the state of a virtual machine or disk volume. Differential backups include files modified since the last full backup. Full backups include all files, modified or not, since the last backup.

24. Which type of backup contains only those files modified since the last full backup?
    A. Snapshot
    B. Incremental
    C. Differential
    D. Full

    ☑ **C.** Differential backups include only files modified since the last full backup.
    ☒ **A, B,** and **D** are incorrect. Snapshots provide a point-in-time picture of the state of a virtual machine or disk volume. Incremental backups include files modified since the last full or incremental backup. Full backups include all files, modified or not, since the last backup.

25. Which type of backup does not modify the archive bit?

A. Snapshot

B. Incremental

C. Differential

D. Full

☑   **C.** Differential backups include files created or modified since the last full backup. The archive bit is not cleared with this type of backup so that the next differential backup will still include all files since the last full backup.

☒   **A, B,** and **D** are incorrect. Snapshots provide a point-in-time picture of the state of a virtual machine or disk volume. New and modified files have the archive bit enabled, or set to 1, or "on", which means it needs to be backed up. This is a flag used by backup software to determine what should be included in the backup. Incremental backups include files modified since the last full or incremental backup. Full backups include all files, modified or not, since the last backup.

26. While creating a DRP, you are concerned with how long the restoration of data files will take. You conclude the restoration cannot exceed three hours. What is another way of stating this?

A. RPO = 3 hours

B. Backup = 3 hours

C. RTO = 3 hours

D. Restore = 3 hours

☑   **C.** The recovery time objective (RTO) is the maximum amount of tolerable downtime.

☒   **A, B,** and **D** are incorrect. The recovery point objective (RPO) is the maximum tolerable amount of data loss. RTO and RPO are terms used in business continuity parlance, not backup and restore.

27. What is the purpose of a backup catalog?

A. It is an index of the data on backup media.

B. It contains decryption keys.

C. It contains software licenses.

D. It lists backup sources available on the network.

☑   **A.** Backup catalogs are an index of the contents of backup media.

☒   **B, C,** and **D** are incorrect. The listed items are not stored in a backup catalog.

28. Which term is best associated with data backups?

A. Performance

B. Integrity

C. Availability

D. Confidentiality

☑   **C.** Data is more available if there are backups of it.

☒   **A, B,** and **D** are incorrect. The listed items are not as related to data backups as availability is.

29. Your network link to the public cloud is 80 percent utilized by other services. On-premises files must be replicated to the public cloud while minimizing bandwidth usage. What type of replication method should you use?

  A. Asynchronous

  B. Synchronous

  C. Block-level backup

  D. Content delivery network

  ☑ **C.** Block-level backup detects file block changes and replicates only those items.

  ☒ **A, B,** and **D** are incorrect. Asynchronous and synchronous replication are related to acknowledgments of disk writes. Content delivery networks (CDNs) place content so that it is geographically near end users.

30. Which type of snapshot technology has the least computational requirements?

  A. Copy-on-write

  B. Deduplication

  C. Compression

  D. Redirect-on-write

  ☑ **D.** Redirect-on-write snapshots redirect write requests to alternate locations so that the original data continues to be available.

  ☒ **A, B,** and **C** are incorrect. Copy-on-write makes a copy of blocks before changes overwrite them; this is more computationally expensive than redirection when writing. Deduplication and compression are not snapshot technologies.

31. What is another name for a cloud backup?

  A. Snapshot

  B. Clone

  C. Online backup

  D. Offline backup

  ☑ **C.** Online backups are always readily available as is the case with cloud backups.

  ☒ **A, B,** and **D** are incorrect. The listed terms are not synonymous with cloud backup.

32. You need to ensure that critical on-premises virtual machines are immediately available in the event of a regional disaster. What should you configure?

  A. Cloud failover

  B. Failover cluster

  C. Hourly backups

  D. Virtual machine clones

  ☑ **A.** Cloud failover allows on-premises services to be failed over to a cloud provider.

  ☒ **B, C,** and **D** are incorrect. A regular failover cluster will not solve the issue of a regional disaster. Backups and virtual machine clones are not designed for immediate access when an outage occurs.

33. Due to a short RTO of five minutes, you need to ensure a mission-critical website is available in the event of a regional disaster. What should you configure?

A. Mirrored site

B. Staged site

C. Container site

D. Zone site

☑ **A.** A mirrored site is a copy of a website (in this case) that provides high availability.

☒ **B, C,** and **D** are incorrect. The listed site types are invalid.

34. A custom application draws insights from big data analytics. Due to the large volume of data transmitted between application components, you need to minimize computational and network latency. Which pair of options should you consider?

A. Distributed processing, jumbo frames

B. Jumbo frames, NIC teaming

C. Clustering, edge sites

D. Scaling in, edge sites

☑ **A.** Distributed processing uses multiple computers working together to solve large, complex problems. Jumbo frames are larger than normal network frames that can contain more data while reducing the number of frames that need to be processed. Network devices such as routers must be configured with an appropriate maximum transmission unit (MTU) size to properly support jumbo frames.

☒ **B, C** and **D** are incorrect. Jumbo frames are oversized network packets that allow more data to be sent in a single transmission, while NIC teaming groups two or more network interface cards (NICs) together for the purpose of redundancy or aggregated bandwidth, but these do not address computational latency. Clustering is used to make applications highly available but does not reduce computational or network latency. Edge sites can reduce network latency by keeping application components close together. Scaling in reduces the number of virtual machine nodes that support an application.

35. You need to ensure that server backups have a minimal impact on user productivity. When should you schedule backups to occur?

A. During maintenance windows

B. 12 A.M.–5 A.M.

C. During failback windows

D. 6 P.M.–12 A.M.

☑ **A.** Maintenance windows are built around times of minimal computing requirements.

☒ **B, C,** and **D** are incorrect. Not every company has the same productivity schedules. Failback windows is an invalid term.

36. Which action could have resulted in the state of the file depicted in Figure 12-2?

    A. A change was made to the file.

    B. Block-level snapshots were enabled.

    C. A full backup was just performed.

    D. An incremental backup was just performed.

FIGURE 12-2

Windows file properties

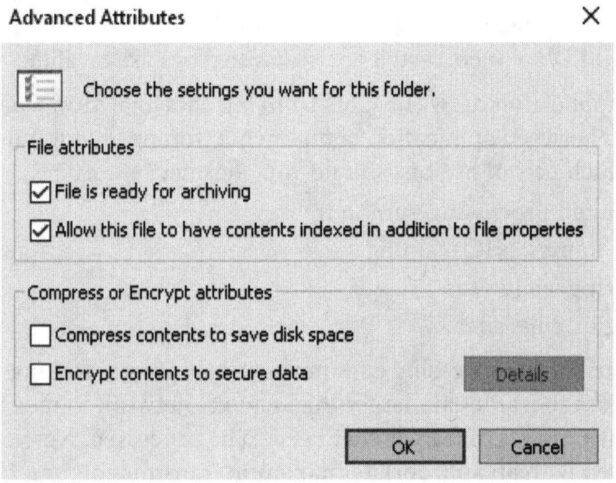

    ☑ **A.** You know the file was changed because it is flagged as being ready for archiving.

    ☒ **B, C,** and **D** are incorrect. The archive bit is not related to snapshots. You know a backup has not occurred since the archive bit is enabled.

37. Which benefits are realized by using a content delivery network? Choose two.

    A. Enhanced security

    B. Dynamic website content

    C. Increased performance

    D. Data availability

    ☑ **C** and **D.** Content delivery networks (CDNs) place content so that it is geographically near end users, which increases performance and data availability.

    ☒ **A** and **B** are incorrect. Accounts do not need delegated cloud administrative privileges of any kind. CDNs do not increase security nor do they enable dynamic website content.

38. What can be done to adhere to the RPO?

    A. Enable deduplication.

    B. Increase backup storage capacity.

    C. Increase backup frequency.

    D. Use SSD storage.

☑ **C.** The recovery point objective (RPO) is the maximum tolerable amount of data loss, and it is related to the backup frequency.

☒ **A, B,** and **D** are incorrect. Deduplication reduces disk space consumption. Additional backup space and fast SSD storage do not have a direct impact on the RPO.

39. How is the DRP different from the BCP?

    A. The DRP is specific to a system.
    B. The BCP is specific to a system.
    C. The DRP is related to business continuity.
    D. The BCP is related business continuity.

    ☑ **A.** Whereas business continuity plans (BCPs) ensure the overall continued meeting of business objectives, disaster recovery plans (DRPs) apply to restoration procedures of specific systems.

    ☒ **B, C,** and **D** are incorrect. Both DRPs and BCPs are related to business continuity.

40. Which of the following items can reduce the RTO? Choose two.

    A. Runbooks
    B. Increased network bandwidth
    C. Decreased network bandwidth
    D. Content delivery networks

    ☑ **A** and **B.** Runbooks are used to automate workflows; this along with more network bandwidth can reduce the time to restore a failed service.

    ☒ **C** and **D** are incorrect. The listed items will not reduce the recovery time objective (RTO).

41. Which communication method is used for inter-node cluster communication?

    A. Shared storage
    B. LUN
    C. iSCSI
    D. Heartbeat

    ☑ **D.** The cluster heartbeat is constant cluster node intercommunication.

    ☒ **A, B,** and **C** are incorrect. The listed items are not specifically designated as cluster heartbeat mechanisms.

42. What do cluster nodes use to conclude that a member is no longer available?

    A. Heartbeat
    B. Ping
    C. Tracert
    D. DNS TTL

    ☑ **A.** When a cluster node does not send a heartbeat within a configured timeframe, other nodes discard the silent node and take over its services.

    ☒ **B, C,** and **D** are incorrect. Ping and tracert are TCP/IP connectivity tools. The DNS time-to-live (TTL) determines how long DNS entries remain cached.

43. Which type of alternative disaster recovery site contains equipment but lacks up-to-date data?

A. Cold site

B. Warm site

C. Hot site

D. Lukewarm site

☑ **B.** Warm sites lack only up-to-date data.

☒ **A, C,** and **D** are incorrect. Cold site are empty facilities. Hot sites are fully equipped and contain up-to-date data. Lukewarm sites do not exist.

44. Which type of redundancy allows nodes to reside on different sides of a WAN?

A. WAN clustering

B. Geo-clustering

C. Disparate clustering

D. Long-haul clustering

☑ **B.** Geo-clustering provides high availability across long distances.

☒ **A, C,** and **D** are incorrect. The listed items are not valid clustering terms.

45. Which of the following is a common SAN redundancy configuration?

A. Failover clustering

B. Regional replication

C. Multipathing

D. RAID 0

☑ **C.** Multipathing uses redundancy (HBAs, Fibre Channel switches) to remove single points of failure in a storage area network (SAN).

☒ **A, B,** and **D** are incorrect. The listed solutions are not directly related to SANs.

46. You are about to apply a new batch of updates to a Linux virtual machine. What should you do before performing this task?

A. Take a snapshot.

B. Create a clone.

C. Enable RAID 0.

D. Enable RAID 1.

☑ **A.** Virtual machine snapshots are useful for quick point-in-time copies of a virtual machine's state that will be kept for a short time.

☒ **B, C,** and **D** are incorrect. Creating a clone or enabling RAID takes much longer and does not provide additional benefits.

Chapter 13

Testing, Automation, and Changes

CERTIFICATION OBJECTIVES

13.01   Testing Techniques

13.02   Automation and Orchestration

13.03   Change and Configuration Management

QUESTIONS

The cloud presents software and system testers with a very convenient infrastructure. Entire cloud networks, virtual machines, and databases can be deployed in a matter of minutes using scripts or templates.

Change management systems present a centralized and structured method for taking change requests to the implementation level. Runbook automation uses activities to automate even the most complex tasks related to all administrative functions.

1. Which performance metric represents the amount of data that has been paged to disk?
   A. Page faults
   B. Peak memory usage
   C. Paged pool
   D. Memory IOPS

2. You are using testing automation software to send normal data loads to an application. What type of testing is this?
   A. Stress testing
   B. Load testing
   C. Regression testing
   D. Penetration testing

3. You are using testing automation software to send excessive data loads to an application. What type of testing is this?
   A. Stress testing
   B. Load testing
   C. Regression testing
   D. Penetration testing

4. Which technique is used by the hypervisor to map host memory to virtual machines?
   A. Shadow page tables
   B. Page faults
   C. Peak memory usage
   D. Paged pool

5. Why are shadow page tables necessary?
   A. VMs don't always support dynamic memory.
   B. VMs cannot access host memory directly.
   C. RAM depletion means writing pages to disk.
   D. They trigger page faults.

6. You are planning a new testing strategy for your software development team. The ideal solution will be portable, allow the app to be isolated from other software, and provide the fastest possible startup time. Which testing solution should you select for your team?
   A. Virtual machines
   B. Containerization
   C. Virtual machine snapshots
   D. Cloud computing

7. While assessing public cloud providers, you decide to review SLAs. Which of the following statements accurately describes SLAs?
   A. Each cloud provider has an all-encompassing SLA.
   B. Each cloud service has its own SLA.
   C. SLAs cannot be negotiated.
   D. SLAs contain cloud service best practices.

8. Which function ensures data is correct and has not been tampered with?
   A. Encryption
   B. Availability
   C. Integrity
   D. Confidentiality

9. What are orchestration workflow automations called?
   A. Scriptbooks
   B. Runbooks
   C. Workflowbooks
   D. Automationbooks

10. Which term is used to describe a specific runbook task?
    A. Constructor
    B. Initiator
    C. Event
    D. Activity

11. Which organizational role determines whether IT changes get approved or rejected?
    A. CEO
    B. CIO
    C. Server administrator
    D. Change manager

12. Which term describes the selection of computing power for a virtual machine?

   A. Sizing

   B. Scaling out

   C. Scaling in

   D. Scaling up

13. Which group or role provides input to the change manager?

   A. Server administrators

   B. Cloud administrators

   C. Change advisory board

   D. CIO

14. Which of the following are examples of items stored in a configuration management database? Choose two.

   A. Baselines

   B. Customer transactions

   C. Web server logs

   D. Software licenses

15. Which of the following is related to auto-scaling?

   A. Adding vCPUs

   B. Enabling virtual machine dynamic memory

   C. Enabling a virtual machine load balancer

   D. Virtual machine template

16. Which body decides upon effective tests for a specific application?

   A. Resource advisory board

   B. Testing advisory board

   C. Change advisory board

   D. Quality assurance team

17. Which test ultimately determines whether an application meets functional design requirements?

   A. Load testing

   B. User acceptance testing

   C. Stress testing

   D. Penetration testing

18. You are planning load tests against a cloud web application. What do you use to determine normal activity levels for the application?

   A. Previous load test result

   B. Baseline

   C. Previous stress test results

   D. Performance metrics

19. You are troubleshooting performance problems on a development virtual machine. Based on the following metrics, which solution would best improve performance?

> % CPU utilization – 70
> % Average IOPS – 90
> Page faults/sec – 1425

A. Add CPUs.
B. Add RAM.
C. Add more disks.
D. Add faster disks.

20. You are determining the maximum dynamic memory limit for a new virtual machine. Which metric should you consult?

A. Paged pool
B. Page faults
C. Average memory usage
D. Peak memory usage

21. An application uses multiple background processes to read data from a cloud MySQL database. You need to determine the average application read IOPS for performance adjustments. What should you do?

A. Add process IOPS read values together.
B. Add MySQL read values together.
C. Add process IOPS write values together.
D. Add MySQL write values together.

22. You notice excessive network traffic initiated from a server named Hypervisor1. Traffic destined for Hypervisor1 falls within normal limits. Hypervisor1 hosts two database servers and a virtual machine load balancer for virtual machine web applications all running on Hypervisor1. The source of the excessive network traffic must be identified. What should you do?

A. Monitor inbound network traffic for Hypervisor1 NICs.
B. Monitor outbound network traffic for Hypervisor1 NICs.
C. Monitor inbound network traffic for each virtual machine vNIC.
D. Monitor outbound network traffic for each virtual machine vNIC.

23. You need to audit Help Desk user's cloud MySQL database searches for a particular table. Security and performance levels must be maintained while conducting the audit. What should you do?

A. Enable read auditing for all users.
B. Enable write auditing for all users.
C. Enable table-specific read auditing for the Help Desk group.
D. Enable table-specific write auditing for the Help Desk group.

24. Which tool provides a visual representation of performance metrics?
    A. Management report
    B. Management dashboard
    C. .CSV file
    D. .XML file

25. Which metric measures the amount of time a virtual machine has to wait for physical CPU to become available?
    A. CPU wait time
    B. % average CPU utilization
    C. % CPU utilization
    D. CPU ready

26. Which of the following metrics is directly related to CDN testing?
    A. % CPU utilization
    B. Free disk space
    C. CPU wait time
    D. Network latency

27. You are deploying secure Linux application containers to a cloud network called VNet1. What is required on each virtual machine in VNet1?
    A. Linux
    B. PKI
    C. Containerization software
    D. Hypervisor

28. Which functional testing step occurs immediately before defining expected output?
    A. Define test input.
    B. Compare actual output against expected output.
    C. Identify program actions.
    D. Run through each test case.

29. Which functional testing step is best suited for automation?
    A. Define test input.
    B. Define expected output.
    C. Identify program actions.
    D. Run through each test case.

30. Which type of cloud provider document provides a similar solution to different customer types?
    A. Standard SLA
    B. Multilevel SLA
    C. Corporate SLA
    D. Community SLA

31. Which term best relates to an SLA?

    A. Discount

    B. Security

    C. Availability

    D. Delegated administration

32. Which attribute applies to both hypervisor hosts and virtual machine guests?

    A. Sizing

    B. vNIC

    C. vCPU

    D. Dynamic memory

33. Which of the following terms best relates to high availability?

    A. Replication

    B. IOPS

    C. Snapshot

    D. Runbook

34. You are using Microsoft System Center Orchestrator for workflow automation. You notice that support for Microsoft Azure cloud computing is missing. What should you do?

    A. Recognize that Orchestrator does not support Azure automation.

    B. Upgrade Orchestrator to a newer version.

    C. Install the Azure integration pack.

    D. Create PowerShell scripts instead.

35. As the department head for the Marketing team, you would like Android smartphones used by team members to have VPN access to corporate networks. What should you do?

    A. Create a runbook.

    B. Submit an RFC.

    C. Create a PowerShell script.

    D. Create a shell script.

36. The IT director in your organization suggests the gradual adoption of public cloud computing for selected IT workloads. What formal process should be followed to make this modification organization-wide?

    A. Change proposal

    B. Troubleshooting process

    C. RFC

    D. Runbook submission

37. Currently your automation environment consists of one runbook server. You need to ensure a critical weekly runbook executes on schedule. What should you do?

    A. Take a snapshot of the runbook.

    B. Enable the runbook to run on multiple runbook servers.

    C. Enable a runbook load balancer.

    D. Create a second runbook that performs the same tasks.

38. While creating a runbook to automate the deployment and verification of server software patches, you decided to build more resilience into the workflow. In the event of the failed application of patches, you would like the system to return to its prior state. What type of activity should you build into your runbook?

    A. System restore point

    B. Backup

    C. Snapshot

    D. Rollback

39. You are troubleshooting the installation of an app on a user smartphone. After testing the first solution theory, you realize the problem has not been solved. What options are available for your next action? Choose two.

    A. Escalate.

    B. Document the solution.

    C. Verify system functionality.

    D. Establish another theory.

40. Which type of testing is most likely to require written permission from the system owner?

    A. Vulnerability

    B. Penetration

    C. Functional

    D. Regression

41. You are scripting the testing of a load-balanced, cloud-based web application that uses a backend MySQL data store. You need to verify the quality of rows stored in MySQL database tables. What type of testing will the script perform?

    A. Functional

    B. Data integrity

    C. Regression

    D. Penetration

42. You need a way to verify that tested applications are performing well under normal load conditions. How can you do this?

    A. Compare test results to logs.

    B. Compare test results to the baseline.

    C. Compare current test results to previous test results.

    D. Compare current logs to previous logs.

43. Which statements are correct? Choose two.

    A. Testing is reactive.

    B. Testing is proactive.

    C. Troubleshooting is reactive.

    D. Troubleshooting is proactive.

44. What reduces the amount of time spent on administrative tasks?

    A. Snapshots

    B. Backups

    C. Runbooks

    D. Load balancing

45. After solving a unique user connectivity issue to the Internet, you move on to the next helpdesk ticket. Which troubleshooting step did you miss?

    A. Escalate.

    B. Document the solution.

    C. Identify the problem.

    D. Verify system functionality.

46. You are troubleshooting a scheduled runbook that is not executing. You discover that NTP traffic is blocked on the affected host. After allowing NTP traffic, you move on to the next helpdesk ticket. Which troubleshooting step did you miss?

    A. Escalate.

    B. Document the solution.

    C. Identify the problem.

    D. Verify system functionality.

47. Users complain they do not have access to search a database server. You connect to the database host and set user read permissions to all database tables. Which troubleshooting step did you miss?

    A. Escalate.

    B. Document the solution.

    C. Identify the problem.

    D. Verify system functionality.

A QUICK ANSWER KEY

1.	C	**13.**	C	**25.**	D	**37.**	B
2.	B	**14.**	A, D	**26.**	D	**38.**	D
3.	A	**15.**	D	**27.**	C	**39.**	A, D
4.	A	**16.**	D	**28.**	A	**40.**	B
5.	B	**17.**	B	**29.**	D	**41.**	B
6.	B	**18.**	B	**30.**	B	**42.**	B
7.	B	**19.**	B	**31.**	C	**43.**	B, C
8.	C	**20.**	D	**32.**	A	**44.**	C
9.	B	**21.**	A	**33.**	A	**45.**	B
10.	D	**22.**	D	**34.**	C	**46.**	D
11.	D	**23.**	C	**35.**	B	**47.**	C
12.	A	**24.**	B	**36.**	A		

IN-DEPTH ANSWERS

1. Which performance metric represents the amount of data that has been paged to disk?
   A. Page faults
   B. Peak memory usage
   C. Paged pool
   D. Memory IOPS

   ☑ **C.** The paged pool metric represents the amount of data swapped from RAM to disk.
   ☒ **A, B,** and **D** are incorrect. Page faults occur when data is read from disk rather than memory. Peak memory usage represents the high-water mark for memory consumption. There is no such thing as memory IOPS.

2. You are using testing automation software to send normal data loads to an application. What type of testing is this?
   A. Stress testing
   B. Load testing
   C. Regression testing
   D. Penetration testing

   ☑ **B.** Load testing presents a system with normal activity.
   ☒ **A, C,** and **D** are incorrect. Stress testing presents an application with excessive activity. Regression testing ensures changes have not broken previously working functionality. Penetration testing detects and exploits vulnerabilities.

3. You are using testing automation software to send excessive data loads to an application. What type of testing is this?
   A. Stress testing
   B. Load testing
   C. Regression testing
   D. Penetration testing

   ☑ **A.** Stress testing presents an application with excessive activity.
   ☒ **B, C,** and **D** are incorrect. Load testing presents a system with normal activity. Regression testing ensures changes have not broken previously working functionality. Penetration testing detects and exploits vulnerabilities.

4. Which technique is used by the hypervisor to map host memory to virtual machines?

   A. Shadow page tables
   B. Page faults
   C. Peak memory usage
   D. Paged pool

   ☑ **A.** Hypervisors make their physical memory available to virtual machines through shadow page tables.

   ☒ **B, C,** and **D** are incorrect. Page faults occur when data is read from disk rather than memory. Peak memory usage represents the high-water mark for memory consumption. The paged pool metric represents the amount of data swapped from RAM to disk.

5. Why are shadow page tables necessary?

   A. VMs don't always support dynamic memory.
   B. VMs cannot access host memory directly.
   C. RAM depletion means writing pages to disk.
   D. They trigger page faults.

   ☑ **B.** Shadow page tables make memory available to virtual machines without allowing direct access to host memory.

   ☒ **A, C,** and **D** are incorrect. The listed items are not directly related to shadow page tables.

6. You are planning a new testing strategy for your software development team. The ideal solution will be portable, allow the app to be isolated from other software, and provide the fastest possible startup time. Which testing solution should you select for your team?

   A. Virtual machines
   B. Containerization
   C. Virtual machine snapshots
   D. Cloud computing

   ☑ **B.** Application containers isolate an app from other apps on the same host while providing a very fast startup time since they normally do not contain an operating system.

   ☒ **A, C,** and **D** are incorrect. Virtual machines do not start up as quickly as application containers. Snapshots do not provide application isolation; they are a point-in-time copy of data. Cloud computing is a generic term that does not address the specific needs of the scenario.

7. While assessing public cloud providers, you decide to review SLAs. Which of the following statements accurately describes SLAs?

   A. Each cloud provider has an all-encompassing SLA.
   B. Each cloud service has its own SLA.
   C. SLAs cannot be negotiated.
   D. SLAs contain cloud service best practices.

☑ **B.** Service level agreements (SLAs) are contracts between service providers and consumers concerning expected levels of service. SLAs exist for specific cloud services such as storage versus virtual machines.

☒ **A, C,** and **D** are incorrect. SLAs exist for each cloud service and can be negotiated in some cases. Best practices are not contained within SLAs.

8. Which function ensures data is correct and has not been tampered with?

A. Encryption
B. Availability
C. Integrity
D. Confidentiality

☑ **C.** Data integrity ensures information is accurate and has not been tampered with.

☒ **A, B,** and **D** are incorrect. Encryption provides data confidentiality. Backups and replication provide data availability.

9. What are orchestration workflow automations called?

A. Scriptbooks
B. Runbooks
C. Workflowbooks
D. Automationbooks

☑ **B.** Runbooks are used to automate workflows.

☒ **A, C,** and **D** are incorrect. The listed terms are invalid.

10. Which term is used to describe a specific runbook task?

A. Constructor
B. Initiator
C. Event
D. Activity

☑ **D.** Runbooks contain activities that are used to automate workflows.

☒ **A, B,** and **C** are incorrect. The listed terms are not used to execute runbook tasks.

11. Which organizational role determines whether IT changes get approved or rejected?

A. CEO
B. CIO
C. Server administrator
D. Change manager

☑ **D.** Modifications to systems must be approved by the change manager.

☒ **A, B,** and **C** are incorrect. The listed organizational roles do not approve or reject changes.

12. Which term describes the selection of computing power for a virtual machine?

A. Sizing

B. Scaling out

C. Scaling in

D. Scaling up

☑ **A.** The virtual machine "size" determines how powerful it is in terms of CPU, RAM, and disk subsystem, whether scaling up or down.

☒ **B, C,** and **D** are incorrect. Scaling out adds virtual machines to support an app. Scaling in removes unnecessary virtual machines to reduce costs. Scaling up means resizing the virtual machine to increase its computing power.

13. Which group or role provides input to the change manager?

A. Server administrators

B. Cloud administrators

C. Change advisory board

D. CIO

☑ **C.** The change manager role accepts input from the change advisory board (CAB).

☒ **A, B,** and **D** are incorrect. The listed groups and role do not provide direct input to the change manager.

14. Which of the following are examples of items stored in a configuration management database? Choose two.

A. Baselines

B. Customer transactions

C. Web server logs

D. Software licenses

☑ **A** and **D.** The configuration management database (CMDB) contains configuration items (CIs) such as baseline configurations and software licenses.

☒ **B** and **C** are incorrect. Customer transactions and logs are not stored in the CMDB.

15. Which of the following is related to auto-scaling?

A. Adding vCPUs

B. Enabling virtual machine dynamic memory

C. Enabling a virtual machine load balancer

D. Virtual machine template

☑ **D.** Virtual machine templates identify the necessary details to spin up new virtual machine instances to meet application demand.

☒ **A, B,** and **C** are incorrect. Adding vCPUs is one aspect of virtual machine resizing. Dynamic memory is not related to auto-scaling. Enabling a load balancer does not always imply auto-scaling.

16. Which body decides upon effective tests for a specific application?

- A. Resource advisory board
- B. Testing advisory board
- C. Change advisory board
- D. Quality assurance team

☑ **D.** The quality assurance (QA) team determines which tests should be run.

☒ **A, B,** and **C** are incorrect. The listed entities are not responsible for determining which tests should be run.

17. Which test ultimately determines whether an application meets functional design requirements?

- A. Load testing
- B. User acceptance testing
- C. Stress testing
- D. Penetration testing

☑ **B.** There are many different types of application testing. In the end, users must accept the application before it can be rolled out into production to solve issues it was designed to solve.

☒ **A, C,** and **D** are incorrect. Load testing simulates normal activity against an app, while stress testing simulates excessive activity. Pen testing finds weaknesses and attempts to exploit them.

18. You are planning load tests against a cloud web application. What do you use to determine normal activity levels for the application?

- A. Previous load test result
- B. Baseline
- C. Previous stress test results
- D. Performance metrics

☑ **B.** A baseline is required to determine what normal activity looks like.

☒ **A, C,** and **D** are incorrect. The listed items are not required prior to running a load test.

19. You are troubleshooting performance problems on a development virtual machine. Based on the following metrics, which solution would best improve performance?

> % CPU utilization – 70
> % Average IOPS – 90
> Page faults/sec – 1425

- A. Add CPUs.
- B. Add RAM.
- C. Add more disks.
- D. Add faster disks.

☑ **B.** More RAM would mean fewer page faults, which would result in less CPU and disk usage.

☒ **A, C,** and **D** are incorrect. Since a lack of RAM seems to be the root cause, the listed items would not improve performance as much.

20. You are determining the maximum dynamic memory limit for a new virtual machine. Which metric should you consult?
   A. Paged pool
   B. Page faults
   C. Average memory usage
   D. Peak memory usage

   ☑ **D.** Knowledge of the highest amount of memory used (peak) is used to determine the dynamic memory high watermark setting.
   ☒ **A, B,** and **C** are incorrect. The listed metrics will not help determine the maximum dynamic memory limit.

21. An application uses multiple background processes to read data from a cloud MySQL database. You need to determine the average application read IOPS for performance adjustments. What should you do?
   A. Add process IOPS read values together.
   B. Add MySQL read values together.
   C. Add process IOPS write values together.
   D. Add MySQL write values together.

   ☑ **A.** Since each process has an IOPS metric, make sure to add them together to determine the average application read IOPS.
   ☒ **B, C,** and **D** are incorrect. The listed solutions will not determine the average application read IOPS for an app using multiple processes.

22. You notice excessive network traffic initiated from a server named Hypervisor1. Traffic destined for Hypervisor1 falls within normal limits. Hypervisor1 hosts two database servers and a virtual machine load balancer for virtual machine web applications all running on Hypervisor1. The source of the excessive network traffic must be identified. What should you do?
   A. Monitor inbound network traffic for Hypervisor1 NICs.
   B. Monitor outbound network traffic for Hypervisor1 NICs.
   C. Monitor inbound network traffic for each virtual machine vNIC.
   D. Monitor outbound network traffic for each virtual machine vNIC.

   ☑ **D.** Traffic initiated from Hypervisor 1 is the problem; each virtual machine vNIC must be monitored in order to identify the culprit.
   ☒ **A, B,** and **C** are incorrect. Outbound traffic from Hypervisor1 is the problem, not inbound.

23. You need to audit Help Desk user's cloud MySQL database searches for a particular table. Security and performance levels must be maintained while conducting the audit. What should you do?
   A. Enable read auditing for all users.
   B. Enable write auditing for all users.

C. Enable table-specific read auditing for the Help Desk group.

D. Enable table-specific write auditing for the Help Desk group.

☑ **C.** Do not audit more resources or users than is absolutely necessary. Otherwise, performance and disk space consumption are negatively affected.

☒ **A, C,** and **D** are incorrect. Auditing all users generates too much unnecessary activity. Reads must be audited, not writes.

24. Which tool provides a visual representation of performance metrics?

A. Management report

B. Management dashboard

C. .CSV file

D. .XML file

☑ **B.** Many tools allow the creation of customized dashboards as a visual representation of graphs or metrics that are important to a specific administrator.

☒ **A, C,** and **D** are incorrect. Reports and export files are not as visual as dashboards.

25. Which metric measures the amount of time a virtual machine has to wait for physical CPU to become available?

A. CPU wait time

B. % average CPU utilization

C. % CPU utilization

D. CPU ready

☑ **D.** The CPU ready metric represents how long virtual machines wait for physical hypervisor CPU time.

☒ **A, B,** and **C** are incorrect. The CPU wait time measures how long a process thread waits before it is processed. The CPU utilization metrics show utilization, not how long CPU processing takes.

26. Which of the following metrics is directly related to CDN testing?

A. % CPU utilization

B. Free disk space

C. CPU wait time

D. Network latency

☑ **D.** Content delivery networks (CDNs) replicate web app content so that it is geographically near users, with the purpose of reducing network latency. Therefore, network latency is the most important metric to evaluate when CDN testing.

☒ **A, B,** and **C** are incorrect. While CPU utilization and storage space consumption have an impact on CDNs, the major purpose of using a CND is reduced network latency.

27. You are deploying secure Linux application containers to a cloud network called VNet1. What is required on each virtual machine in VNet1?

    A. Linux

    B. PKI

    C. Containerization software

    D. Hypervisor

    ☑ **C.** Application containers can only run if the correct container host software is running.

    ☒ **A, B,** and **D** are incorrect. The listed items are not required to run containers.

28. Which functional testing step occurs immediately before defining expected output?

    A. Define test input.

    B. Compare actual output against expected output.

    C. Identify program actions.

    D. Run through each test case.

    ☑ **A.** With functional testing, test inputs must be defined before test outputs.

    ☒ **B, C,** and **D** are incorrect. The listed functional testing steps do not occur before defining the expected output.

29. Which functional testing step is best suited for automation?

    A. Define test input.

    B. Define expected output.

    C. Identify program actions.

    D. Run through each test case.

    ☑ **D.** Automation is key for running a series of tests efficiently.

    ☒ **A, B,** and **C** are incorrect. The listed steps are not as well suited for automation.

30. Which type of cloud provider document provides a similar solution to different customer types?

    A. Standard SLA

    B. Multilevel SLA

    C. Corporate SLA

    D. Community SLA

    ☑ **B.** Multilevel SLAs apply to the same service used by different types of cloud customers.

    ☒ **A, C,** and **D** are incorrect. The listed SLAs do not differ between client types.

31. Which term best relates to an SLA?

    A. Discount

    B. Security

    C. Availability

    D. Delegated administration

    ☑ **C.** Service level agreements (SLAs) deal primarily with service uptime, which relates to availability.

    ☒ **A, B,** and **D** are incorrect. The listed terms are not the primary focus of SLAs.

32. Which attribute applies to both hypervisor hosts and virtual machine guests?

    A. Sizing
    B. vNIC
    C. vCPU
    D. Dynamic memory

    ☑ **A.** Sizing determines the underlying machine horsepower including CPUs, RAM, and storage and applies to physical and virtual machines.
    ☒ **B, C,** and **D** are incorrect. vNICs, vCPUs, and dynamic memory do not apply directly to hypervisor hosts.

33. Which of the following terms best relates to high availability?

    A. Replication
    B. IOPS
    C. Snapshot
    D. Runbook

    ☑ **A.** High availability for data can be achieved by replicating it to another host or location.
    ☒ **B, C,** and **D** are incorrect. Input/output operations per second (IOPS) and runbook automation are not directly related to availability. While snapshots make data available in the event of a disaster, replication is more applicable since it continues to receive updates.

34. You are using Microsoft System Center Orchestrator for workflow automation. You notice that support for Microsoft Azure cloud computing is missing. What should you do?

    A. Recognize that Orchestrator does not support Azure automation.
    B. Upgrade Orchestrator to a newer version.
    C. Install the Azure integration pack.
    D. Create PowerShell scripts instead.

    ☑ **C.** Modern tools are modular and support the installation of components that add functionality, such as the Azure integration pack for Orchestrator.
    ☒ **A, B,** and **D** are incorrect. Orchestrator supports Azure automation though the integration pack. Upgrading Orchestrator or creating PowerShell scripts is unnecessary when a simple installation of an integration pack is all that is needed.

35. As the department head for the Marketing team, you would like Android smartphones used by team members to have VPN access to corporate networks. What should you do?

    A. Create a runbook.
    B. Submit an RFC.
    C. Create a PowerShell script.
    D. Create a shell script.

    ☑ **B.** A request for change (RFC) is the formal way of submitting change requests.
    ☒ **A, C,** and **D** are incorrect. The listed items are directly related to automation but not changes.

36. The IT director in your organization suggests the gradual adoption of public cloud computing for selected IT workloads. What formal process should be followed to make this modification organization-wide?

    A. Change proposal
    B. Troubleshooting process
    C. RFC
    D. Runbook submission

    ☑ **A.** Change proposals are used for larger-scale, complex modifications, such as public cloud computing adoption.

    ☒ **B, C,** and **D** are incorrect. Troubleshooting is not required since there is no specific problem. Request for changes (RFCs) are for smaller modifications such as configuration changes on smartphones. Runbooks are used for automation and are not specifically related to change.

37. Currently your automation environment consists of one runbook server. You need to ensure a critical weekly runbook executes on schedule. What should you do?

    A. Take a snapshot of the runbook.
    B. Enable the runbook to run on multiple runbook servers.
    C. Enable a runbook load balancer.
    D. Create a second runbook that performs the same tasks.

    ☑ **B.** Using multiple runbook nodes can improve performance and availability of runbooks.

    ☒ **A, C,** and **D** are incorrect. Runbooks do not support snapshots. A load balancer does not ensure a runbook runs on schedule. A second similar runbook is useless with one runbook server.

38. While creating a runbook to automate the deployment and verification of server software patches, you decided to build more resilience into the workflow. In the event of the failed application of patches, you would like the system to return to its prior state. What type of activity should you build into your runbook?

    A. System restore point
    B. Backup
    C. Snapshot
    D. Rollback

    ☑ **D.** The runbook should roll back failed updates.

    ☒ **A, B,** and **C** are incorrect. System restore points work only on Windows clients, not servers. Backups and snapshots take much longer to create when the quicker existing patch rollback feature can be used.

39. You are troubleshooting the installation of an app on a user smartphone. After testing the first solution theory, you realize the problem has not been solved. What options are available for your next action? Choose two.

    A. Escalate.

    B. Document the solution.

    C. Verify system functionality.

    D. Establish another theory.

    ☑ **A** and **D.** When the first solution theory fails, either escalate the issue to be handled elsewhere or come up with new solution theories to solve the problem.

    ☒ **B** and **C** are incorrect. There is not yet a solution to document or verify.

40. Which type of testing is most likely to require written permission from the system owner?

    A. Vulnerability

    B. Penetration

    C. Functional

    D. Regression

    ☑ **B.** Because penetration tests are active and invasive and could bring systems down, written permission is required prior to test execution.

    ☒ **A, C,** and **D** are incorrect. The other listed test types are not as likely to require written permission from the system owner.

41. You are scripting the testing of a load-balanced, cloud-based web application that uses a backend MySQL data store. You need to verify the quality of rows stored in MySQL database tables. What type of testing will the script perform?

    A. Functional

    B. Data integrity

    C. Regression

    D. Penetration

    ☑ **B.** Data integrity testing ensures the validity of data.

    ☒ **A, C,** and **D** are incorrect. Functional testing verifies that the solution meets design requirements. Regression testing ensures new changes do not break previously working functionality. Penetration testing finds weaknesses and attempts to exploit them.

42. You need a way to verify that tested applications are performing well under normal load conditions. How can you do this?

    A. Compare test results to logs.

    B. Compare test results to the baseline.

    C. Compare current test results to previous test results.

    D. Compare current logs to previous logs.

    ☑ **B.** "Normal" can only be determined over time with a baseline.

    ☒ **A, C,** and **D** are incorrect. The listed items are not used to determine whether test results are normal or not; a baseline is required.

43. Which statements are correct? Choose two.

A. Testing is reactive.

B. Testing is proactive.

C. Troubleshooting is reactive.

D. Troubleshooting is proactive.

☑ **B** and **C.** Testing attempts to find flaws before a solution is rolled out to production. Troubleshooting occurs in reaction to a problem.

☒ **A** and **D** are incorrect. The statements are incorrect.

44. What reduces the amount of time spent on administrative tasks?

A. Snapshots

B. Backups

C. Runbooks

D. Load balancing

☑ **C.** Runbooks are an automation solution that reduces the amount of time spent on administrative tasks.

☒ **A, B,** and **D** are incorrect. Snapshots, backups, and load balancing are not automation solutions that can save time.

45. After solving a unique user connectivity issue to the Internet, you move on to the next helpdesk ticket. Which troubleshooting step did you miss?

A. Escalate.

B. Document the solution.

C. Identify the problem.

D. Verify system functionality.

☑ **B.** Solutions must be documented.

☒ **A, C,** and **D** are incorrect. The listed troubleshooting steps have been executed.

46. You are troubleshooting a scheduled runbook that is not executing. You discover that NTP traffic is blocked on the affected host. After allowing NTP traffic, you move on to the next helpdesk ticket. Which troubleshooting step did you miss?

A. Escalate.

B. Document the solution.

C. Identify the problem.

D. Verify system functionality.

☑ **D.** After implementing a solution to a problem, verify that the issue is addressed and that no new problems have been introduced.

☒ **A, B,** and **C** are incorrect. Escalation is not necessary since a solution was found. Documentation occurs only after a successful solution verification. Problem identification has already occurred.

47. Users complain they do not have access to search a database server. You connect to the database host and set user read permissions to all database tables. Which troubleshooting step did you miss?

    A. Escalate.

    B. Document the solution.

    C. Identify the problem.

    D. Verify system functionality.

    ☑ **C.** The specific problem was not even identified before changes were made.

    ☒ **A, B,** and **D** are incorrect. The listed steps can occur only after the proper identification of the problem.

Chapter 14

Troubleshooting

CERTIFICATION OBJECTIVES

14.01   Troubleshooting Tools

14.02   Documentation and Analysis

14.03   Troubleshooting Methodology

QUESTIONS

Solving problems over time is inevitable with even the best-planned IT systems. The CompTIA six-step troubleshooting methodology aids in resolving issues efficiently from problem identification all the way to documenting the solution.

Tools such as ping, nslookup, and tracert can pinpoint network configuration problems. Technicians can also look to log files for data related to performance and issues.

1. You are configuring a cloud network firewall. The firewall must permit ping traffic from your administrative on-premises station. What type of traffic should you allow?

    A. SSH

    B. ICMP

    C. RDP

    D. UDP

2. Which command resulted in the output shown in Figure 14-1?

    A. ipconfig

    B. tracert

    C. nslookup

    D. ping

FIGURE 14-1

Command output for question 2

```
Reply from 192.168.0.1: bytes=32 time=7ms TTL=64
Reply from 192.168.0.1: bytes=32 time=9ms TTL=64
Reply from 192.168.0.1: bytes=32 time=13ms TTL=64
Reply from 192.168.0.1: bytes=32 time=7ms TTL=64
```

3. Which Windows command shows the path a packet takes as it traverses routers?

    A. ipconfig

    B. tracert

    C. nslookup

    D. ping

4. Which command resulted in the output shown in Figure 14-2?
   A. ipconfig
   B. tracert
   C. nslookup
   D. ping

FIGURE 14-2

```
9     *        *        *       Request timed out.
10    *        *        *       Request timed out.
11    41 ms    36 ms    37 ms   yyz10s06-in-f3.1e100.net [172.217.2.163]
```

Command
output for
question 4

5. Which of the following tools can be used specifically to verify DNS functionality? Choose two.
   A. dig
   B. tracert
   C. ipconfig
   D. nslookup

6. Which command resulted in the output shown in Figure 14-3?
   A. dig
   B. tracert
   C. ipconfig
   D. nslookup

FIGURE 14-3

Command
output for
question 6

```
Default Server:  cns01.eastlink.ca
Address:  24.222.0.94

> www.google.com
Server:  cns01.eastlink.ca
Address:  24.222.0.94

Non-authoritative answer:
Name:    www.google.com
Addresses:  2607:f8b0:400b:80d::2004
            172.217.2.164
```

7. You need to view network interface settings for a cloud-based Linux virtual machine. Which command should you issue?
   A. ifconfig
   B. tracert
   C. ipconfig
   D. nslookup

8. You are testing cloud-provided DNS name resolution. You need to clear the local DNS cache for a cloud-based virtual machine. Which command should you issue?

   A. ifconfig /flushdns

   B. ifconfig /clearcache

   C. ipconfig /flushdns

   D. ipconfig /clearcache

9. Which command resulted in the output shown in Figure 14-4?

   A. ipconfig

   B. netstat

   C. nslookup

   D. dig

FIGURE 14-4	Proto	Local Address	Foreign Address	State
	TCP	192.168.0.10:52295	qh-in-f188:5228	ESTABLISHED
Command	TCP	192.168.0.10:52312	13.107.42.11:https	ESTABLISHED
output for	TCP	192.168.0.10:52369	40.69.169.176:https	ESTABLISHED
question 9	TCP	192.168.0.10:52643	edge-star-mini-shv-01-yyz1:https ESTABLISHED	
	TCP	192.168.0.10:52648	edge-star-shv-01-yyz1:https ESTABLISHED	

10. Which protocol resolves IP addresses to MAC addresses?

    A. TCP

    B. UDP

    C. ARP

    D. ICMP

11. Your network consists of industrial computer systems along with standard office productivity tools running on desktop computers. You need a threat detection solution that will examine all device log file entries to identify correlations. What should you use?

    A. Syslog

    B. SIEM

    C. IDS

    D. IPS

12. What is the first step in a troubleshooting methodology?

    A. Identify assets.

    B. Identify the problem.

    C. Identify the solution.

    D. Identify threats.

13. You have been troubleshooting startup issues related to a cloud virtual machine. After investigating server log files, you determine the problem was due to a misconfiguration by an assistant administrator. After you fix the configuration, the server starts up without issues. You implement stricter controls to limit server configuration access. What should you do next?

    A. Reboot the server.
    B. Document the solution.
    C. Patch the server.
    D. Reimage the server.

14. After deploying a custom web application to an existing application server, you determine the change has negatively affected the stability of both servers. Performance metrics indicate the server is not overwhelmed. You need to ensure the stability of both servers while minimizing resource utilization. What should you do?

    A. Implement application containers.
    B. Deploy the new app in a new virtual machine.
    C. Deploy an image and install the new app.
    D. Scale up the existing server.

15. Using Figure 14-5, match the troubleshooting steps listed on the left to the correct order of steps on the right.

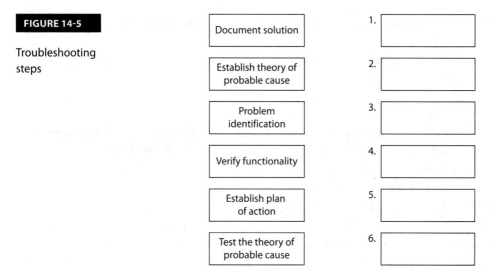

FIGURE 14-5

Troubleshooting steps

16. Trinity is a developer in your organization. A custom application has not been functioning properly and Trinity has been assigned to the support request. After applying code changes and checking in the code, she runs a series of regression tests using a script called regtest.sh. To which troubleshooting step does regtest.sh apply?

    A. Document the solution.

    B. Verify full system functionality.

    C. Establish a plan of action.

    D. Test the theory.

17. Which protocol is used to synchronize system clocks over a network?

    A. ICMP

    B. NTP

    C. ARP

    D. TCP

18. Which two items are used to control compute resource usage by cloud consumers?

    A. Thresholds

    B. SLA

    C. Quotas

    D. Limits

19. Which disk performance unit of measurement is best suited for use in establishing a performance baseline?

    A. GB storage space consumed

    B. % CPU utilization

    C. IOPS

    D. % network utilization

20. A runbook that previously ran without issues is no longer functioning. The runbook uses cloud APIs to query cloud service log entries. What is the most likely cause of the failure?

    A. The cloud APIs are unavailable.

    B. There has been a change in the runbook workflow.

    C. The runbook is not calling the APIs correctly.

    D. RBAC settings are configured incorrectly.

21. API request limits are normally applied to which of the following items? Choose two.

    A. IP address

    B. MAC address

    C. Subnet

    D. Hostname

22. You are troubleshooting network connectivity from a user desktop to a remote website. What is the first device you should ping?
    A. DHCP host
    B. DNS server
    C. Default gateway
    D. Website

23. Refer to the network diagram in Figure 14-6. You are troubleshooting user desktop connectivity to the listed website. What is the problem?
    A. The default gateway IP address is unreachable.
    B. The DNS server must be on the user desktop subnet.
    C. The DHCP server must be on the user desktop subnet.
    D. The website DNS name is invalid.

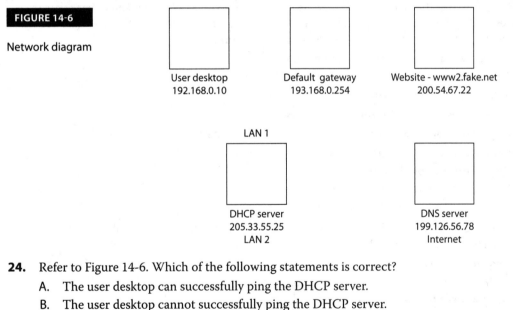

FIGURE 14-6

Network diagram

User desktop
192.168.0.10

Default gateway
193.168.0.254

Website - www2.fake.net
200.54.67.22

LAN 1

DHCP server
205.33.55.25
LAN 2

DNS server
199.126.56.78
Internet

24. Refer to Figure 14-6. Which of the following statements is correct?
    A. The user desktop can successfully ping the DHCP server.
    B. The user desktop cannot successfully ping the DHCP server.
    C. The user desktop can successfully ping the DNS server.
    D. The user desktop cannot successfully ping 127.0.0.1.

25. Refer to Figure 14-6.

    A. A DNS A record for www2.fake.net will potentially allow connectivity by name.

    B. A DNS PTR record for www2.fake.net will potentially allow connectivity by name.

    C. The DHCP server must reside on the subnet with user desktops.

    D. The DNS server must reside on the subnet with user desktops.

26. Using an internal CA, you have issued a new TLS certificate for a custom website and configured the server to use it. Users complain that they cannot successfully connect to the website. What is the most likely cause of the problem?

    A. The server certificate has expired.

    B. The client certificate has expired.

    C. The server certificate is untrusted.

    D. The client certificate is untrusted.

27. Roman is a user in the HelpDesk_East group. Roman complains that he no longer has access to a restricted file server share on a Windows server. You verify that HelpDesk_East has the necessary permissions. What is the most likely cause of the problem?

    A. HelpDesk_East has insufficient permissions.

    B. The server folder is corrupt.

    C. Roman's private key has expired.

    D. Roman's user account permissions have been changed.

28. Which plan of action best addresses an infected corporate desktop computer?

    A. Update the virus signatures on the host.

    B. Disable updates on the host.

    C. Run a virus scan on the host.

    D. Disable network connectivity for the host.

29. An internal CA-issued certificate has been configured for an internal website. What is the next task that should be completed?

    A. Update device certificate expiration dates.

    B. Add the website name to the certificate.

    C. Add the website IP address to the certificate.

    D. Update device trusted authority lists.

30. When attempting an SSH connection to a newly deployed Linux virtual machine called linux1.fakedomain.net in the cloud, you are unable to make a connection. What should you verify? Choose two.

    A. linux1.fakedomain.net is pingable by IP address

    B. nslookup resolution of linux1.fakedomain.net to the correct IP address

    C. ping resolution of linux1.fakedomain.net to the correct IP address

    D. Firewall ACLs

31. Which Windows command shows current network port connections?

    A. nslookup

    B. netstat

    C. ipconfig

    D. arp

32. Which troubleshooting step follows problem identification?

    A. Establish a theory of probable cause.

    B. Documentation.

    C. Test the theory.

    D. Verify system functionality.

33. You have selected a new public cloud provider for e-mail services. The current provider does not have an API that supports the migration of user contact lists. What should you do?

    A. Stay with the current provider.

    B. Select a different new provider.

    C. Export contacts to a standard format.

    D. Develop a new API to migrate contacts.

34. Users complain about the poor performance of a newly deployed internal web application that has been deployed to the public cloud. After investigating the issue, you notice that three other busy web applications are also being used in the cloud with excessive network traffic. You need to improve application performance. What should you do?

    A. Enable a content delivery network.

    B. Scale up.

    C. Deploy a new cloud virtual network.

    D. Enable centralized logging.

35. Which of the following is most likely to be addressed by an SLA?

    A. RBAC settings

    B. Cloud archive encryption

    C. Default user credentials

    D. Cloud service provider outage

36. You are deploying a cloud-based Microsoft SQL Server relational database for which you have existing licenses. Which cloud deployment option should you choose?

    A. BYOD

    B. BYOL

    C. Database replication

    D. Minimal vCPUs

37. After creating and testing a new cloud deployment, you notice a remote administration flaw in the Linux deployment template shown here. What is the flaw?

```
"IpProtocol": "udp",
"ToPort": "22",
"CidrIp": "0.0.0.0/0"
```

A. "ToPort" should be 3389.

B. "ToPort" should be 443.

C. "IpProtocol" should be tcp.

D. "IpProtocol" should be icmp.

38. Which of the following is most likely to result in problematic network time synchronization?

A. Incorrect RBAC permissions

B. Lack of virtual machine guest tools

C. Incorrect VLAN association

D. Lack of a default gateway

39. Which of the following is most likely to result in problematic runbook automation?

A. Incorrect RBAC permissions

B. Lack of language support

C. Incorrect VLAN association

D. Lack of a default gateway

40. Which option should be exercised when adding more underlying computer power is no longer available?

A. Dedicated hosting

B. Increase backup storage capacity

C. Scaling out

D. Use SSD storage

41. After deploying a new virtual machine in the cloud, you notice that although it has received a public IP address, it has not received a private IP address. What is the most likely cause of the problem?

A. The cloud DHCP provider is unavailable.

B. Incorrect RBAC permissions were assigned to the virtual machine.

C. The DHCP configuration has run out of IP addresses.

D. The virtual machine has run out of disk space.

42. Batch jobs handling on-premises backups to the cloud are failing on some occasions. What is the most likely reason for this?

A. Incorrect RBAC permissions

B. Not enough time to complete backup

C. Expired PKI certificate

D. Cloud NTP misconfiguration

43. Your on-premises network has been experiencing more IT resource demands than usual. As a result, storage capacity has been depleted. You need to ensure that future storage demands are met despite having exhausted on-premises resources. What should you enable?

    A. Shared storage

    B. LUN masking

    C. Cloud bursting

    D. Cloud zoning

44. You are configuring RBAC permissions used by a cloud template. What should you configure to ensure the future success of template deployments?

    A. Use the cloud root account.

    B. Use the cloud administrator account.

    C. Use cloud account MFA.

    D. Use a cloud service account.

45. Your centralized cloud policy configuration prohibits the installation of mobile device apps. Some smartphones are unable to apply the policy settings. Which term best describes the scenario?

    A. Change management failure

    B. Security control failure

    C. RBAC failure

    D. MFA failure

46. Which command captures all types of network traffic?

    A. nslookup

    B. arp

    C. netstat

    D. tcpdump

47. You are automating cloud resource deployment through a template. You need to ensure that cloud resource changes do not prevent services from running. Which of the following attributes is the least likely to change?

    A. Server name

    B. IP address

    C. Location

    D. GUID

48. As a developer, you plan to use Microsoft Visual Studio to manage cloud resources through cloud APIs. When you begin testing cloud connectivity in Visual Studio, you realize cloud options are not supported. What should you do?

    A. Write shell scripts instead.

    B. Write PowerShell scripts instead.

    C. Create custom APIs.

    D. Install a newer version of Visual Studio.

A

QUICK ANSWER KEY

1.	B	**14.**	A	**26.**	C	**39.**	A
2.	D	**15.**	See "In-Depth	**27.**	D	**40.**	C
3.	B		Answers."	**28.**	D	**41.**	C
4.	B	**16.**	B	**29.**	D	**42.**	B
5.	A, D	**17.**	B	**30.**	B, D	**43.**	C
6.	D	**18.**	C, D	**31.**	B	**44.**	D
7.	A	**19.**	C	**32.**	A	**45.**	A
8.	C	**20.**	B	**33.**	C	**46.**	D
9.	B	**21.**	A, C	**34.**	C	**47.**	D
10.	C	**22.**	C	**35.**	D	**48.**	D
11.	B	**23.**	A	**36.**	B		
12.	B	**24.**	B	**37.**	C		
13.	B	**25.**	A	**38.**	B		

IN-DEPTH ANSWERS

1. You are configuring a cloud network firewall. The firewall must permit ping traffic from your administrative on-premises station. What type of traffic should you allow?
   A. SSH
   B. ICMP
   C. RDP
   D. UDP

   ☑ **B.** The Internet Control Message Protocol (ICMP) is used for TCP/IP connectivity testing with commands such as ping and tracert.

   ☒ **A, C,** and **D** are incorrect. Secure Shell (SSH) is a secure remote administration tool used most often for managing network devices and Unix and Linux hosts. Remote Desktop Protocol (RDP) is used for remote Windows management. User Datagram Protocol (UDP) is a connectionless network transport protocol.

2. Which command resulted in the output shown in Figure 14-1?
   A. ipconfig
   B. tracert
   C. nslookup
   D. ping

   FIGURE 14-1

   Command output for question 2

   ```
   Reply from 192.168.0.1: bytes=32 time=7ms TTL=64
   Reply from 192.168.0.1: bytes=32 time=9ms TTL=64
   Reply from 192.168.0.1: bytes=32 time=13ms TTL=64
   Reply from 192.168.0.1: bytes=32 time=7ms TTL=64
   ```

   ☑ **D.** The ping command sends echo requests to a remote device; if the device is running and firewalls allow the ICMP traffic, echo replies are sent back to the originator.

   ☒ **A, B,** and **C** are incorrect. Ipconfig shows TCP/IP settings for each Windows interface. Tracert uses ICMP to send traffic through each router on the path to a target and displays each router that reports back to the originator. Name server lookup (nslookup) is used to test and query DNS servers.

3. Which Windows command shows the path a packet takes as it traverses routers?
   A. ipconfig
   B. tracert
   C. nslookup
   D. ping

   ☑ **B.** Tracert uses ICMP to send traffic through each router on the path to a target and displays each router that reports back to the originator.

   ☒ **A, C,** and **D** are incorrect. Ipconfig shows TCP/IP settings for each Windows interface. Name server lookup (nslookup) is used to test and query DNS servers. The ping command sends echo requests to a remote device; if the device is running and firewalls allow the ICMP traffic, echo replies are sent back to the originator.

4. Which command resulted in the output shown in Figure 14-2?
   A. ipconfig
   B. tracert
   C. nslookup
   D. ping

FIGURE 14-2

```
 9     *         *         *      Request timed out.
10     *         *         *      Request timed out.
11    41 ms     36 ms     37 ms  yyz10s06-in-f3.1e100.net [172.217.2.163]
```

Command
output for
question 4

   ☑ **B.** Tracert uses ICMP to send traffic through each router on the path to a target and displays each router that reports back to the originator.

   ☒ **A, C,** and **D** are incorrect. Ipconfig shows TCP/IP settings for each Windows interface. Name server lookup (nslookup) is used to test and query DNS servers. The ping command sends echo requests to a remote device; if the device is running and firewalls allow the ICMP traffic, echo replies are sent back to the originator.

5. Which of the following tools can be used specifically to verify DNS functionality? Choose two.
   A. dig
   B. tracert
   C. ipconfig
   D. nslookup

   ☑ **A** and **D.** Domain information gopher (dig) and name server lookup (nslookup) are DNS testing tools.

   ☒ **B** and **C** are incorrect. Tracert uses ICMP to send traffic through each router on the path to a target and displays each router that reports back to the originator. Ipconfig shows TCP/IP settings for each Windows interface.

6. Which command resulted in the output shown in Figure 14-3?

   A. dig

   B. tracert

   C. ipconfig

   D. nslookup

FIGURE 14-3

Command
output for
question 6

```
Default Server:  cns01.eastlink.ca
Address:  24.222.0.94

> www.google.com
Server:  cns01.eastlink.ca
Address:  24.222.0.94

Non-authoritative answer:
Name:    www.google.com
Addresses:  2607:f8b0:400b:80d::2004
            172.217.2.164
```

   ☑ **D.** Name server lookup (nslookup) is used to test and query DNS servers.

   ☒ **A, B,** and **C** are incorrect. Domain information gopher (dig) is a DNS testing tool, and the output does not match what results when using dig. Tracert uses ICMP to send traffic through each router on the path to a target and displays each router that reports back to the originator. Ipconfig shows TCP/IP settings for each Windows interface.

7. You need to view network interface settings for a cloud-based Linux virtual machine. Which command should you issue?

   A. ifconfig

   B. tracert

   C. ipconfig

   D. nslookup

   ☑ **A.** ifconfig is a Unix and Linux command that shows network interfaces along with TCP/IP values such as IP address and subnet mask.

   ☒ **B, C,** and **D** are incorrect. Tracert uses ICMP to send traffic through each router on the path to a target and displays each router that reports back to the originator. Ipconfig shows TCP/IP settings for each Windows interface. Name server lookup (nslookup) is used to test and query DNS servers.

8. You are testing cloud-provided DNS name resolution. You need to clear the local DNS cache for a cloud-based virtual machine. Which command should you issue?

   A. ifconfig /flushdns

   B. ifconfig /clearcache

   C. ipconfig /flushdns

   D. ipconfig /clearcache

   ☑ **C.** Ipconfig shows TCP/IP settings for each Windows interface; the /flushdns parameter clears the local DNS memory cache, which is useful when testing DNS server record changes.

   ☒ **A, B,** and **D** are incorrect. The listed syntax for each is invalid.

9. Which command resulted in the output shown in Figure 14-4?
   A. ipconfig
   B. netstat
   C. nslookup
   D. dig

FIGURE 14-4	Proto	Local Address	Foreign Address	State
	TCP	192.168.0.10:52295	qh-in-f188:5228	ESTABLISHED
Command	TCP	192.168.0.10:52312	13.107.42.11:https	ESTABLISHED
output for	TCP	192.168.0.10:52369	40.69.169.176:https	ESTABLISHED
question 9	TCP	192.168.0.10:52643	edge-star-mini-shv-01-yyz1:https	ESTABLISHED
	TCP	192.168.0.10:52648	edge-star-shv-01-yyz1:https	ESTABLISHED

☑ **B.** The netstat command shows statistics for various protocols, such as TCP in this case.
☒ **A, C,** and **D** are incorrect. Ipconfig shows TCP/IP settings for each Windows interface. Name server lookup (nslookup) is used to test and query DNS servers. Domain information gopher (dig) is a DNS testing tool.

10. Which protocol resolves IP addresses to MAC addresses?
    A. TCP
    B. UDP
    C. ARP
    D. ICMP

☑ **C.** Address Resolution Protocol (ARP) is a TCP/IP suite protocol that resolves IP addresses to MAC addresses on a local area network.
☒ **A, B,** and **D** are incorrect. Transmission Control Protocol (TCP) is an acknowledged connection-oriented packet transmission protocol. User Datagram Protocol (UDP) is a connectionless network transport protocol. The Internet Control Message Protocol (ICMP) is used for TCP/IP connectivity testing with commands such as ping and tracert.

11. Your network consists of industrial computer systems along with standard office productivity tools running on desktop computers. You need a threat detection solution that will examine all device log file entries to identify correlations. What should you use?
    A. Syslog
    B. SIEM
    C. IDS
    D. IPS

☑ **B.** Security Information and Event Management (SIEM) systems identify correlations from data acquired from network devices to identify security issues.

    ☒   **A, C,** and **D** are incorrect. Syslog is a Unix and Linux logging standard that allows customized log event filtering and forwarding. Intrusion detection systems (IDSs) and intrusion prevention systems (IPSs) identify host and network abnormalities, but IPSs can also take steps to stop suspicious activity.

12. What is the first step in a troubleshooting methodology?
    A. Identify assets.
    B. Identify the problem.
    C. Identify the solution.
    D. Identify threats.

        ☑   **B.** Problem identification is the first step in the six-step CompTIA troubleshooting model.
        ☒   **A, C,** and **D** are incorrect. Asset and threat identification are not part of the troubleshooting model but are related to a business impact analysis (BIA). Identifying the solution is not a part of the troubleshooting model; verifying system functionality, which is loosely related, is.

13. You have been troubleshooting startup issues related to a cloud virtual machine. After investigating server log files, you determine the problem was due to a misconfiguration by an assistant administrator. After you fix the configuration, the server starts up without issues. You implement stricter controls to limit server configuration access. What should you do next?
    A. Reboot the server.
    B. Document the solution.
    C. Patch the server.
    D. Reimage the server.

        ☑   **B.** After verifying that a change has solved the problem, document the solution.
        ☒   **A, C,** and **D** are incorrect. The listed items are not required and do not map to the CompTIA troubleshooting model.

14. After deploying a custom web application to an existing application server, you determine the change has negatively affected the stability of both servers. Performance metrics indicate the server is not overwhelmed. You need to ensure the stability of both servers while minimizing resource utilization. What should you do?
    A. Implement application containers.
    B. Deploy the new app in a new virtual machine.
    C. Deploy an image and install the new app.
    D. Scale up the existing server.

        ☑   **A.** Application containers isolate apps from one another on the same host while, in most cases, sharing the underlying operating system.
        ☒   **B, C,** and **D** are incorrect. Deploying a new VM and deploying an image are not as efficient as using containers since they contain an entire operating system. Scaling up (adding underlying compute power) will not solve app instability issues in this case since performance is normal.

15. Using Figure 14-5, match the troubleshooting steps listed on the left to the correct order of steps on the right.

FIGURE 14-5

Troubleshooting steps

Document solution

Establish theory of probable cause

Problem identification

Verify functionality

Establish plan of action

Test the theory of probable cause

1.

2.

3.

4.

5.

6.

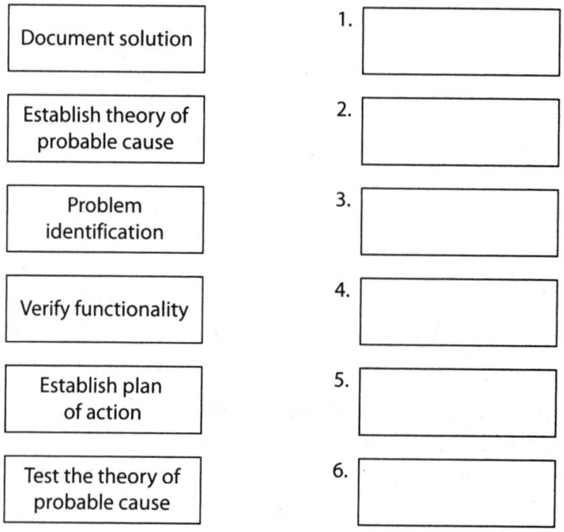

☑ Figure 14-7 shows the correct order of the troubleshooting steps. Troubleshooting begins with identifying the problem, followed by coming up with a plausible theory as to the cause. Next, the theory is tested to determine if it correctly identifies the cause of the problem. If not, either escalate or come up with and test additional theories. Once a theory is correct, a plan of action is established and the solution is implemented. After the solution is implemented, system functionality must be verified, and finally the solution must be documented.

FIGURE 14-7

Troubleshooting steps—the answer

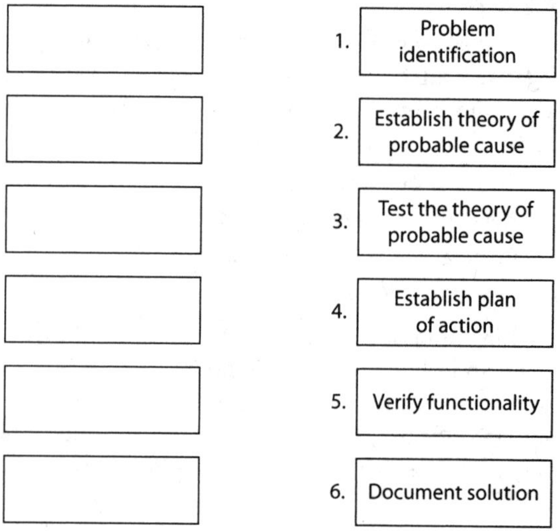

1. Problem identification

2. Establish theory of probable cause

3. Test the theory of probable cause

4. Establish plan of action

5. Verify functionality

6. Document solution

16. Trinity is a developer in your organization. A custom application has not been functioning properly and Trinity has been assigned to the support request. After applying code changes and checking in the code, she runs a series of regression tests using a script called regtest.sh. To which troubleshooting step does regtest.sh apply?

    A.   Document the solution.

    B.   Verify full system functionality.

    C.   Establish a plan of action.

    D.   Test the theory.

    ☑   **B.** Regression testing verifies that a change has not affected previously working functionality. This is part of verifying system functionality.

    ☒   **A, C,** and **D** are incorrect. The listed troubleshooting steps are not applicable to regression testing.

17. Which protocol is used to synchronize system clocks over a network?

    A.   ICMP

    B.   NTP

    C.   ARP

    D.   TCP

    ☑   **B.** The Network Time Protocol (NTP) uses UDP 123 to synchronize clocks over a network.

    ☒   **A, C,** and **D** are incorrect. The Internet Control Message Protocol (ICMP) is used for TCP/IP connectivity testing with commands such as ping and tracert. Address Resolution Protocol (ARP) resolves IP addresses to MAC addresses. Transmission Control Protocol (TCP) is an acknowledged connection-oriented packet transmission protocol.

18. Which two items are used to control compute resource usage by cloud consumers?

    A.   Thresholds

    B.   SLA

    C.   Quotas

    D.   Limits

    ☑   **C** and **D.** Quotas and limits can throttle resource usage.

    ☒   **A** and **B** are incorrect. Thresholds and service level agreements (SLAs) do not limit resource usage by cloud consumers; SLAs contains service uptime information. The terms "quotas" and "limits" are used with cloud computing, not "thresholds."

19. Which disk performance unit of measurement is best suited for use in establishing a performance baseline?

A. GB storage space consumed

B. % CPU utilization

C. IOPS

D. % network utilization

☑ **C.** Input/output operations per second (IOPS) is a standard disk performance unit of measurement that can be used to set a performance baseline related to storage activity.

☒ **A, B,** and **D** are incorrect. The listed metrics are either not disk related or not performance related.

20. A runbook that previously ran without issues is no longer functioning. The runbook uses cloud APIs to query cloud service log entries. What is the most likely cause of the failure?

A. The cloud APIs are unavailable.

B. There has been a change in the runbook workflow.

C. The runbook is not calling the APIs correctly.

D. RBAC settings are configured incorrectly.

☑ **B.** Runbooks automate workflows. Changes such as those to URLs or API entry points can break runbooks.

☒ **A, C,** and **D** are incorrect. Cloud APIs are very reliable and are very rarely unavailable. The APIs are being called correctly since the runbook ran before; if the API changed, then answer B is more applicable. Role-based access control (RBAC) permissions are not likely an issue since the runbook executed previously.

21. API request limits are normally applied to which of the following items? Choose two.

A. IP address

B. MAC address

C. Subnet

D. Hostname

☑ **A** and **C.** Application programming interface (API) request limits prevent APIs from being overwhelmed by requests from a specific IP address or subnet.

☒ **B** and **D** are incorrect. MAC addresses and hostnames are not used to limit API calls.

22. You are troubleshooting network connectivity from a user desktop to a remote website. What is the first device you should ping?

A. DHCP host

B. DNS server

C. Default gateway

D. Website

☑ **C.** Ensure the default gateway (router) is reachable first.

☒ **A, B,** and **D** are incorrect. The listed items should not be pinged before the default gateway.

23. Refer to the network diagram in Figure 14-6. You are troubleshooting user desktop connectivity to the listed website. What is the problem?

A. The default gateway IP address is unreachable.

B. The DNS server must be on the user desktop subnet.

C. The DHCP server must be on the user desktop subnet.

D. The website DNS name is invalid.

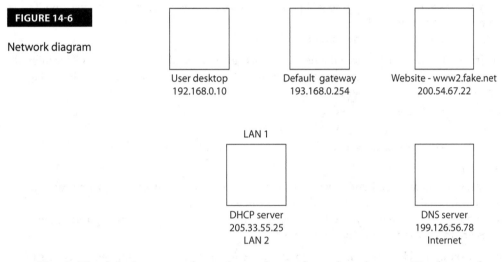

FIGURE 14-6

Network diagram

User desktop
192.168.0.10

Default gateway
193.168.0.254

Website - www2.fake.net
200.54.67.22

LAN 1

DHCP server
205.33.55.25
LAN 2

DNS server
199.126.56.78
Internet

☑ **A.** The default gateway (router) must be configured on the same IP subnet as hosts.

☒ **B, C,** and **D** are incorrect. DNS and DHCP servers do not have to reside on the same subnet with user devices. The listed website DNS name is valid.

24. Refer to Figure 14-6. Which of the following statements is correct?

A. The user desktop can successfully ping the DHCP server.

B. The user desktop cannot successfully ping the DHCP server.

C. The user desktop can successfully ping the DNS server.

D. The user desktop cannot successfully ping 127.0.0.1.

☑ **B.** Connectivity to remote hosts is not possible from the user desktop since it does not have a way out (default gateway on the same subnet).

☒ **A, C,** and **D** are incorrect. The listed items are incorrect statements.

25. Refer to Figure 14-6.

    A. A DNS A record for www2.fake.net will potentially allow connectivity by name.
    B. A DNS PTR record for www2.fake.net will potentially allow connectivity by name.
    C. The DHCP server must reside on the subnet with user desktops.
    D. The DNS server must reside on the subnet with user desktops.

    ☑ **A.** A DNS A record resolves names such as www2.fake.net to IP addresses. This would potentially allow connections by name if clients are pointing to the correct DNS server, and if clients can connect to the IP address.
    ☒ **B, C,** and **D** are incorrect. The listed items are incorrect statements.

26. Using an internal CA, you have issued a new TLS certificate for a custom website and configured the server to use it. Users complain that they cannot successfully connect to the website. What is the most likely cause of the problem?

    A. The server certificate has expired.
    B. The client certificate has expired.
    C. The server certificate is untrusted.
    D. The client certificate is untrusted.

    ☑ **C.** Unless certificates are issued by a trusted public certificate authority (CA), devices will have to be configured with the CA trusted root certificate.
    ☒ **A, B,** and **D** are incorrect. The certificate is new and will not have already expired. Client certificates are rarely used with secure websites.

27. Roman is a user in the HelpDesk_East group. Roman complains that he no longer has access to a restricted file server share on a Windows server. You verify that HelpDesk_East has the necessary permissions. What is the most likely cause of the problem?

    A. HelpDesk_East has insufficient permissions.
    B. The server folder is corrupt.
    C. Roman's private key has expired.
    D. Roman's user account permissions have been changed.

    ☑ **D.** On Windows hosts, the most restrictive permission applies. In this case, Roman's individual permissions must be more restrictive than the group permissions.
    ☒ **A, B,** and **C** are incorrect. The question states the group has the correct permissions. Corruption would most likely prevent all access to the folder, not just for Roman. The private key is not used to access shared network folders.

28. Which plan of action best addresses an infected corporate desktop computer?

    A. Update the virus signatures on the host.
    B. Disable updates on the host.
    C. Run a virus scan on the host.
    D. Disable network connectivity for the host.

    ☑ **D.** Infected devices should be removed from the network immediately.
    ☒ **A, B,** and **C** are incorrect. Applying updates and running virus scans should be done normally, not in response to an incident. Updates should never be disabled.

29. An internal CA-issued certificate has been configured for an internal website. What is the next task that should be completed?

A. Update device certificate expiration dates.

B. Add the website name to the certificate.

C. Add the website IP address to the certificate.

D. Update device trusted authority lists.

☑ **D.** The trusted root certificate for the internal CA must be added to devices so that they trust certificates issued by that CA.

☒ **A, B,** and **C** are incorrect. Device certificates are not part of this scenario. The certificate has already been issued and most likely contains the website name and possibly the IP address.

30. When attempting an SSH connection to a newly deployed Linux virtual machine called linux1.fakedomain.net in the cloud, you are unable to make a connection. What should you verify? Choose two.

A. linux1.fakedomain.net is pingable by IP address

B. nslookup resolution of linux1.fakedomain.net to the correct IP address

C. ping resolution of linux1.fakedomain.net to the correct IP address

D. Firewall ACLs

☑ **B** and **D.** The name must resolve to the correct IP address, and firewall ACLs must allow TCP port 22 traffic.

☒ **A** and **C** are incorrect. Ping traffic (ICMP) might be blocked while SSH traffic might be allowed; ping may not be reliable in this case.

31. Which Windows command shows current network port connections?

A. nslookup

B. netstat

C. ipconfig

D. arp

☑ **B.** The Windows netstat command shows protocol statistics for that host.

☒ **A, C,** and **D** are incorrect. Name server lookup (nslookup) is used to test and query DNS servers. Ipconfig shows TCP/IP settings for each Windows interface. Address Resolution Protocol (ARP) resolves IP addresses to MAC addresses on a local area network.

32. Which troubleshooting step follows problem identification?

A. Establish a theory of probable cause.

B. Documentation.

C. Test the theory.

D. Verify system functionality.

☑ **A.** After identifying the problem, come up with a probable cause of the problem.

☒ **B, C,** and **D** are incorrect. Documentation of the solution is the last step of the troubleshooting process. A theory of probable cause is first required before testing the theory and verifying system functionality.

33. You have selected a new public cloud provider for e-mail services. The current provider does not have an API that supports the migration of user contact lists. What should you do?

A. Stay with the current provider.

B. Select a different new provider.

C. Export contacts to a standard format.

D. Develop a new API to migrate contacts.

☑ **C.** Most public cloud providers allow data to be exported to a standard file format such as CSV or XML.

☒ **A, B,** and **D** are incorrect. Exporting contacts is the best option.

34. Users complain about the poor performance of a newly deployed internal web application that has been deployed to the public cloud. After investigating the issue, you notice that three other busy web applications are also being used in the cloud with excessive network traffic. You need to improve application performance. What should you do?

A. Enable a content delivery network.

B. Scale up.

C. Deploy a new cloud virtual network.

D. Enable centralized logging.

☑ **C.** Network isolation in the cloud can improve application performance.

☒ **A, B,** and **D** are incorrect. Content delivery networks (CDNs) are useful for public, not private, websites. Scaling up and centralized logging will not improve application performance when network traffic is the problem.

35. Which of the following is most likely to be addressed by an SLA?

A. RBAC settings

B. Cloud archive encryption

C. Default user credentials

D. Cloud service provider outage

☑ **D.** Service level agreements (SLAs) are contracts between service providers and consumers that detail items such as expected uptime and the consequences if the stated uptime values are violated due to cloud provider outages.

☒ **A, B,** and **C** are incorrect. The listed items are not contained in an SLA.

36. You are deploying a cloud-based Microsoft SQL Server relational database for which you have existing licenses. Which cloud deployment option should you choose?

A. BYOD

B. BYOL

C. Database replication

D. Minimal vCPUs

☑ **B.** Bring your own license (BYOL) allows cloud customers to use previously purchased licenses with compatible cloud service offerings such as databases.

☒ **A, C,** and **D** are incorrect. Bring your own device (BYOD) allows the use of personal mobile devices on a corporate network. Database replication and vCPUs are not as prevalent configuration options as is the reuse of licenses.

37. After creating and testing a new cloud deployment, you notice a remote administration flaw in the Linux deployment template shown here. What is the flaw?

```
"IpProtocol": "udp",
"ToPort": "22",
"CidrIp": "0.0.0.0/0"
```

A. "ToPort" should be 3389.
B. "ToPort" should be 443.
C. "IpProtocol" should be tcp.
D. "IpProtocol" should be icmp.

☑ **C.** SSH uses TCP port 22, not UDP so the template should use "tcp" for the "IpProtocol" directive.

☒ **A, B,** and **D** are incorrect. The listed items do not apply to the template code.

38. Which of the following is most likely to result in problematic network time synchronization?

A. Incorrect RBAC permissions
B. Lack of virtual machine guest tools
C. Incorrect VLAN association
D. Lack of a default gateway

☑ **B.** Virtual machine guest tools provide many services to virtual machines, including time synchronization.

☒ **A, C,** and **D** are incorrect. The listed items do not affect network time synchronization.

39. Which of the following is most likely to result in problematic runbook automation?

A. Incorrect RBAC permissions
B. Lack of language support
C. Incorrect VLAN association
D. Lack of a default gateway

☑ **A.** Role-based access control (RBAC) permissions can be applied to cloud resources; if done incorrectly, it can prevent proper runbook execution.

☒ **B, C,** and **D** are incorrect. The listed items are not likely to prevent runbook automation.

40. Which option should be exercised when adding more underlying computer power is no longer available?

A. Dedicated hosting

B. Increase backup storage capacity

C. Scaling out

D. Use SSD storage

☑ **C.** Scaling out adds virtual machine instances to support an increased IT workload.

☒ **A, B,** and **D** are incorrect. Dedicated hosting is offered by some cloud providers and should be avoided where possible due to prohibitive costs. Storage options will not help when more processing power is required.

41. After deploying a new virtual machine in the cloud, you notice that although it has received a public IP address, it has not received a private IP address. What is the most likely cause of the problem?

A. The cloud DHCP provider is unavailable.

B. Incorrect RBAC permissions were assigned to the virtual machine.

C. The DHCP configuration has run out of IP addresses.

D. The virtual machine has run out of disk space.

☑ **C.** Dynamic Host Configuration Protocol (DHCP) provides TCP/IP settings to devices. This is often a provided service for cloud networks. Depending on the addressing, there could be an easily reached limit to the number of available IP addresses.

☒ **A, B,** and **D** are incorrect. The listed items are not as likely as IP address depletion.

42. Batch jobs handling on-premises backups to the cloud are failing on some occasions. What is the most likely reason for this?

A. Incorrect RBAC permissions

B. Not enough time to complete backup

C. Expired PKI certificate

D. Cloud NTP misconfiguration

☑ **B.** Care must be taken to ensure the backup time windows allow sufficient time to complete large backups.

☒ **A, C,** and **D** are incorrect. Since backups work on some occasions, it is not an RBAC permission issue. PKI certificates are not required for backups. NTP is not misconfigured if backups work on some occasions.

43. Your on-premises network has been experiencing more IT resource demands than usual. As a result, storage capacity has been depleted. You need to ensure that future storage demands are met despite having exhausted on-premises resources. What should you enable?

A. Shared storage

B. LUN masking

C. Cloud bursting

D. Cloud zoning

☑   **C.** Cloud bursting reaches into the cloud when on-premises IT resources are depleted.
☒   **A, B,** and **D** are incorrect. The listed options are storage configuration options, but will not address the need for more storage when storage resources are depleted on premises.

44. You are configuring RBAC permissions used by a cloud template. What should you configure to ensure the future success of template deployments?
   A.   Use the cloud root account.
   B.   Use the cloud administrator account.
   C.   Use cloud account MFA.
   D.   Use a cloud service account.

☑   **D.** Specific cloud service accounts should be created and used for cloud services; regular user accounts should not be used.
☒   **A, B,** and **C** are incorrect. The listed options are incorrect; specific cloud service accounts should be created.

45. Your centralized cloud policy configuration prohibits the installation of mobile device apps. Some smartphones are unable to apply the policy settings. Which term best describes the scenario?
   A.   Change management failure
   B.   Security control failure
   C.   RBAC failure
   D.   MFA failure

☑   **A.** Centralized policy settings that cannot be applied are called change management failures.
☒   **B, C,** and **D** are incorrect. The scenario is not a security, role-based access control (RBAC), or multifactor authentication (MFA) failure.

46. Which command captures all types of network traffic?
   A.   nslookup
   B.   arp
   C.   netstat
   D.   tcpdump

☑   **D.** tcpdump is a Unix and Linux packet capturing command.
☒   **A, B,** and **C** are incorrect. The listed commands do not capture network traffic.

47. You are automating cloud resource deployment through a template. You need to ensure that cloud resource changes do not prevent services from running. Which of the following attributes is the least likely to change?
   A.   Server name
   B.   IP address
   C.   Location
   D.   GUID

☑   **D.** Cloud providers assign unchanging globally unique identifiers (GUIDs) to cloud resources.
☒   **A, B,** and **C** are incorrect. Name, locations, and IP addresses can change.

48. As a developer, you plan to use Microsoft Visual Studio to manage cloud resources through cloud APIs. When you begin testing cloud connectivity in Visual Studio, you realize cloud options are not supported. What should you do?

    A. Write shell scripts instead.

    B. Write PowerShell scripts instead.

    C. Create custom APIs.

    D. Install a newer version of Visual Studio.

    ☑ **D.** Sometimes tools themselves need to be upgraded to support the latest cloud features.

    ☒ **A, B,** and **C** are incorrect. The listed items are not necessary; all that is needed is a tool update.

Appendix

About the Online Content

This book comes complete with Total Tester Online customizable practice exam software with 200 practice exam questions, as well as a separate quiz containing 10 performance-based questions.

System Requirements

We recommend and support the current and previous major versions of the following desktop browsers: Chrome, Firefox, Edge, and Safari. These browsers update frequently, and sometimes an update may cause compatibility issues with the Total Tester Online or other content hosted on the Training Hub. If you run into a problem using one of these browsers, please try using another until the problem is resolved.

Single User License Terms and Conditions

Online access to the digital content included with this book is governed by the McGraw-Hill Education License Agreement outlined next. By using this digital content you agree to the terms of that license.

Access   To register and activate your Total Seminars Training Hub account, simply follow these easy steps.

1. Go to **hub.totalsem.com/mheclaim**.
2. To Register and create a new Training Hub account, enter your e-mail address, name, and password. No further information (such as credit card number) is required to create an account.
3. If you already have a Total Seminars Training Hub account, select "Log in" and enter your e-mail and password.
4. Enter your Product Key: `j67d-z4zp-zx67`
5. Click to accept the user license terms.
6. Click "Register and Claim" to create your account. You will be taken to the Training Hub and have access to the content for this book.

Duration of License   Access to your online content through the Total Seminars Training Hub will expire one year from the date the publisher declares the book out of print.

Your purchase of this McGraw-Hill Education product, including its access code, through a retail store is subject to the refund policy of that store.

The Content is a copyrighted work of McGraw-Hill Education and McGraw-Hill Education reserves all rights in and to the Content. The Work is © 2018 by McGraw-Hill Education, LLC.

Restrictions on Transfer   The user is receiving only a limited right to use the Content for user's own internal and personal use, dependent on purchase and continued ownership of this book. The user may not reproduce, forward, modify, create derivative works based upon, transmit, distribute, disseminate, sell, publish, or sublicense the Content or in any way commingle the Content with other third-party content, without McGraw-Hill Education's consent.

Limited Warranty   The McGraw-Hill Education Content is provided on an "as is" basis. Neither McGraw-Hill Education nor its licensors make any guarantees or warranties of any kind, either express or implied, including, but not limited to, implied warranties of merchantability or fitness for a particular purpose or use as to any McGraw-Hill Education Content or the information therein or any warranties as to the accuracy, completeness, currentness, or results to be obtained from, accessing or using the McGraw-Hill Education content, or any material referenced in such content or any information entered into licensee's product by users or other persons and/or any material available on or that can be accessed through the licensee's product (including via any hyperlink or otherwise) or as to non-infringement of third-party rights. Any warranties of any kind, whether express or implied, are disclaimed. Any material or data obtained through use of the McGraw-Hill Education content is at your own discretion and risk and user understands that it will be solely responsible for any resulting damage to its computer system or loss of data.

Neither McGraw-Hill Education nor its licensors shall be liable to any subscriber or to any user or anyone else for any inaccuracy, delay, interruption in service, error or omission, regardless of cause, or for any damage resulting therefrom.

In no event will McGraw-Hill Education or its licensors be liable for any indirect, special or consequential damages, including but not limited to, lost time, lost money, lost profits or good will, whether in contract, tort, strict liability or otherwise, and whether or not such damages are foreseen or unforeseen with respect to any use of the McGraw-Hill Education content.

Total Tester Online

Total Tester Online provides you with a simulation of the CompTIA Cloud+ CV0-002 exam. Exams can be taken in Practice Mode or Exam Mode. Practice Mode provides an assistance window with hints, references to the book, explanations of the correct and incorrect answers, and the option to check your answer as you take the test. Exam Mode provides a simulation of the actual exam. The number of questions, the types of questions, and the time allowed are intended to be an accurate representation of the exam environment. The option to customize your quiz allows you to create custom exams from selected domains or chapters, and you can further customize the number of questions and time allowed.

To take a test, follow the instructions provided in the previous section to register and activate your Total Seminars Training Hub account. When you register, you will be taken to the Total Seminars Training Hub. From the Training Hub Home page, select the Total Tester from the "Study" drop-down at the top of the page, or from the list of "Products You Own" on the Home page. You can then select the option to customize your quiz and begin testing yourself in Practice Mode or Exam Mode. All exams provide an overall grade and a grade broken down by domain.

Performance-Based Questions

In addition to multiple-choice questions, the CompTIA Cloud+ CV0-002 exam includes performance-based questions (PBQs), which are designed to test your ability to solve problems in a simulated environment. You can access the performance-based questions included with this book by selecting the PBQs from the list of "Products You Own" on the Training Hub Home page.

Technical Support

For questions regarding the Total Tester software or operation of the Training Hub, visit **www.totalsem.com** or e-mail **support@totalsem.com**.

For questions regarding book content, e-mail **hep_customer-service@mheducation.com**. For customers outside the United States, e-mail **international_cs@mheducation.com**.